To Mother
Christmas 1988
Love Richard x

Chapter 22 page 193.

I am sure this was
fathers quote.
He once told it to
me in one of his
stories!

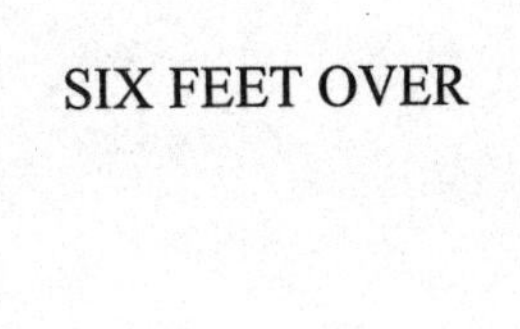

SIX FEET OVER

SIX FEET OVER

Pleasures and Perils of Aerial Crop Spraying

Peter Charles

UNITED WRITERS
Cornwall

UNITED WRITERS PUBLICATIONS LTD
Ailsa, Castle Gate, Penzance, Cornwall.

British Library Cataloguing in Publication Data:
A catalogue record for this book is
available from the British Library.

ISBN 1 85200 077 5

Printed in Great Britain by
United Writers Publications Ltd
Cornwall.

To my late brother, Max, without
whose encouragement this book
would not have been written.

CONTENTS

Chapter		Page
1	Too Old for Airlines	9
2	Early Days	10
3	Aeroplanes at Last	14
4	A Licensed Aircraft Engineer in Jersey	22
5	In the Footsteps of Rhodes	31
6	The Berlin Airlift	37
7	Ten Pounds Well Spent	47
8	Learning to Fly	59
9	The Art of Crop Spraying	65
10	Caterpillar Crisis	77
11	The Lure of Africa	86
12	Bananas and Jungle	97
13	South American Venture	103
14	Landing Problems	110
15	Some Pigeon!	118
16	Return to the Sudan	125
17	Eating Humble Pie	142
18	Africa Wins Again	150
19	Deep Flying in Austria	159
20	Snowbound in Scotland	169
21	Some Unorthodox Landings	176
22	Going Solo Again	184
23	Avalanche of Work	194
24	Complaints and Controls	199
25	Problems With Fruit	205
26	A Tragic Accident	213
27	Enforced Retirement	223

1

Too Old for Airlines

"Crop spraying!"
"Crop spraying!"
"Another one, crop spraying!"
"Again, crop spraying!"

Laurie Bond, examiner of airmen, Dept. of Civil Aviation, Melbourne, Australia, was pointing to the chart of air accidents on the wall of his office.

I had just told him that, with my grand total of 200 flying hours, I had got a job as a pilot with a new crop spraying company.

"You're mad," he said. "Look at all the accidents and some of them are experienced pilots."

"Where else can I get a job as a pilot?" I asked. "I'm thirty, too old for the airlines, and besides I have no instrument rating."

I had written to all the airlines in Australia without success. One replied that their minimum requirement was not over twenty-four years of age and 2,000 hours jet experience. They added that if in the future I should meet these requirements I could apply again. It was possible that I might acquire 2,000 hours jet experience, but to regress to an under twenty-four year old was well nigh impossible.

"Well, I wish you luck," said Laurie.

So began a career as a crop spraying pilot that was to last thirty years, taking me to many countries where I flew at six feet over the crops and had a great deal of fun.

2

Early Days

My first experience of aviation was when I was six years old. Playing in the garden, I looked up to see a long, silver, cigar shaped object moving across the sky, quite low. It was an airship! I stood fascinated, while it moved slowly along and disappeared behind some trees. I found out later that it was the R100. (I wonder if Nevil Shute was on board?)

Some time later my father, who managed a book and newspaper shop, came home early in the morning. Our neighbour's son was one of the crew of another airship, the R101. He was a radio operator I believe, and my father had seen the report of it crashing in France in the daily papers before they were delivered. There was no television in those days and few radios and telephones, so my father came back to break the news to the parents before they saw it in the paper.

My mother came from Farnborough, Hants, and used to tell me of the exploits of the early aviator, S. F. Cody, sometimes known as Colonel Cody, who built and flew his primitive aeroplanes from Laffins Plain, and how he crashed to his death near her home. He was quite a hero, locally and nationally, and was given an impressive funeral in Farnborough. There were photos of his funeral in the family album. One wreath I remember was in the shape of a four-bladed propeller.

Along with my friends I built model aeroplanes, replicas of World War I aircraft from both sides and we used to play at dog fights. I also built flying models driven by elastic, but they never flew very well.

I left school soon after war broke out. I can remember the headmaster announcing at morning prayers that a chap named Colwell, who had been my house captain and whom I had admired very much, had been killed on a flying mission to Norway.

My academic achievements at school were poor. I left at sixteen in the form below School Certificate (GCSE). Seeing the academic qualifications my grandchildren now have to achieve in order to get a job, I realise that if I left school today, I would have difficulty getting a job as a road sweeper!

With the war on and my poor scholastic achievements my job prospects were limited, but I wanted to work on aeroplanes. I got a job as a 'boy' with Weyburn Engineering at Elstead, Surrey. It was still in existence a few years ago. They made various components for the aircraft industry which did not mean much to me at the time, but later, working on aircraft engines I recognised them as being parts of the Gipsy Major engine.

The Battle of Britain was being fought while I was at Elstead. We watched the fight high in the summer sky. The sky would be covered in vapour trails and sometimes an aircraft glinted in the sun. Then, suddenly, it would all be over, leaving only the vapour trails drifting in the sky. The Royal Aircraft Establishment at Farnborough was bombed as I was cycling home from work. I could see the smoke caused by the bombing and the planes climbing away, heading for home. I felt very exposed and a little scared to see the enemy so close.

This job was not getting me very far. With the help of family friends I was taken on by Swain and Jones, a garage in Farnham. Due to the war I could only be an 'unindentured' apprentice. At least I was working on complete engines even if they were in cars. My wage was five shillings (25 pence) a week!

I came home every night covered in oil and grease and very happy. I was put with a senior mechanic called Dedman. As his son was also an apprentice, everyone called him 'Dad', like his son. We used to do bearing replacements, re-bores and de-cokes, all good stuff.

Many of the nuts were locked by split pins, as they are today. If they were a tight fit or in an awkward place, they were difficult to remove. After we had both struggled to remove a difficult pin

'Dad' would remark, "Split pins are the invention of the devil." I have often remembered this when, in later years I struggled to remove a difficult pin.

I was taught to ride the firm's motor-cycle and often sent on it to collect spare parts. The sales manager, Mr Brockhurst, also taught me to drive on his Austin 7. It had a hand crank start and a fierce clutch. With my inexperience I was prone to stall the engine on starting off. When this happened he had to get out and crank it. Once, on a bad day, I stalled it six times and each time he had to get out, crank it and get back in, when I promptly stalled it again. Every time I did this his temper and language got worse and worse!

Due to the labour shortage through military call-up, I found I was being given jobs usually done by improvers after a five-year apprenticeship, but under the watchful eye of 'Dad'. This was all very good experience. My wage was now seven shillings (35 pence) a week. About this time the firm got a government contract to repair army vehicles, but this meant they had to pay union rates. Because of my age my pay went up to 18 shillings (90 pence) a week. I was rich!

I was taken on one side by the owner, Mr Jones, who was really a nice person and rather a father figure to the young employees. He explained the position to me, pointing out that he was obliged to pay me this very high wage. Really I was not worth the rate, but he would expect me to try and earn it. Since I was doing the work of an improver I thought I warranted it, but did not say so.

Walking to work each day I passed a garage called the Tourist Trophy Garage, which specialised in sports cars. On many occasions I saw a man in a dark blue uniform with wings over his breast pocket. He was obviously a pilot, but I did not recognise the uniform. One day I plucked up courage and asked him to what service he belonged. He told me he flew for Air Transport Auxiliary, which delivered aircraft from the factories to RAF aerodromes. I told him I was keen to work on aircraft and he suggested I wrote for a job, as they were short of engineers.

This resulted in an interview at ATA headquarters at White Waltham aerodrome, near Maidenhead, Berks, and being offered a job as a semi-skilled fitter at £2.10/- (£2.50) a week. Now I was going to work on aeroplanes and earn enough to support myself away from home.

My elder brother, Max, came with me for the interview at my mother's insistence. He had been discharged from the RAF after being wounded flying as an air gunner in Blenheims over France in the early days of the war.

We went to the police station to enquire if they could recommend lodgings for me. They sent me to a Mrs Pinchin, a motherly widow, where I stayed for most of the time I was with ATA.

3

Aeroplanes at Last

Air Transport Auxiliary was an organisation started by a few pre-war amateur pilots to ferry aircraft from the factories to RAF bases, releasing RAF pilots for more warlike duties. It expanded rapidly and experienced pilots and engineers were seconded from Imperial Airways, whose activities were restricted by the war.

Pilots unfit for duties with the RAF, due to age or physical handicaps, were recruited. Some had only one hand or one eye or wore spectacles. Amongst the women who joined, one was a grandmother! One pilot had no left arm at all, but flew single engined aircraft, such as Spitfires. I was told that to take off he held the control stick back between his knees, while applying the brakes. Then he opened the throttle with his right hand, locked it in the fully opened position, released the brakes, grabbed the control stick and was away. I was not told his technique for landing, but it could have been equally interesting. No wonder they were referred to as Ancient and Tattered Airmen!

ATA became a mini-airline. Ferry pools were located around the country, near centres of aircraft production. The headquarters at White Waltham, as well as being a ferry pool, ran a flying school to convert pilots to twin engined aircraft, using Oxfords and Wellingtons.

Every morning the pilots climbed into the air taxis, Avro Ansons and the four-seater American Fairchild Argus, and were dropped off at various aerodromes to collect and ferry aircraft to the RAF. In the evening the air taxis collected them from their final destinations and brought them back to base.

As the organisation grew, so the engineering side expanded to maintain the aircraft. Some engineers came from other industries, such as motor, marine and construction. Others, butchers, bakers and candlestick makers had been trained at six-month courses at government schools, set up to provide manpower for the war industries. Eventually ATA ran its own engineering school, where engineers attended to update their knowledge on the new aircraft types being produced.

This was the organisation I entered one Monday morning, ushered into a large hangar full of all sorts of aircraft; Tiger Moths, Masters, Oxfords, Ansons, Wellingtons, Hudsons, and out on the airfield in the transit bays, Spitfires, Hurricanes, Mosquitos.

Every aircraft that served in the RAF passed through the hands of ATA. Working on such a variety of aircraft types was a wonderful experience, which stood me in good stead when I entered civil aviation at the end of the war.

Everyone was keen to learn more about their job. As well as courses at the ATA engineering school, senior engineers would run voluntary courses out of working hours. One inspector, John Williams, went through engine systems in the lunch hour. We took our sandwiches and thermos flasks to his office. Sitting on the floor, eating our lunch, we studied and discussed oil, fuel and ignition systems of various engines. Two foremen, Jim England and Percy Adams, who came from Imperial Airways, ran an informal meeting once a week after work, where problems that had arisen were discussed. The enthusiasm of everyone to improve their knowledge and skill was remarkable.

There was still time for some fun. The Cheetah engine had an oil filter made up of six separate round discs of fine mesh, which were located on a central shaft. When a fitter was working on this engine for the first time, the other fitters would wait until he had refitted the filter to the engine after cleaning it, then unobserved, leave one of these discs on his bench. The fitter would find it and a worried, puzzled look would appear on his face. Thinking he had left off one of the discs when he assembled the filter, he would seize his pliers, undo the wire locking, rush to the stores for a spanner and remove the filter, only to find that it was correctly assembled. He would then hear the laughter of his mates. It was amazing how often this trick could be successfully perpetrated.

Even at this young age I had developed a dislike of needless 'bull' and bureaucracy, which led to brushes with authority. Some tools drawn from the stores were not being returned, so a ruling was made that if a fitter was unable to account for a tool, he would have to pay for a replacement.

I had drawn a drill from the stores and the tool storeman asked me to return it as they were taking stock. I could not find it and told the storeman. A couple of days later I was called into the chief storeman's office. "There is a drill signed out by you," he said, "and I understand you can't return it."

"That's right," I replied. "I can't find it, so I suppose I shall have to pay for it."

He passed me a form. "You'd better fill this in."

The form had a lot of questions on it. 'Had the tool been returned?' 'Why not?' 'Had it been broken?' 'Had it been lost?' 'If so, how had it been lost?' This I thought was a silly question, so I wrote 'Just lost', and handed back the form.

The chief storeman looked at the form. "You can't say that!" he exclaimed.

"Why not?" I replied. "I drew the drill from the stores, now I can't find it, so I shall have to pay for it."

"You can't say 'Just lost'. Can't you say you left it on your bench and when you came back from lunch it had gone?"

"No, I can't say that," I replied, "because that's not what happened."

"Well, I can't accept the form like this," said the chief storeman.

I shrugged my shoulders. "That's my answer." I left the office and went back to work. Half an hour later I went to the stores to draw a tool.

"I'm sorry, Peter," said the tool storeman, "but I've been instructed not to issue you with any tools."

I went to the foreman. "I can't get any tools from the stores; will you go and see about it?"

He came back. "That's right, you can't get any tools."

"If I can't get any tools to do my work, there is not much point in my being here, is there?" I said.

The foreman shrugged his shoulders and went into his office, so I shut my toolbox and went home. After three days I thought I had better go back, as absenteeism in wartime was taken quite seriously. No one said a word about my absence and when I went to draw tools, they were issued to me. What happened in the meantime I do not know, but I felt I had won. Later I was charged for the drill.

On a fine summer's day, the hangar was almost empty. The fitters, normally working on dozens of aircraft, had melted away. I was standing at my bench reading a newspaper, when the charge-hand came up. "Good lord, Peter, don't stand in the middle of the hangar reading a newspaper."

"Have you got a job for me?" I asked.

"No, but you are right under the Chief Engineer's office; what is he going to think if he comes out and sees you reading a newspaper?"

"If I was the Chief Engineer," I replied, "and I came out of my office and saw the hangar empty, and all the aircraft serviceable and flying, which is what they are supposed to do, I would be delighted."

"Maybe," he said, "but be a good chap and go for a walk round the airfield." So I took myself off to a quiet spot, out of sight, and finished my paper.

Soon after I joined ATA, another engineer about my age, also joined. Johnny Ratchford had been apprenticed to an aero club in Carlisle, and lost his right leg when knocked down by a car. We became great friends, a friendship that has lasted to this day - over fifty years. Johnny was a very determined young man, and in spite of an artificial leg, clambered up steps and trestles and all over aeroplanes, carried his toolbox and would have no assistance from anyone. After a short time, everyone forgot he had an artificial leg. The main trouble he had was when he joined the lads for a few beers in the evening and his artificial leg remained sober!

I had never flown, and I badgered the foreman for a flight. Eventually he got me one when an Anson was on a routine test flight. The pilot told me that my job was to wind the undercarriage up and down. This involved about 100 turns on a small crank beside the pilot's seat.

After we took off, I started to raise the undercarriage. As I was sitting in the right-hand seat, I had to wind with my left hand. It was very awkward and we reached the top of the climb before it was retracted. This was the first chance I had to look around.

The pilot carried out his test routine, and then descended back to the airfield. "OK," he said, "lower the undercarriage."

I started to wind away, my head buried in the cockpit, while we descended and joined the airfield circuit. I was able to look around again on the landing. I was so busy during this short flight that I could not recall any sensation of flying. I think I was only taken up by the pilot to relieve him of the arduous task of raising and lowering the undercarriage!

The first helicopter I saw, an early Bell, arrived and flew up and down the tarmac in front of the hangar, looking for a place to put down, like a car looking for a parking slot. I laughed with delight at its antics, so new and amusing.

Then one of our aircraft crashed, which was not so amusing. The crash bell sounded and from the hangar door, I saw a column of black smoke rising outside the airfield boundary. The fire tender and ambulance were racing across the airfield. A Fairchild Argus had crashed after take off, killing all four pilots on board, one of them a young woman.

Going to lunch later I passed the sick bay as the ambulance was unloading the bodies, lying on stretchers covered with blankets. It was the first time I had been close to death and it gave me a sad feeling.

Another crash occurred, but with a happier ending. A Halifax bomber was seen approaching the airfield, obviously intending to land. It was returning from a raid and was in trouble. White Waltham was not a large airfield and only had a grass surface. On landing it overshot the boundary and came to rest on the far slope of the railway cutting. Out rushed the fire tender and ambulance and a lot of people to help the crew.

All the crew jumped out and shouted that there was still a bomb aboard. Those about to be brave jumped into an air raid slit trench - including me, to watch events. When nothing happened for some time we all went back to work. Next day the RAF came and salvaged the aircraft. It was exciting at the time.

The war was ebbing and flowing. Battles in North Africa, Pearl Harbour, the sinking of the *Repulse* and *Prince of Wales*, the loss of Singapore, the invasion of Burma. And the air-raids over England.

While I was home one night, the air-raid siren went. We

watched the searchlights weaving over the sky. Then the sky lit up, and every few minutes a big flash occurred. London must be having a bad time we thought. The all-clear went, but the glow in the sky continued, with flashes every now and then. We could not understand this as the all-clear had sounded, but eventually went to bed. A single track railway line went from Farnham to Guildford. Apparently an ammunition train was in a siding at a little village called Tongham. A bomber had jettisoned its bombs and by Murphy's Law had hit the train.

Things then changed for the better. The Battle of El Alamein, the invasion of North Africa and Italy, and then D-Day and the invasion of Europe. The bombing of Germany had built up. Bomber streams, hundreds of aircraft, would sometimes join up over Maidenhead, before setting course for Germany. Gliders, towed by Dakotas and Halifaxes passed over on their way to Arnhem.

The flying bomb (Doodle Bug) arrived. One landed half a mile from where I was living, luckily in an open field, but it shook the house and rattled the windows. Then people coming to work from London talked of big explosions, without any warning. The V2 rocket had arrived. The Allied advance in Europe captured the launching sights of these weapons and soon the war in Europe was over.

With the end of the European war ATA was disbanded. They wanted to have an Open Day at White Waltham, to show their war work to the public, with a static and flying display. The flying display was not allowed, but as ATA had so many contacts with aircraft manufacturers and their test pilots, an unofficial display was arranged.

Various test pilots 'just happened' to be over White Waltham at a particular time on that day and put their aircraft through their paces. The pilot of a Mosquito put on a unique display. He did a low pass over the crowd with one engine stopped and the propeller feathered. Then he swooped over the crowd again with both engines stopped and both propellers feathered! As he climbed away a voice in the crowd remarked, "I hope his battery terminal does not fall off." (The propeller is unfeathered by an electric motor.)

Now I gave some thought to my future in civil aviation.

Leaving ATA, I joined Flight Refuelling at Staverton airfield, near Gloucester, where several ex-ATA engineers had found jobs, including Johnny Ratchford. Flight Refuelling operated Avro Lancasters carrying out aerial refuelling trials under government contract. This was Sir Alan Cobham's company. Cobham had pioneered aerial refuelling before the war, when he ran his flying circus, and it had got to the development stage. With the aid of navigational equipment developed during the war, it was now a practical proposition for two aircraft to meet in most weather conditions and carry out refuelling.

The system used at this time was rather primitive, but effective. Later it was improved by the probe and drogue method. The tanker aircraft would fly behind and below the receiver aircraft, which let out a line with a sinker weight attached. The tanker fired a harpoon with a line attached which intertwined with the receiver line. The line was wound in by the tanker and attached to the delivery hose.

The receiver wound the hose in and connected it to its fuel system. The tanker then rose above the receiver and the fuel flowed by gravity into the receiver's fuel tanks. With refuelling completed, the hose was wound back into the tanker and the lines disconnected.

Sometimes things would go wrong. The sinker weight would fall off or the lines break. On one occasion the clutch failed on the hose drum and the hose wound out and disappeared over the Gloucestershire countryside!

When these incidents happened, the old hands who had been with Cobham in the pre-war circus days would wander round the hangar muttering; "And they tell us the circus days are over."

One day there was a visit by Cobham and several Ministry officials. A Lancaster was parked on the taxiway and they were all standing by it in deep discussion. Cobham was a keen gardener and the areas around the hangars were landscaped with nicely cut lawns and shrubs.

A tractor driver, a real Gloucester lad, nicknamed Cobley Coo, could not get past, so he drove his tractor on to the grass. He was stopped and reprimanded by Cobham. As he walked back to his tractor he was heard to grumble, "What do they expect me to do, carry the bloody thing across?"

Many parts of the Lancaster that needed frequent inspection were covered with fabric strips or patches, held on with aircraft dope. We had a boisterous inspector who delighted in removing these patches with a little scenario. He would call out in a deep voice, “Take ’em down! Take ’em down!” He would change to a falsetto voice, “No! No! Not that!” In a deep voice again, “Take ’em down! Take ’em down!” then he would rip off a fabric patch which made a noise similar to the ripping of female underwear.

He loved to do this when one of the women office workers was walking across the hangar. The more mature ladies would give as good as they got. “Yah, you and whose army?” But the younger girls would flee, blushing, back into the office. Today, I suppose this would be called sexual harassment!

I had now got my aircraft engineer’s licence. The atom bomb brought the war with Japan to an end. The need for aerial refuelling in that war theatre ceased, together with the government contract. I was made redundant.

4

A Licensed Aircraft Engineer in Jersey

Answering an advertisement in *Flight* magazine from a charter company in Jersey, for a licensed aircraft engineer, I applied and was offered the job.

Air Transport Charter (CI) Ltd., had four ex-service directors. One an army captain, one a major, a naval commander and a wing commander. When all four directors visited the hangar the cry would go out, "Look out, here come Combined Operations!"

The company had only been operating for a few months when I joined and I found that I was the only licensed engineer. There were two ex-RAF fitters, both local lads, Maurice Holly and Jock Paignal. There was also another man called Charles Wacket-Evans, who had the title of Chief Inspector, but held no engineer's licence. He was a pleasant, extrovert type and a bit of a 'bull' artist. He told me that he had applied for his licences but the Air Registration Board considered him too well qualified to be given one!

The company expanded rapidly to five D.H. Rapides and three Douglas Dakotas. Both the engineering and flying staff increased and a chief engineer, A.P. Hunt arrived, holding a fistful of licences.

Charles, with no licence, did not fit into the engineering organisation, so he had the job of going to government surplus auctions buying spares and equipment.

Most of his buys were very good, but sometimes he got carried away with his bidding. Opening one box we found it contained fuel gauges for a Douglas Boston bomber. "Charlie," we said, "we are operating Douglas Dakotas, not Douglas Bostons."

"Oh," said Charlie, "it was only £5 for 50 gauges, it was so cheap I couldn't resist it and they might come in useful."

In the hangar Charlie was facetiously referred to as Charles 'Bucket' Evans.

The national airlines had the monopoly of flying scheduled services, the other operators could only fly charter flights. The whole aircraft had to be chartered by someone, who could then sell individual seats. ATC ran services from Jersey to the mainland; although they were supposed to be charter flights they ran to a company schedule and individual seats were sold. To conform to the regulations someone had to sign the charter form. Along with other engineers, office girls and hangar sweepers, I chartered an aircraft on many occasions.

Jersey was a pleasant island on which to live after the austerities of wartime England, and in spite of having not long been liberated, had a holiday atmosphere about it. Nearly all the ground and flying staff were young and new to civil aviation and we had a lot of fun. I had an old Hillman tourer; it was big and roomy and could carry seven or eight bodies carousing around the island sampling Mary Ann ales. Four of us, all young, vocal and sure of ourselves had a long lunch in a seaside restaurant, well lubricated with wine. As the meal progressed the conversation got more animated, covering our views on religion, politics and life in general. We ended up as the last customers, except for an elderly couple sitting at a nearby table. While making a boisterous departure the lady remarked to us: "Thank you for giving us such an entertaining lunch, we've listened to your conversation, absolutely fascinated."

I went with the crew to collect our first Dakota from Scottish Aviation at Prestwick airport. Scottish Aviation must have converted hundreds of ex-military Dakotas for airline use.

New aircraft, such as the Vickers Viking, were only coming into service slowly, and many airlines all over the world were starting up and using ex-military aircraft. The hangar was full of aircraft with the insignia of many companies. Ethiopian Airways had a flamboyant colour scheme, with the 'Lion of Judah' painted on the tail. The figure was hand painted by an artist and spread over both the fin and rudder. I wondered what they would do if they had to change a rudder. Fly out the artist to match it up with the fin, I suppose!

With the arrival of the Dakotas, charter flights started to Europe, the Middle East and Africa. As the company had no depots overseas all ground handling had to be done by the crew or agents. So in addition to the pilot, co-pilot and radio operator, they carried an engineer, whose job was to refuel the aircraft and fix or arrange to be fixed, any defects that occurred en route. It says something for the design of the Dakota and for the standard of maintenance of the companies I flew with over several years, that I never experienced any serious trouble.

I flew on many of these charters, and as it was my first experience of life outside England, many impressions were made on my mind: the different food; the taste of butter made from goat's milk; the heavily chlorinated water of Malta; journeys to and from African airfields in dilapidated taxis, the African driver clashing the gears and constantly sounding the horn; the overpowering heat after a midday refuelling stop and the noise of cicadas in the night.

I recall cool, smooth night flights after turbulent daytime flights over the desert. Driving through Uganda villages, lush with greenery, with almost the atmosphere of an English village. Refuelling at night on desert airfields, I would watch Arabs walk out of the darkness of the desert - from where, and disappear into the darkness - to where? At isolated African airfields, immigration and customs officers sat at fold-up tables in front of thatched, open sided terminal buildings. When the aircraft departed, they folded the tables, put their papers and rubber stamps into battered cases and left the airfield empty and sleeping in the sun.

My first flight was to Brest to pick up cauliflowers for the English market. The pilot was Don Greenhalgh, the Chief Pilot. We left Brest in the evening, bound for Croydon. Soon afterwards the radio failed, luckily it was a clear starlit night. With the aid of an aeronautical map, I checked our progress along the French coast by the morse flashes from the lighthouses. We arrived over Jersey at about 11 o'clock. "Now to wake someone up," said Don as he made a low pass over the house of the Traffic Manager, with the landing lights on. Circling the airfield we saw lights on the road, and then lights came on in the hangar and offices. As there was bright moonlight, Don landed without waiting for a flare path. The radio engineer was fetched and soon the radio was repaired and we went on to Croydon. An interesting first flight. The next charter was to West Africa. The band of the Gold Coast, now Ghana, was returning home after a ceremonial visit to London. We flew across Europe and down the West African coast. One refuelling stop was at Villa Cisneros, a desert airstrip and a Beau Geste fort in a Spanish colony. The commander invited us to stay, but we had no time to stop. I am sure he would have liked some company for a brief time, living in such an isolated outpost. A priest, dressed in white and carrying a cross came and blessed the aircraft.

I saw little of Africa from the ground on our journey down the West Coast. On the night-stops we arrived late and left early, only having time to eat and sleep. Only the humid oppressive heat registered with me. After leaving Dakar, the desert gave way to savannah type countryside. I looked down on villages of round straw huts, surrounded by thorn fences to keep the cattle safely in at night or maybe to keep the lions out! Then turning east towards Accra this became thick tropical forest.

We spent a day in Accra, before the flight home. It seemed a pleasant town at that time, full of colonial type houses with cool verandahs, green lawns and lush vegetation. We bargained with the local traders and I bought a pair of bookends, the bust of a man and a woman, carved from local wood, which now prop up my books. With the advent of air travel the quality of local crafts has declined and the price has risen. There is now no time to inspect goods closely or haggle too long over the price.

We made five trips to Villafranca in Northern Italy to pick up fruit and vegetables. I was asked by the foreman of the loading gang if I would bring back some articles which were in short supply in Italy, such as razor blades, lighters, elastic and a glass cutter. I used to set up a little stall under the wing of the aircraft and barter for silk stockings and bottles of wine. On one trip we had to night stop in Verona and I was amazed how prosperous it appeared in spite of the shortage of mundane articles. The town was full of Lambretta scooters and both the men and women were smartly dressed, as if they had all bought new clothes that day. What shops I saw seemed to be full of high class goods. Such a change from post-war austerity England.

Collecting early strawberries from Valencia, in Spain was

another charter. We stopped overnight and the agent took us for a drink in a café. During the conversation the pilot asked him about the civil war. The agent looked distressed. "Ooh, we don't talk about that," he said. I was not sure whether he was afraid of Franco's police or if it was too frightful to talk about,

In the hotel no one spoke English, so we ordered our meal by signs and drawings. I have found in my travels, that providing people are 'sympatico' it is possible to have a simple conversation even if neither person can speak the other's language. Here I saw for the first time real poverty. People were living in huts and shacks on the river bank right next to the city.

Loading the aircraft in the morning, the captain was counting on the boxes to check his take off weight. When he called a halt there were still six boxes left on the lorry. "What about one for the crew?" he asked the agent.

"Si, si, captain," he answered, and handed over another box.

At Croydon we were to leave the aircraft there for some maintenance and take another one back to Jersey. While the crew were dealing with the agent and flying control, I moved all the overnight bags and our box of strawberries to the other aircraft. Meeting the crew in the coffee shop, the captain said, "Peter, we are one box short in the consignment." I told him that I had put our gift box in the other aircraft. This was a ticklish situation for if we went and fetched it, it would look like stealing. We decided to keep quiet and put it down to a mistake in the loading. I do not know if this was a genuine mistake in Spain or a bit of sharp practice.

One of the company's contracts was to fly out spares and equipment for the Iraq Petroleum Company (IPC). A pipeline ran from oil fields in the Persian Gulf and Kirkuk to terminals at Tripoli in the Lebanon and Haifa in Palestine. At intervals on the long pipeline were booster stations to help the oil on its way. These were stuck out in the desert and serviced by a fleet of D.H. Dove aircraft based at Tripoli and operated under contract with Airwork. Many of our flights terminated at Tripoli, but sometimes we took freight to H3 (one of the pumping stations), Baghdad, Basra and Bahrain Island.

On night stops in Tripoli I would have a few beers with Johnny Ratchford who was now working there for Airwork. I also met Bob Pearson, who later was to be my house building partner in

Australia. Tripoli was a pleasant town, with tree-lined streets, an interesting 'souk' and open air cafés. The cafés were always full of men playing backgammon, sipping Turkish coffee and smoking hookahs, and I suspect completing a few business deals.

On one occasion a problem was expected with the return load from Tripoli, affecting the aircraft centre of gravity, and possibly causing a nose heavy situation. An empty 45 gallon drum was put on board, and if necessary this could be filled with water and positioned to counteract the forward load. As it happened this load did not materialise, so we flew back with the empty drum and four crankshafts for repair. These items were secured by light rope to stop them moving around.

Flying back over the Mediterranean Sea towards Malta, the captain, Don Greenhalgh, was at the navigator's table, the aircraft on automatic pilot with the co-pilot keeping watch. I went into the cabin to have a sleep.

I was woken up by severe turbulence, lifting me off the floor a few feet and dumping me down again. I looked out of the window and saw we were flying in swirling black cloud. I could see the wings flexing and all the aluminium panels were drumming like flexing biscuit tin lids.

It got worse and I had to hang on to the side of the fuselage to avoid being thrown around. Then the drum broke loose from its mooring and started floating about in the fuselage. This was getting serious. I tried to grab the drum and tie it down again, which resulted in me floating around the fuselage, clutching the drum, alternately hitting the floor and the roof, while the aircraft bucked all over the sky! I thought: "If the crankshafts get loose and start flying around too, they could do serious damage to me and even punch holes in the fuselage skin." Then the turbulence decreased and I was able to lash the drum down. Looking out of the window I saw we had broken cloud and were flying at about 2,000 feet over a stormy sea, in heavy rain.

A few minutes later the radio operator, Bert Gladwin, came back to see if I was all right. "We thought you had jumped overboard." he grinned. "The rear door warning light came on." Bert always had an odd sense of humour!

Apparently we had flown into a turbulent line squall at 8,000 feet. The co-pilot did not recognise it and took no avoiding action. Don Greenhalgh had to struggle back to his seat, disengage the automatic pilot, and ease the aircraft down through the storm. It was so turbulent that he could not strap himself in, and had to fly the aircraft with one hand, while holding on to his seat with the other. We landed at Malta with a very frightened engineer on board. Before we flew on the next morning I had a good look over the aircraft for damage, but it had stood the test very well.

When the engineers in the hangar heard of my predicament, floating around the fuselage, clutching a barrel, they thought it was the joke of the year!

Soon after this Johnny Ratchford and Bob Pearson, having finished their contracts in the Middle East joined ATC in Jersey. Johnny did several charter flights with the deputy chief pilot, John Wright, called Wilbur, of course.

Wilbur was a very experienced pilot having been on the trans-Atlantic ferry service in the war. Whereas Don Greenhalgh was a natural pilot, Wilbur tended to fly by the book. He loved flying in bad weather and looked on it as a challenge.

Johnny was on a charter to the Middle East with Wilbur. Leaving Tripoli, in the Lebanon for Malta they encountered very strong head-winds. Abeam the RAF staging post at El Adem, it looked as if they would be short on fuel by the time they reached Malta, but Wilbur decided to go on. Arriving over Malta all the fuel gauges were registering zero. To the crew's consternation Wilbur, instead of asking the control tower for a straight-in approach, carried out a full procedure circuit. When Johnny refuelled the aircraft next morning, he found there was only a few gallons of petrol left. The finger-biting was justified.

I was on another flight with Wilbur. The co-pilot was Sam Pover and I think he may have saved my life. We landed at Marseilles to refuel. It was a dirty night, rain and low cloud. After refuelling, I found Wilbur and Sam having a serious discussion about the weather. Looking at the route forecast, with my limited knowledge, it seemed awesome, and Sam was not happy at all.

In spite of the weather Wilbur wanted to go on. Eventually Sam said, "Well, you can go on if you like, but I'm staying here." As the aircraft could not be flown without the co-pilot, we stayed the night.

When we got to Croydon the next day, we found the weather had been terrible that night. Storms, snow and low cloud. One of the newspaper planes, that used to fly in all weathers, had crashed and killed the crew.

A year or so later, tragically Wilbur was killed when he crashed taking off in a snowstorm. He fought the weather once too often.

Several engineers were in the Chief Engineer's office doing paper work. The Chief Engineer had left for a meeting in St. Helier and I was working at his desk. Leaning back in the chair and putting my feet on the desk I declared, "I think I will be Chief Engineer for the day. You are a lazy, incompetent lot and you are all sacked." Just then the door opened and the Chief Engineer came in for his brief-case. I took my feet down and rather sheepishly returned to my work. He said nothing at the time, but he was overheard to say to someone, "And there was Peter Charles sitting in my chair with his feet on my desk, like an Eastern potentate!" For a long time I was referred to as the Grand Vizier!

One of the pilots was well up in the Salvation Army, and as he was going to a meeting in London after flying the passengers to the mainland, he wore his Salvation Army uniform, One of the passengers was heard to remark, "This is the first time I have been flown by a real sky pilot!"

The engineers' pay structure had become haphazard as the staff increased and there were several anomalies, so we asked the Chief Engineer if it could be reviewed. Discussion went on between the directors and the engineers through the Chief Engineer. Although he had the knowledge and the authority he took no active part, acting only as an intermediary. All this took a long time. It could have all been settled by an hour's meeting of all parties, but the directors, being military types, were probably not used to dealing directly with 'the other ranks', and it was making me a bit bolshie.

It came round for my turn to be duty engineer for the early morning departures. I had been out on the town with my pals the night before and was not feeling my best when the alarm clock went off. Being both bolshie and under the weather, I turned the alarm off and went back to sleep. Eventually I arrived at the airfield an hour late, to find the aircraft on the tarmac, passengers waiting in the lounge and the traffic officer Les Cotteral, and the pilot Sam Pover, waiting in the office. "Where the devil have you been?" they asked impatiently. I muttered something about being fed up with the company and went out to check the aircraft. Returning to the office to sign the Daily Certificate of Safety for

Flight, they both took me on one side. "We don't know what your argument is with the company," said Sam, "but we have both got up early to do our job, the passengers are now late and no doubt have business to do on the mainland. You have messed up everyone's day, all innocent people who have nothing to do with your disagreement with the company." After seeing the aircraft off, I went for a coffee in the airport restaurant and thought about what Sam had said and realised he was right.

I had upset everyone's day because I was solely involved in my own problems and was not attending to my job. As this came from my own contemporaries, with whom I drank and played darts, it had far more effect on me than a reprimand from the boss.

I resolved that in future, whatever I thought of a company or a boss, if I was taking his wages I would do my job. If things got too bad, rather than be bolshie, I would leave. This view I maintained from then on, and I can say that I could always go back to a company I had left. I was starting to grow up!

A good thing about civil aviation at that time was that if you wanted to be a pilot, a navigator, a radio operator or an engineer, obtained the necessary qualifying experience and passed the examination, then you could be issued with a licence. No one was interested in what school you went to, or how many 'O' or 'A' levels you had. If you could prove that you could do the job you got the qualification.

Johnny and I decided it was time we moved on and got experience on more modern aircraft. With civil aviation starting up again there were plenty of jobs. The world was our oyster!

We decided to leave Jersey, and while having a little holiday see what the world had to offer us.

5

In the Footsteps of Rhodes

Reading *Flight* magazine, starting at the back where all the jobs were advertised, I saw that British West Indian Airways required 'A' and 'C' licensed engineers for their Viking fleet. I did not have the Viking on my 'A' licence, but at that time a type could be added to the licence if it was already endorsed with a similar type, providing the engineer attended the manufacturer's course and passed their examination. It was only possible to attend this course if you were sponsored by an operator.

As I had a similar type on my 'A' licence, the Dakota, I applied to BWIA, pointing out that if they sponsored me on a Viking course, I could get it added to my licence and meet their requirements. I would attend the course at my own expense and realised that any offer of a job would be dependent on my obtaining the licence.

In due course I got a letter from the Personnel Officer of BOAC subsidiary companies asking me to come to London for an interview. At their offices in Victoria I was ushered into a large room, where the man behind an imposing desk introduced himself as the Personnel Officer. He glanced down at a paper on his desk. "You are applying for the vacancy for an 'A' and 'C' licensed engineer with British West Indian Airways."

"That's right."

"Have you an 'A' and 'C' licence on the Viking?"

"I have a 'C' licence on the Viking and I have an 'A' licence on a similar type."

"But you have not got an 'A' licence on the Viking now?"

"No, but as I explained in my letter, if I could be sponsored on a course at Vickers, I could easily get it, but I cannot get on a course unless I am sponsored by an operator. And, of course, I understand that any offer of a job would depend on my obtaining this licence."

He shuffled his papers around again. "But it says here they require 'A' and 'C' licensed engineers on the Viking and you have not got an 'A' licence."

I suspected that in spite of his title, he had little knowledge of the licensing system. I stood up. "I don't seem to be getting my point across to you, so we are both wasting our time. Good afternoon."

I thought then that there was probably an overworked chief engineer in the West Indies being baulked from getting staff by a man sitting in an office 4,000 miles away, who had no detailed knowledge of his requirements. It was the first time I had come across this trend, where job applicants are interviewed by personnel officers and not by the person they would have to work with and under. Later I heard of a case where the applicant was interviewed and accepted by the union shop steward!

During this time Johnny and I kept in touch by telephone, discussing the job market and the conversation would go something like this:

"Johnny, I hear ------- Air Services are looking for engineers."

"Oh, no, you know who their chief engineer is - that idiot -----"

"Is that where he has got to. What about ------ Airways?"

"I heard they have problems with the Air Registration Board and they may have to close down. There is ------- Charter."

"That's run by that awful bloke ----- "

"Is it? We want to keep well away from there!"

And so the conversation would go on. When Johnny put the telephone down his father lowered his paper and said, "It appears to me that you and Peter Charles are the only sensible people in the aircraft industry."

I reminded Johnny of this about forty years later. "I'm not so sure that it does not still apply!" he remarked.

By chance I met an engineer from Central African Airways on leave in England. His name was Tom Iveson - later he was killed when a Viking lost a wing in Africa. He extolled life in Rhodesia

(Zimbabwe); wonderful climate and wide open spaces, and suggested I applied for a job. It sounded good to me and I told Johnny about it. We both wrote and were offered jobs.

Johnny flew out in a D. H. Dove being delivered to the airline. I followed later on CAA's scheduled service, after attending a Viking course and getting it added to my licence. Much of the route out was familiar to me from previous charter flights, but I had never been to Rhodesia.

Salisbury (Harare) reminded me of a wild west American town. The streets were wide, buildings low and the sidewalks covered. The cars parked nose to the pavement, and you could imagine that not long ago horses were tied to the railings instead.

Accommodation was difficult. Hotels had to keep rooms for transient travellers, and you could not stay longer than three nights. Until we found permanent accommodation this meant continual moving, wondering whether you would end up without a bed for the night.

We soon found permanent accommodation near the airfield. It comprised two rondavels joined together to give a living-room, bedroom and a bathroom. The rondavel is an improved version of the native round hut. The walls are adobe, plastered inside and out, with a tiled floor and a conical thatched roof. Very cool and airy. They were in the garden of a house belonging to a Dutch South African who worked on the railway. He had a family of young children and the youngest, a boy of about four years old was tri-lingual; he spoke Afrikaans to his parents, Swahili to the servants and English to us, and never got them mixed up.

Central African Airways were having trouble with the Bristol Hercules engines fitted in the Viking due to incorrect power settings being used. They carried an engineer who kept a log of power settings, temperatures and pressures and also, from a chart advised the pilot the correct combination of boost and engine speed to use. He also supervised refuelling and rectified minor defects where there was no station engineer.

As we were air-crew we were sent to the tailor to be measured for uniforms. These were a gabardine tunic and slacks and a bush jacket and shorts. When we were being measured, I heard Johnny ask the tailor to make him all slacks.

I said, "What do you want slacks for in this climate, shorts are just the job?"

He looked at me with a pathetic expression on his face. “Don’t be an idiot,” he said, “how can I wear shorts?”

I had forgotten all about his leg!

As well as flying on the Vikings, I was sent on other jobs. One was to relieve the station engineer at Blantyre in Nyasaland (Malawi), while he was on leave. It was an easy number, re-fuelling and turning round a daily service from Salisbury. There was also a D.H. Rapide, with a resident pilot, who flew to Beira in Portuguese East Africa (Mozambique). As there were only three services a week he had plenty of spare time which he put to good use by running several businesses, including a store and a brickworks. Due to company reorganisation he was posted back to Salisbury, which would have meant the end of his businesses, so he resigned. Certainly a case of part-time flying!

The company had a D.H. Dove fitted out for aerial photography and survey work. It was sent to the Sabi valley and I went along as engineer. It was not an arduous assignment as the light suitable for aerial photography was restricted to a few hours a day and only if the weather was favourable. We were based at a landing strip on a sugar plantation in the valley. The manager’s house, where we stayed, was built on the only hill for miles. Here, too, the guest bedrooms were rondavels in the grounds.

Reached by a narrow path down the side of the hill was the best lavatory I have ever sat on. Built over a crack in the side of the hill, many feet deep, it needed no servicing. It faced east and had no door, so you sat there in the warm morning sun, looking over the valley to the faraway hills in Mozambique. Most civilised.

There was no water supply on the hill, so a tank drawn by two oxen, came each day to replenish the domestic water tank. A little work, plenty of sunshine, a cold beer in the cool of the evening, a congenial way to spend a month.

Life was pleasant in Rhodesia and living was cheap. Tobacco, as it was locally grown, was very cheap. Two shillings would buy a carton of 25 cigarettes or a quarter pound packet of pipe tobacco. We had a favourite restaurant in Salisbury which served a magnificent mixed grill with everything in it. Chops, steak. liver, kidney, tomatoes, mushrooms and chips. When at home we lunched on local Roquefort cheese, fresh pineapple and new bread and butter.

Coming home one day I found Johnny sitting on his bed looking glum and worried. "A bolt in my knee joint has broken," he said, "and I can't walk." He rolled up his trouser leg and I examined the joint. One of the pivot bolts had sheared and the threaded part was still in the leg.

"Wait here," I said. "I'll go to the airfield and get some tools."

"I wasn't thinking of going anywhere," said Johnny with a rueful grin.

When I got back I drilled a hole in the centre of the broken bolt and with the tang end of a file managed to unscrew it. Back at the airfield I walked into the foreman's office and said to Ian Hepburn, "Johnny's broken his leg."

"Oh, I am sorry," he said, "which hospital is he in?"

"No, no, it's his other leg," I explained, "and he needs a bolt like this," showing him the two halves.

"Well, that's easy," he said. "Let's go down to the machine shop and see what we can do."

Half an hour later he gave me a new bolt which I fitted to Johnny's leg, and he was mobile again. The next day Ian said to him, "You've had something out of CAA that no one else has had!"

Johnny flew to England on the monthly service. On the return flight the pilot decided to take on extra fuel at Khartoum and overfly Juba, in the southern Sudan, as there was some problem on the airfield. The extra fuel, however, put him above his authorised take-off weight.

This would have gone unnoticed, but on arrival at Nairobi the undercarriage would not come down. In spite of every effort, including using the emergency system, it remained retracted and the pilot had to make a wheels up landing. During the investigation later, the pilot was questioned on how he managed to fly so far on the fuel he was supposed to carry. I gather he talked of tail winds and weak mixture cruise, but I never heard the outcome. What is known as 'Sod's law'.

The problems on the Hercules engine having been sorted out, the company decided not to carry engineers on the aircraft, but to put them out as station engineers. I was asked to go to Livingstone, near Victoria Falls. Being young and ambitious I had no desire to end up in a malaria ridden part of the country, turning round three aircraft a week, so I resigned.

Johnny was the engineer on the flight back to England on which I was a passenger. South of Juba we passed over a large herd of elephants and the pilot circled round them, giving us a wonderful bird's eye view of African wild life. I expect they are now ivory ornaments on someone's mantlepiece.

Soon after Johnny came home and married Carol, the girl he met when we were at Flight Refuelling and I was his best man.

6

The Berlin Airlift

I was due to start work with Westminster Airways at Blackbushe Airport in the New Year, but two days before Christmas the Chief Engineer, Mike Moore, asked me to come in and assist in changing a carburettor on a DC3. This job went over into Christmas Day. At lunch time Mike came up to the airfield and said, "Clean yourselves up and come home for Christmas lunch." That was my introduction to Westminster Airways where I spent a very happy and interesting two years until I went to Australia.

I had a room in the White Hart Hotel in Blackwater, which has now been pulled down and replaced with a row of shops. It was a time after the war, when people did not have much money and the pub was only busy on Saturday night and Sunday lunchtime. In the week, some evenings would go by without a single customer, and Mr Truelove, the landlord, and I would sit each side of the bar playing cribbage and buying each other halves of beer. When a customer did come in we would be quite resentful as it interrupted our game.

It became a company pub, frequented by air-crew and ground staff. This used to liven up some of the evenings. Going to my room after an evening in the bar I found that my bed was missing. After a search I discovered it, neatly made up on the back lawn. The efforts of my drinking partners trying to get the bed up two flights of stairs was hilarious.

A favourite game was fire drill. The bedrooms were on the top floor of this three storey hotel with a fire escape at the end of the passage. It consisted of a rope attached to an inertia reel. You buckled a belt round your waist, let yourself out of the window and were lowered to the ground at a steady pace.

On some evenings, as things warmed up, someone would cry, "Let's bale out of the fire escape!" Everyone would rush upstairs and jump out of the window, one after the other, then upstairs again for another go. Some of the customers must have thought us completely mad.

The Berlin Airlift was on at this time and DC3s were being withdrawn to be replaced by aircraft with a greater payload. BOAC was disposing of its fleet of Haltons (converted Halifax bombers) and charter companies were buying them to put on the airlift. Westminster Airways operated a freighter version from Hamburg and added three more as fuel tankers operating from Schleswigland, near the Danish border.

The Berlin Airlift was a marvellous operation. The minimum needs of a city of two million people were supplied by air for over 12 months. The bulk of the operation was carried out by the US Air Force, flying DC4s, under the code name Operation Vittles.

After the DC3s were withdrawn, the British operation, named Plainfare, was carried out with RAF Hastings and 25 charter companies operating mainly Halton and Lancastrian aircraft. For a time Short flying boats landed on Lake Havel in Berlin until winter froze the lake. Large and ungainly loads such as electrical generators were carried in Bristol Freighters.

When the airlift was fully operational, aircraft flew from their bases in West Germany along three narrow corridors to three airfields in Berlin. Several bases fed each corridor, so very precise navigation and timing was essential to ensure correct separation and track along the narrow corridor over East Germany.

Navigation aids developed in the war were used and the airfields in Berlin were equipped with radar for blind landings in bad weather. Landings were at two minute intervals in fine weather and at five minute intervals in bad weather.

This went on for 24 hours a day, seven days a week for over 12 months. Nothing was allowed to interrupt the flow of aircraft. If an aircraft missed its allotted take-off slot, the flight was cancelled. If it failed to land at the first attempt it was routed back to base with its load. The airfields in Berlin were kept open at all times. If an aircraft blocked the runway for any reason after landing it was unceremoniously pushed off, by bulldozer if necessary.

Soon I was sent to Hamburg, to assist in the maintenance of the Halton. Several of the engineers had been there several months looking after the DC3s and were well organised with their social life.

The engineers worked a 24 hour on, 24 hour off, shift system. Although the hours were long, the work was not hard as the aircraft were away for some hours on each sortie and usually only required a visual check and refuelling between flights.

Coming off duty at 6 am they would go back to the mess on the airfield for a few hours sleep. In the afternoon they were off into Hamburg to meet their girlfriends, returning on the early morning tram they would start another shift at 6 am. All the German workers on the early morning tram carried small identical cases holding their lunch and cigarettes. One of the engineers felt very conspicuous without a similar case, so he bought one to carry empty on these journeys.

The only currency we were allowed was BAFO (British Armed Forces of Occupation) which could only be spent in messes, canteens, and NAAFI, run by the military. The way to obtain German marks to spend in the bars and nightclubs of Hamburg was to deal in the well organised black market. BAFO notes, cigarettes and whisky were the most popular items and the exchange rate would vary from day to day and dealer to dealer. Black marketeers operated in many parts of the city and deals could be struck. Almost anything could be bought or sold.

One engineer got involved in a deal with whisky and arranged to meet his contact in a dubious quarter of Hamburg. He was uneasy entering the Hamburg underworld, a bar full of tough looking characters and had problems dealing with his black market contact. "I don't want any funny business," he threatened his contact. "I have a gun in my pocket."

"Is that so," answered the contact, "how much do you want for it?"

The company was now operating all its aircraft in the role of tankers, flying diesel oil into Berlin. I flew back to England when the freighter version operating from Hamburg returned for conversion.

The bomb doors were removed and a large oval tank, similar to that on a road tanker, was strapped into the Halton bomb bay. It protruded below the fuselage and was faired in back and front. The installation was a rush job due to the urgency of the airlift requirements and no provision was made to dump the fuel in an emergency. The Chief Pilot, Tom Freer, resigned: I believe he could not accept the lack of this safety measure in the event of a wheels-up landing.

Some months later, while refuelling at Rome on a DC3 charter, I heard someone call my name. It was Tom Freer, in the uniform of a British European Airways junior pilot. He held out his sleeve with one gold ring on it, "What do you think of this?" he said. When I last saw him he carried four gold rings.

"You seem to have gone off the Gold Standard, Tom," I remarked. It must have been difficult for an experienced pilot to start at the bottom again. BEA, like many airlines promoted on length of service, not experience.

After spending some time at Blackbushe converting Haltons into tankers I flew back to Germany, landing at the company base in Schleswigland. It was a windswept, wet, cold and desolate part of the country in winter. The crews flew for months without seeing the ground between Schleswig and Berlin.

The aircraft were dispersed round the airfield and maintenance had to be done in the open. A nissen hut acted as store, workshop and engineers' crew room. Frequent recourse to the RAF coal burning stove in the hut was needed to thaw frozen fingers.

Both the air-crew and engineers had a difficult time under these conditions. Very different from the fleshpots of Hamburg!

Tom Freer's fears became reality when, as one of our aircraft was approaching Berlin, an undercarriage light failed to indicate that one of the legs was locked down. The aircraft aborted the landing and returned to Schleswig with a full load of diesel. Although visually the leg appeared to be down, the pilot could not be sure that it was positively locked.

On the way back the engineer leaned into the bomb bay, with the second pilot holding his legs, and tried to punch a hole in the diesel tank with the aircraft fire axe to dump the oil. The tank was too strong and the axe too blunt to succeed.

A gentle landing was made in the hope that it was an electrical fault and that the leg was in fact, locked down. Luckily this was the case and the aircraft landed safely.

The difficulty was finding the fault as a test retraction had to be made. This was not possible on dispersal, but we found a hangar large enough to take the aircraft and some big hydraulic lifting jacks. But these were only just big enough to get the wheels clear of the ground when extended to their limit.

When lifted the aircraft swayed ominously. An engineer was sent into the cockpit to raise the undercarriage on the hand pump. As he pumped the aircraft swayed. "God," I thought, "if the aircraft falls off the jacks I shall be in real trouble!"

The electrician found and repaired the fault. The undercarriage was selected 'down', the wheels dropped with a thump, locked, swaying the aircraft and the green light came on. With a sigh of relief the aircraft was lowered back on to its wheels.

The turn-round time at Tegel airport in Berlin, was just long enough for the crew to get a cup of tea at the NAAFI. Finishing their tea the captain and engineer went out to the aircraft to start the engines ready for the departure time. Since they had landed other Haltons had departed and arrived.

The co-pilot was still chatting to the tea girl, when he heard the engines start. He dashed out into the dark, rainy night, rushed up to the line of aircraft and scrambled into the rear door against the slipstream of the engines. He worked his way up the fuselage to the cockpit to find a stranger sitting in his seat. "What the hell are you doing here!" he exclaimed. "What the hell are YOU doing here!" replied the occupant. He looked at the captain, who he did not recognise, and at the engineer who was a stranger. He realised then, that in the dark he had got into the wrong aircraft!

Someone composed the lyrics for an airlift song, sung to the tune of *Lili Marlene*:

Flying down to Tegel with a load of derv,
Calls for lots of courage and bags and bags of nerve,
And when we get there, so they say,
We'll have to do a GCA,
We're on the Berlin airlift, out in Germany.

With the end of the airlift many of the engineers, who had lived a hectic working and social life for several months, were glad to return to a more mundane life in England. It was rather an anti-climax flying home in the DC3 sent to collect us.

The company reverted to its pre-airlift role of charter flights with its two DC3s. Many of the flights were taking servicemen's families to Cyprus, Egypt, Aden and other areas where British troops were stationed. Some had young children, who for the first few hours sat quietly with their mothers, but as soon as they became familiar with flying, rushed up and down the gangway and jumped over the seats, turning the cabin into a children's playground.

One of the Haltons had a moment of glory as a film star in the film of Nevil Shute's book, *No Highway*. It was sold to the film company for the scene when the 'boffin' from Farnborough, Mr Honey, played by James Stewart, retracts the undercarriage of the 'Reindeer' aircraft on the ground in Newfoundland.

The film company property men came to convert a dirty old tramp into an elegant, modern airliner. They were very clever, removing the round Hercules engines and the tailplane, and replacing them with new streamlined engine nacelles and a high fin carrying the tailplane. A wooden frame was built over the square fuselage and covered in aluminium sheets, converting it into a round cabin. The sheets were nailed to the frame and close up it seemed very crude, but from a distance the nail heads were just like rivets, and it all looked real.

Electric motors were put in the nacelles, driving four-bladed, wooden propellers. As the scene was to be shot at night, the crude details would not show.

When it was finished dozens of caravans appeared and parked round the hangar, changing rooms, director's offices, workshops; they literally took over the place.

On the night of the action, the aircraft was towed to a taxiway, with an engineer in the cockpit to raise the undercarriage at the appropriate time. It had to be right, there was no second chance!

The floodlights were switched on, the cameras positioned and the electric motors turned on to rotate the propellers. Now there was a problem. The propeller blades were flat pieces of wood and when they revolved it was not possible to see them to show that the engines were running.

There was much discussion between the director, the cameramen and the technicians. The engines were stopped, and a property man painted a black strip along the leading edge of each blade. The engines were started again, and lo! you could see the disc formed by the rotating propeller. Clever, these property men.

Now all was set. The propellers turned, the cameras rolled, the engineer raised the undercarriage and the aircraft settled gracefully on its belly. A workhorse of the airlift bowed out in a moment of glory. When I saw the film, the whole scene only lasted a few seconds!

The company had a contract to service Avro Tudor aircraft operated by a new company, Dempster Airways, who flew charter flights to South Africa. This was the most modern and also the biggest aircraft I had worked on. Viewing the empty passenger cabin from the entrance door it looked as big as a ballroom.

A DC3 belonging to Pan African Air Charter was stuck at Juba, in the southern Sudan with an unserviceable engine. Dempsters were going to deliver a replacement engine on their way to South Africa. The Pratt and Whitney engine arrived late one night, with a crane and Dempster's engineering manager, Bill Meacock. The engine had to be loaded into the front freight compartment behind the cockpit. The only way in was through the crew door, which was very small and high off the ground, as the Tudor was a tail-wheel aircraft.

The engine was lifted up by the crane, but would not go through the small door. "Take off the reduction gear," said Bill. "It's got to go in."

We took off the reduction gear and offered it up again. It was still too wide to go through the door. "Take off the starter and generator," said Bill. "It's got to go in."

Again it was lifted up, but the magnetos stuck out too far. "Take off the magnetos," said Bill. "It's got to go in."

Off came the magnetos. It would now go in width-wise but was two inches too high. "Take off the top cylinder," said Bill. "It's got to go in."

We took off the top cylinder and the engine just squeezed through the door. We boxed the components we had taken off and put them in with the engine. Bill was satisfied, but I thought of the poor engineer at Juba who would have to assemble it all before he could fit it to the aircraft.

Air Vice-Marshal Don Bennett, of Pathfinder fame, bought the company's Airspeed Consul. He sent his radio engineer to fit additional radio equipment and drill holes in the fuselage for the aerials. On the day of delivery the aircraft was taken to the apron by the terminal building and I was given the job of handing it over. Our Chief Engineer, Mike Moore, told me no Certificate of Fitness for Flight could be issued, as there was no paperwork for the new radio equipment.

I went to the terminal building to meet Bennett, give him the log books and other papers and refuel the aircraft to his requirements. We went through the paperwork together and he asked for the Daily Certificate. I told him the position regarding the radio installation. There was a pause for a few seconds while Bennett went red in the face before giving his views on bureaucracy, paperwork and the pettiness of Westminster Airways. I suggested he rang the Chief Engineer and discuss the matter with him. Some compromise must have been reached as he came back in a better mood.

I checked over and refuelled the aircraft and met Bennett in the departure lounge for the final handover. A charter flight of forces families had just left and on one of the tables was a bowl of half eaten Farley's rusks. Bennett looked at it and commented, "Westminster Airways breakfast, I presume."

He asked me a few questions about the aircraft as he had not flown this type before. I offered to explain the cockpit layout to him, but he did not think it necessary. He commented, "Aviation will not have arrived until you can get in an aeroplane and fly away, just as you get into a car." On that basis aviation has certainly not arrived yet!

I stayed to watch him take off. It was an interesting meeting. Bennett was certainly one of the country's best pilots, but a difficult man to work with as he hated red tape and could do any job on an aircraft as well, if not better, than most people.

On my 25th, birthday I inherited a small legacy and decided to realise my ambition and learn to fly. I went to Fairoaks Airfield where under the instruction of Wing Commander Arthur, the Chief Flying Instructor, I was taught the technique of flying a Tiger Moth.

I found it most exhilarating, flying in an open cockpit aircraft on fine summer evenings, a warm wind blowing in my face. Wing Commander Arthur was an excellent instructor. He kept his 'patter' in the air to a minimum, restricted to brief remarks such as "Keep the wings level," or "Watch your airspeed," and on landing, "Pull the stick right back NOW!" Unless you were doing something stupid or dangerous he allowed you to sort out problems in your own time.

After practice at turning, climbing and gliding, we started on circuits. This consisted of take-off, a procedure circuit and landing off a glide approach. This exercise took about 10 minutes and called for a lot of concentration.

Take-off involved opening the throttle smoothly, keeping the aircraft straight with rudder until flying speed had built up, easing the joystick back to lift the aircraft off the ground, climbing away at the correct angle and airspeed and keeping the wings level.

At 500 feet, a gentle turn through 90 degrees. On reaching 1000 feet, another 90 degree turn on to the down wind leg. Throttle back to cruising speed and trim the aircraft for level flight. Look at the runway, and decide the point to turn towards the airfield for a glide approach.

Judging the correct time, turn the aircraft through 90 degrees, close the throttle, trim for gliding speed, then another 90 degree turn to line the aircraft up with the runway, and glide into a landing. About 10 feet off the ground, ease back on the stick, putting the aircraft into the three point attitude. As the speed decreased and the aircraft sank, pull the stick hard back. This should result in a firm three-point landing.

To a novice it all seemed to happen so quickly, as soon as you had executed one manoeuvre, it was time to start the next one. Years later after operating out of farm strips while crop spraying, if I had to land at a controlled airfield, where a procedure circuit was necessary, it seemed to take hours.

After a lesson, when I had done two or three fairly good landings, Wing Commander Arthur climbed out of the front cockpit, removed the joystick and cushions, secured the Sutton harness and said, "Now do a circuit on your own. If you are not happy with your landing, don't be afraid to open the throttle and go round again."

I was both happy and nervous as I taxied back to the end of the runway and took off. My first approach was not good, so I went round again. Perhaps I was nervous or expected perfection, but the second approach did not seem very good either, so I went round again.

This time I said to myself, "You have to get down this time, or you will be up here all evening!" With great concentration I managed a reasonable landing on the third attempt. I went home walking on air, a better 'high' than any drug addict ever achieved, I'm sure.

The only part of my instruction I did not enjoy was spinning. I only had a vague idea what to expect as we climbed to 4,000 feet. The instructor said, "I'll demonstrate a spin to you, then you can do one."

He went on, "I'll talk you through it. First we circle round and look around and below to see that no other aircraft are near us. Then we level the wings, close the throttle and ease the joystick right back. As the airspeed drops off, the aircraft stalls and we apply full rudder, the wing drops and we enter a spin."

Suddenly I was looking straight down at the ground, which was revolving very fast. I was terrified! Then the rotation stopped and we were flying straight and level. I realised that the instructor had been telling me what he was doing to recover from the spin, but I was so tense, and scared and hanging on to the seat like grim death, that I did not take in a word. "OK," he said, "climb back to 4,000 feet and do one yourself." I had not recovered enough from the shock to feel like trying one myself

With a dry mouth I said, "I didn't like that very much, would you do a few more so I can get used to it."

He chuckled, "It is rather frightening at first, but you will soon get used to it."

He did two more spins, then I did one to the left and one to the right. I had now had enough so we returned to the airfield and landed. It was the only flight I did not enjoy and since then I have never liked aerobatics.

I was now really hooked on flying, but it was expensive. Before I had done enough flying to qualify for a Private Pilots Licence I decided to emigrate to Australia. I did not get back to flying again for two years.

7

Ten Pounds Well Spent

After the war the Australian Government was trying to attract immigrants and offering passages to Australia for £10. Another engineer, Jack Bray, and I decided to apply. Having seen much of the world I was rather discontented with the austerity conditions in England. It was the best £10 I ever spent.

Having filled the application forms we were called to Australia House in London to discuss what jobs we could do in Australia. I told the interviewer that I was a licensed aircraft engineer. He pursed his lips, "Not many opportunities in that area, I'm afraid. Lots of ex-RAAF engineers have gone into the aircraft industry, so I don't think you stand much chance." He thought for a while. "There are jobs in the timber industry, I'll put you down for that, then when you get there, if you can get a job with an airline you can change."

As I felt sure that once I was in Australia, I could sort out my own job, I agreed. A few weeks later an advertisement in the daily press asked for aircraft engineers to apply for vacancies with Australian National Airways.

Their Chief Engineer was in London to interview applicants. Jack and I went along and we were both offered jobs. We were told that there was a great shortage of aircraft engineers. So much for the knowledge of the personnel officer at Australia House! I was beginning to have grave doubts about the expertise of some professionals, and further experiences through my life have done nothing to allay this view.

Jack and I left England on a cold, wintry day in January, 1951, aboard the Orient liner *Orcades*. The voyage to Australia was like a holiday cruise, except that the emigrants were in the cheaper cabins below the water line. Otherwise we had the run of the ship apart from the small first class area.

We lazed away the days drinking, sleeping and playing deck games, with the occasional dance and concert. The ship stopped at Ceylon, allowing a day ashore. We took a trip to Kandy, which had a marvellous Buddhist temple and tropical gardens. The journey was by a railway which wound its way up through hills, amid lush tropical scenery.

We berthed at Melbourne after a three week voyage and were met by the Personnel Office of ANA, a Mr Williams. He commiserated with our coming from food-rationed England, assured us that we would have plenty of food and that the national dish was steak and eggs.

I soon discovered that the steak served in most cafés was grey, tough and overcooked! This was before the New Australians - the name given to emigrants from Central Europe - arrived in any number and improved the crude culinary skills of the natives!

Australian National Airways operated a fleet of DC3s and DC4s and three Bristol Fighters. I was familiar with the DC3 and the Bristol Freighter, so I tried to work on the DC4 as often as possible. Eventually I went on a DC4 course at the company engineering school and added it to my licence.

We were housed at first in the company hostel, in adequate but spartan accommodation. It had the advantage of being at the airport, only a short walk to work. As there was a night shift, the canteen was open 24 hours a day.

Soon another engineer, Bob Pearson, arrived. We had worked together in Jersey. The hostel accommodation was only temporary and as decent accommodation was hard to find, Bob and I looked into the possibility of building our own house.

Australians were great do-it-yourself house builders, so we bought a plot of land near the airport, a set of plans and a book called *The Australian Carpenter*, which was a house builders' 'bible', and started to build. ANA ran three shifts on the maintenance section, one from 3pm to 11pm. We both got on this shift, which allowed us to work on the house every morning as well as on days off.

Most of the houses were constructed of timber, and supported on four inch square hardwood pillars, referred to as 'stumps'. raising the house two feet off the ground. There were 110 of these stumps to be sunk 18 inches deep and they all had to be level to take the floor beams.

It was summer when we started to dig the holes for the 'stumps'; the weather was hot and dry and the ground very hard. Every morning and day off we slogged away digging by hand. Our backs got sunburnt and our hands blistered, but after several weeks we got all the 'stumps' in position.

On this estate a great deal of self building was going on around us and another 'Pom' called Ernie, with whom we were friendly, decided to follow our example and took a plot nearby. He bought a caravan for himself and his wife to live in on the plot while he built his house. He was told of a man who would move the caravan for him and we set off one evening to find him. He turned out to be the sort of taciturn Australian you hear about, but do not really believe in.

He was leaning over the gate in front of his house, smoking a pipe. Ernie approached him. "I've been told you move caravans."

He looked at Ernie, took the pipe out of his mouth and said: "Yep."

"It's at Evans caravan yard in Mooney Ponds."

"Yep."

"I want it moved to the estate at Keilor, plot 58."

"Yep."

"I'm off on Friday, could you deliver it in the morning?"

"Yep."

Ernie was a bit disconcerted by this time. "That will be OK, then." Not sure whether he had got through to him.

"Yep."

"Right, see you on Friday."

"Yep."

As we walked away, Ernie was worried. "I wonder how reliable he is?" he muttered.

On the Friday the caravan arrived, the man set it up level on blocks, took his money and left, saying hardly a word.

When Ernie had settled into his caravan, he announced that he was going to dig his 'stump' holes on Saturday. "And jolly good luck to you," we both said, knowing that he was not too keen on hard physical labour. We were working on our house that Saturday, when about midday, Ernie arrived, dressed in his better clothes, saying: "Let's go and have a beer."

"Ah," we jeered. "You've soon given up. You'll never build your house this way."

"All my stump holes are dug," he said smugly. "Come on, let's go for a beer."

He had hired a man with a post-hole digger, who did the whole job in three hours! It made us sick.

"I sometimes think," commented Bob, "that lazy people are the most efficient."

Soon after my arrival I was asked to go to Broken Hill, to relieve the engineer who was going on leave. Broken Hill is a company mining town, serving Broken Hill Pty mining operations. It is in the outback semi-desert area of New South Wales, an isolated oasis set down amid dry scrubland. There is plenty of greenery in the town, kept alive with irrigation, but as soon as you pass the last house it is semi-desert.

The town has a reputation for toughness and independence. As the mines work 24 hours a day, pub licensing laws are ignored, and I was told that when a new Chief of Police arrived from Sydney and tried to stop this unruly behaviour, he was promptly ridden out of town back to Sydney!

The engineer took me to the hotel where I was staying and we had a few beers.

"I must be off now," he said, "or the missus will be after me. I'll pick you up about four and show you the drill." I went up to my room to freshen up for lunch. I put on a pair of slacks and an open neck white shirt and went down to the dining-room. It was in the centre of the hotel, with no windows except in the glass roof. The temperature outside was over 90 degrees, and in spite of several pedestal fans the temperature in the dining-room was about the same.

I sat down at a vacant table. A few minutes later a rather formidable manageress in a black dress came along. "You must wear a jacket in the dining-room," she announced. I thought this rather odd in view of the temperature and the fact that it was a typical Aussie pub.

I went to my room and put on a jacket. Then I thought, "If you wear a jacket, you should wear a tie." I returned to the dining-room, suitably dressed and was shown to a table occupied by another man. He was wearing a jacket, but on looking closer I saw he was wearing a shirt with no collar or tie, just a stud! I looked around and saw people in leather jackets, multi-coloured lumber jackets, bush jackets, no proper jackets and no ties.

This is ridiculous I thought, so I took off my jacket and hung it over the back of my chair. Several times the forbidding manageress approached, I think to reprimand me, but I gave her a fierce stare and she retreated. During my stay I always entered the dining-room in a jacket, but took it off as soon as I sat down.

After a short nap I changed into shorts and was picked up by the engineer. We went out to the airfield to turn round the last aircraft of the day. He explained the work, which was not very demanding, mainly refuelling the aircraft and an in-transit check. The facilities for servicing defects were limited. Tyre and oleo leg inflation and spark plug change about covered it.

"What union are you in?" asked the engineer.

"I'm not in a union."

"Oh, you can't work here unless you are in a union," he declared.

"What, not even for a month, relieving you?" I queried.

"No, we'll have to get you enrolled. My union has a meeting tonight. I'll take you along and get you enrolled before I go."

At the meeting I was introduced to the branch secretary, and my grave omission of not being a union member was explained. The meeting got under way with the usual routine business. Then the secretary announced: "Tonight we have a new prospective member who is relieving the ANA station engineer for a month. The engineer has nominated him, can we have a seconder; good, thank you John."

The secretary turned to me. "Do you agree to abide by the union rules?"

"Yes." I answered.

"Good. Welcome brother Charles to the Broken Hill Branch. Here is a copy of the Rule Book and if you will pay your subscription to the treasurer, that will be all."

I was now a fully paid-up member of the Smelters and Foundrymen's Union, or something like that.

I stayed on for the meeting, as I had never been to a union meeting before. It was most enlightening. Apparently Old Bill was retiring after working a particular machine for the last 25 years. Now Old Bill was a fourth class operator, but the machine was classified as third class. The discussion centred on whether his replacement should be a third class operator, or should the machine be reclassified as a fourth class machine. The discussion was still going on when I left an hour later, so I never knew the outcome, but I did wonder who was running Broken Hill Proprietary!

My duties were not very demanding so I spent plenty of time with the two ex-RAAF pilots who flew for BHP. They had a Noordyn Norseman and a Twin Beech, and flew staff to Sydney and Melbourne and to other mines operated by BHP.

Their duties were not very arduous either, so we would chat over numerous cups of tea. One day I said to them: " Why do you stay in Broken Hill? There is a shortage of pilots and you could work anywhere in the world."

They looked at me in a puzzled way. "But this is our home, we live here." I realised then however unattractive a place may be to an outsider, if you are born there and it is your home, you obviously have a strong attachment to it.

One day, Trevor, the junior pilot, looked up at some dark clouds that were forming at about 12,000 feet. "There is rain potential up there," he announced. He went on to tell me that they were involved in rain making experiments for the Australian Government.

The idea was to seed potential rain clouds with dry ice, to encourage the clouds to turn their moisture into rain, and bring rain to arid parts.

"Well, I can't do anything about it," he said. "There is no one available to throw out the ice."

I volunteered. "If you show me what to do, I'll come up with you." I fancied a flight in a Norseman, anyway.

We drove to the store and loaded crushed dry ice on to the truck and transferred it to the aircraft. There was a chute in the cabin through which the ice could be shovelled. A primitive, but effective arrangement.

We took off and climbed towards the clouds. As we got higher the temperature dropped, and that, together with a cabin full of ice, made things decidedly chilly; I was only wearing shorts and a shirt, but there was nothing I could do about it.

We climbed up level with the clouds, where Trevor flew into a big black one. He called out, "Now!" and I started shovelling ice down the chute. We flew out of the cloud and Trevor did a very steep turn to see the result. The cloud had disappeared, but there was no sign of rain. We tried several more clouds until we ran out of ice.

We glided down to the airfield and thankfully into warmer air. We had dispersed the clouds, but did not make any rain. I think any rain that fell evaporated before it reached the ground.

There was a flying club on the airfield, so I decided to pick up my flying training again, as I had gone solo in England. The club had a Tiger Moth and an instructor named Bruce, who I found was very energetic and talkative. In the air he never stopped talking.

The voice communication in the Tiger Moth is not very good, and not suitable for long detailed explanations while airborne. Bruce kept up a barrage of instructions, criticisms and complaints right round the circuit.

As soon as I got airborne he yelled, "You're drifting to port, look back, the runway is over on the right." Looking back caused me unconsciously to put pressure on the joystick. "Keep the wings level," he yelled. "Look at your airspeed, keep it at 65." I was trying to correct for drift, keep the wings level and maintain a steady climb. "You're at 700 feet," he exclaimed in an exasperated voice, "you should have started your turn at 500 feet." So it went on all round the circuit.

After a couple of circuits, I had got the feel of the aircraft again, so I unplugged the intercom when we took off and reconnected it after landing. I seemed to get round the circuit better that way and he was probably too busy talking to notice. I only had two lessons with Bruce as I did not enjoy it. Then my month was up and I returned to Melbourne.

My years in Australia were busy and rewarding. A new life in a new country; scope to increase my engineering experience and extend my qualifications; new projects such as house building and an opportunity to continue pilot training.

I read all I could about Australian history; its discovery by the early explorers, Cook, Tasman, Dampier; the days of the first convict settlements; the early Australian explorers, such as Stuart, Burke and Wills; and, of course, the early aviation pioneers,

Kingsford-Smith, P. G. Taylor and Charles Ulm.

Some English migrants tended to be critical of life in Australia, complaining of lack of history and culture. I asked one person how often he went to a concert or the theatre in England! Because the language was English and you could buy Cadbury's chocolate they expected it to be like England without the disadvantages. Australian life is as different from England as is France. The city dwellers are like city dwellers everywhere, but people in the 'outback' are warm, hospitable and generous. There are not many mean Australians, though those that are, really are mean. I once asked a work-mate for a lift into Melbourne in his car and he charged me the tram-fare! On the other hand when I was in a country town one of the residents going to Sydney for a few days, lent me his car. "Just leave it in the airport car park when you've finished with it," he said.

The Australians also have a reputation for being lazy, but this is unjust, they have a different work ethic. They are not workaholics, they think there should be time for swimming, surfing and sports, but if there is work to be done they get stuck into it, and when it is done it is down to the pub!

A favourite saying is, "Why stand up when you can sit down, and why sit down, when you can lie down!" The biggest insult you can give an Australian is to suggest that he has descended from the early convicts. But again if he calls you a bastard, it is usually meant affectionately.

There was friendly backchat between the Aussies and the Poms, though I never experienced any animosity towards us. They were very pro American, and favoured American aircraft, cars, refrigerators and equipment. I think they were right as Australian conditions were more comparable to America than England. Discussing this with an Australian of Irish descent, he remarked with typical Irish wit: "What has England ever given us, only rabbits and De Havillands!" (De Havilland's factory in Australia had designed and manufactured an abortion of an aeroplane called the 'Drover'.)

The pubs are open all day, but close at 6 o'clock. The hour before the pub closes is known as the '6 o'clock swill'. After work everyone - males only, of course, flocked to the pub for an hour's hard drinking. The bars were only for drinking, and very spartan, no chairs or any soft comforts like that. You stood, jostled by the crowd, trying to drink cold strong beer. The barman refilled the glasses from a plastic hose with a nozzle on the end, similar to a petrol pump. The noise of everyone talking was astounding. If you closed your eyes, you could imagine yourself in the Tower of Babel!

The beer had a delayed action effect. I would leave the pub quite sober, but by the time I got home I was half drunk. Collapsing on the bed I would wake up at 3 o'clock in the morning, having missed supper and the whole evening. Realising that I was losing much of my life, I cut down my visits to the pub.

Towards the end of my stay in Australia there was a move to allow the pubs to stay open until 10 o'clock. This brought strong opposition from many groups, especially the church. Dire consequences were predicted should this come about, husbands would spend all their time and money in the pub, neglecting their families, the streets would be full of drunks and no woman would be safe out at night.

New South Wales was the first state to introduce this change. I was in Sydney a few weeks later and about 8 o'clock I went into one of the larger bars. It had two long counters down each side, and the area between, as large as a small dance floor, was usually packed tight with drinkers. It was dimly lit and appeared empty. At the far end a small bar was open with about half a dozen men drinking a quiet beer. So much for the predicted mayhem!

Australians still retained some of the pioneering character of the early settlers. Being so far from Europe and America they had to be self-sufficient in many ways. Consequently they were not afraid to tackle anything, building their own houses being a typical example. This attitude influenced me and made me realise that if you were determined enough anything was possible. The attitude could be summed up with two Australian expressions, 'Let's give it a go,' and 'You've got to be in it, to win it.'

Because of this situation and philosophy ANA was very well equipped to carry out extensive repairs to their aircraft, overhaul many components and manufacture parts. When times were quiet on the maintenance side, I asked to go to another department for a few days, so I was able to work for periods in the sheet metal shop and the propeller shop.

As none of the Australians liked working on the Bristol Freighters, the English engineers were allotted to this work, under a charge-hand named Charlie Dixon. We were known as 'Charlie Dixon and his ancient Britons.'

Some time previously a wing had failed on a New Zealand Bristol Freighter due to metal fatigue. After that the centre section was 'lifed', which meant it had to be changed after a certain number of flying hours. One of the Freighters was due for a new centre section. Going into the overhaul hangar, where the work was done, I saw the foreman, standing on a trestle, knocking hell out of one of the two inch bolts attaching it to the fuselage, with a large hammer.

"Joe," I exclaimed. "What on earth are you doing?"

He looked down at me, "Bloody Pommie aircraft. Here it is, 1954, and they are still locking nuts by bashing over the end of the bolt!"

I had to sympathise with him. The DC3 built in 1936 was assembled with all self-locking nuts.

Sometimes aircraft in transit through Melbourne would arrive with a 'mag, drop'; that is some of the spark plugs were not operating. One foreman would take seven or eight engineers, complete with engine trestle, tools and a new set of 36 plugs, to renew the plugs while the passengers waited in the airport lounge.

Everyone would scramble up on the trestle, take off the cowlings, and get in each other's way. Starting to undo the plug leads and remove the plugs, the engine being hot, they burnt their fingers, dropping spanners and plugs. New plugs were fitted before all the old ones had been removed, leads were connected back on to old plugs and general chaos would exist.

When the engine had been cowled up and the scattered plugs collected it would be found that there were 35 old plugs and one new one. It was impossible to tell which plug had not been changed without removing them all again. This happened with such frequency that I used to stand back and take quiet bets that one plug would be missed. I usually won. If half the number of engineers had been put on the job, it would have been done quicker and more efficiently.

An aircraft was in the hangar with a faulty carburettor. The foreman told me to ring up stock control at the main store to locate a replacement. I gave them details of the part and they told me there was one in No. 2 store and one in No. 6 store. I went to No. 2 store. "No, mate," the storeman said, "haven't got one of those." I walked to No. 6 store. "We used to have one in stock," said the storeman, "but we haven't had one for months."

I went to the stock control office. There were a dozen special desks with built in filing systems where all the stock records were kept and brought up to date as spares were used and stock replaced. I told the man in charge that in spite of what his stock cards might say, there was no carburettor in either store. After a long search through the records and several phone calls, he finally located one.

"Sorry about this," he apologised, "but our records are several months out of date."

Looking at all the staff beavering away at this vast filing system, I said, "If that's the case," waving my arm over the office, "all this is pretty useless, you might as well all go home."

He was quite upset, and although it might have been the truth, it was a tactless thing to say.

The propeller overhaul shop only needed a small number of spares, so these were kept in the store serving the sheet metal workshop next door. The storeman found he was getting cramped for space, and as these spares were only used in the propeller shop he suggested to the foreman that he signed a requisition and took all the stock to his office.

This set into motion a chain of events that neither of them realised at the time. When the requisition arrived at the main store it showed the sheet metal store had run out of stock, so it was replaced. When these replacements arrived at the store, the storeman called to the foreman when he passed, "Hey, Bill, here are some more of your spares. The foreman signed another requisition and took them to his office. This went on until the main store ran out of stock, so more were ordered from America.

Eventually an audit showed that many more spares had been used than propellers overhauled. The foreman was asked where they had all gone. "Why," he answered, "they are all here." He opened his cupboard which was crammed full of spares.

These incidents livened up the daily routine. In the meantime the house was nearing completion, at least enough for us to move in. Having never built a house before we did not know what tolerances we could work to, so we paid particular care to get all the levels right, the walls vertical and the rooms square. When we had a problem we went to look at other houses being built to see how it was done. The workmanship in some of the houses built by professionals appalled us. One man told us that he had his house built by a professional. He bought a carpet square to fit one of the rooms and it went six inches up the wall in one corner and left a six inch gap in the other! The water people came along and dug a trench to lay the water main. A few weeks later, the gas people came along and dug up the same trench to lay the gas main!

After much persistence I finally got the maintenance supervisor to agree to my transfer to the airframe overhaul shop, as I wanted to get an engineers 'B' licence covering major repair and overhaul of airframes. In due course I sat and passed the examination. Shortly afterwards I was promoted to the inspection dept. This gave me great scope as it opened up all the departments and workshops to me.

However, it did have its problems. I was called to the Chief Inspector's office. The main stores was falling down on its job to identify incoming stock with a batch number. All aircraft spares have to be identified as they pass from manufacturer to the time they are fitted to the aircraft. In the event of a defect leading to an accident its history can be traced back, even to the manufacturer of the basic material.

Parts were leaving the main store without this information on the label attached to the part. To rectify the problem an inspector was to be put in the store to double check that this procedure was being carried out and I was selected. I did not want to be a storeman, it all sounded very boring.

"This is a case of someone in the stores not doing their job," I protested, "it's the Chief Storekeeper's job to rectify this." My protests were in vain; it had to be done. "What happens if I don't do my job, will you put another inspector behind me to check my work?" I asked. After much argument, I had to accept the situation, but I was promised that it would only be for a month. It was a boring month, but I had some compensation because I resumed my pilot training.

8

Learning to Fly

The Technical Manager of ANA, Don Stewart, was a keen pilot and a qualified flying instructor. The owners of ANA, the Holymans, generously donated some Wacket C6 trainers, so the staff could learn to fly. Under Don's instigation a club called the Aircraft Industries Flying Club was formed and operated from Moorabbin Airport.

It had no paid staff, relying on volunteer instructors and engineers. It had the backing of the airline facilities, such as lecture rooms and a link trainer. A good deal of the overhaul and repair work was carried out in ANA workshops at nil or low cost. In this way flying fees were kept low and I was able to learn to fly out of wages, which was impossible in England.

The Wacket C6 trainer was designed by Wing Commander L.J. Wacket and produced by the Commonwealth Aircraft Corporation during the war. A small wooden aircraft, like a small Harvard, it was used as an elementary trainer. It had a Warner Scarab radial engine, constant speed airscrew and flaps. Quite sophisticated for an elementary trainer.

At every opportunity I went to Moorabbin Airport and started to do 'circuits and bumps' again. Of all the flying sequences I found landings the hardest, right up to the end of my flying days, in spite of thousands of landings, it was always the least polished part of my flying. Rarely did I accomplish what is commonly called a three point 'greaser'.

Don Stewart was a good instructor. As well as teaching the

technicalities, he also taught a philosophy of flying. Like any activity flying had certain risks such as bad weather or an engine failure. He used to lecture us constantly on the need to assess a situation quickly and to select the action with the least risk. What he termed a calculated risk.

If a young, enthusiastic pilot showed signs of over-confidence soon after he had gone solo, Don would give him instruction in aerobatics. "I know very well," he said, "that one day he will sneak off and try a loop or a roll, and if he is not used to the forces and unusual attitudes he might find himself in, he will become disoriented and panic. At least if he has some experience of finding himself upside down, it may save him from killing himself."

He also taught us how to do safe 'beat-ups'. These are frowned upon and are illegal, but every pilot will show off to his girlfriend at some time. Don told us to examine the area for obstructions, especially wires. He warned us not to pull up towards rising ground; not to fly straight at buildings or trees, as a misjudged pull up or an engine failure could result in hitting them. "You can do a very impressive beat-up without endangering yourself or those on the ground," he emphasised, "and you will live to pay the fine!"

I was having some airwork instruction one afternoon, when the weather deteriorated and we could not continue. "Now," said Don, "this is just the situation where you might have to make a precautionary landing in a field."

Heavy, dark clouds were down to 300 feet, it was raining hard and the light was not very good. I had been instructed in precautionary landings on the airfield so I knew the technique, but in an emergency the only fields might be small and have an unknown surface, so it is essential to land slowly. The approach must be accurate to ensure getting in first time, as conditions may not allow a second chance.

The technique is to approach at a low airspeed, in a nose up attitude, under lots of power. The airspeed is controlled with the elevator and the rate of descent with the throttle and the aim is to land just over the fence in the three-point attitude and roll only a short distance.

"Pick a field," said Don, "and make your approach; don't land, but when you know you can, open up, and go round again for another try."

These conditions were not simulated, they were almost real. I did several approaches, some better than others. It was very good experience. After the last approach Don said: "OK, fly back to the airfield." By this time I had no idea of the direction of the airfield. "Fly 260 degrees," said Don. I crept back towards the airfield on this course under low cloud and after a few minutes Moorabbin Airfield showed up. We had only been about three miles away!

I passed the test for my Private Pilot's Licence and with several other members, all younger than me, started to build up hours for a Commercial Pilot's Licence.

The club had begun instruction courses at country towns. At week-ends an instructor would fly to Ararat, Swan Hill or Deniliquin, and this was a good opportunity for pilots to build up hours, flying the aircraft with the instructor as passenger.

These trips were either free or at low cost and were good social occasions. The members in these country towns were very hospitable and Saturday nights were party nights with a barbecue in someone's garden.

Strolling through Deniliquin on a Sunday morning, the town was deserted, not a soul in sight. Passing one of the hotels, which by law was closed on Sunday, I noticed a steady hum coming from the building, rather like the noise of a beehive. I walked round the back, found a door open, and went down the passage towards the source of the noise. On opening the door, the noise increased tenfold. Half the male population of Deniliquin, including the local policeman, were supping ale with great gusto. Needless to say, I joined them!

With three other pilots, I was studying for the written examination for the Commercial Pilot's Licence. It consisted of papers on navigation, meteorology, theory of flight, theory of engines and air law. They were not difficult, but you had to be quick and accurate in the navigation paper. Whenever we got together we would try and identify cloud formations, predict the weather, and test each other on air law.

We did a good deal of 'hangar flying' in the local pub, giving a 'bootful' of rudder, 'hauling' back on the stick and 'banging' the throttle open. While we were building up hours we also started training for an assistant instructor's rating, which we would take at the same time as the commercial licence. This involved learning the instructor's 'patter', explaining to future pupils various sequences, while demonstrating them in the air.

At his first lecture Don started by saying: "I want to emphasise to you all that you do not haul, kick, shove or bang anything. You ease the throttle open, you ease the stick back for take-off, you ease on aileron for a turn." He had obviously overheard our line-shooting!

We had to stand up at evening lectures and explain a flying sequence as if we were talking to a pupil in the air. The 'patter' had to be concise and to the point. No 'ums' and 'ahs'. Don would guide and correct us until we got the 'patter' right. We also went through this 'patter' in the air, taking turns to be instructor and pupil.

At this time Don himself was aiming to take a higher instructor's rating, which involved advanced aerobatics. He had one of the Wackets at Essendon Airport during the week and used to practice after work. As I hated aerobatics I thought if I went along with him as a passenger, I might get used to these frightening manoeuvres.

I strapped myself tightly in the rear seat and hung on to it with both hands, while he flung the aircraft round the sky in loops, rolls and stall turns. I was suspended in the straps when we were upside down and could feel the 'G' force when pulling out of a loop. I never did get used to it; I was nervous and tense the whole time. Aerobatics were not for me!

We all passed the written examination; now we had the air test. Don took us up on simulated tests and polished up our flying. Then the day arrived. The examiner was very good and put me at my ease as far as possible and told me what he wanted me to do.

After an hour in the air we landed and walked into the office. With some apprehension I waited. "How old are you?" he asked.

"I'm thirty," I replied.

"Your instrument flying was a bit rough," he said. "But at your age I doubt if you will be flying for an airline, so I will pass you. If you had been younger I would have failed you on that."

At last I had achieved my ambition. I was a commercial aircraft pilot and an assistant instructor. Yippie, I was on top of the world! I went up country to Ararat as an instructor, not as a pupil, and with all of my 200 hours experience started to teach others. In the land of the blind, one-eye is king! I was really only a few steps in front of my pupils, but I learnt a lot.

Most pupils were average, one or two definitely slow, but I had one who was a natural. After demonstrating a manoeuvre to him, he executed it smoothly and concisely. His name was Falls, and I often wondered if he took up flying professionally.

I became great friends with Owen John and his wife Elizabeth, both members of the Ararat club. Owen had learnt to fly with the club and owned a Fairchild Argus. I gave Elizabeth some of her flying instruction. The club members were an adventurous, hospitable crowd, willing to try anything.

Owen decided to try 'dead stick' landings in his Fairchild. He climbed to 2,000 feet, switched off the engine, slowed the aircraft down so that the propeller stopped windmilling and became stationary, then landed with no motor. On the way down, he primed the engine, set the throttle, and had his finger on the starter button, in case he did not make the airfield. It looked more dangerous and impressive than it really was.

On another occasion, he and a local sheep farmer, Rod Dyer, went to Sydney to pick up a Moth Minor that Rod had bought. It took them longer to fly back than they expected and on the last leg to Ararat they were running out of daylight. There was no cockpit lighting or landing lights on the aircraft and only the needle on the airspeed indicator was luminous.

As it got darker, Rod put his thumb on the instrument glass, below the needle at cruising speed. If the needle disappeared behind his thumb he knew his airspeed had dropped and if the gap between his thumb and the needle increased, he knew his airspeed was too high. They flew the last few miles to Ararat like this and when they arrived it was really dark.

The runway was macadam and did not show up, but a road beside the runway did; and it had a wire fence alongside. Rod mistook this for the runway and made a good approach; it was only when he levelled out and fence posts started to pop through the wing he realised his mistake. The aircraft ended up a shattered heap of plywood and spruce, but amazingly neither Rod or Owen were hurt - only their pride!

Australian National Airways had taken delivery of two Douglas DC6 aircraft. Compared to the DC4, which, though large, was still a simple aircraft, the DC6 was quite sophisticated, with pressurisation and plenty of electronic equipment. After attending a course at the ANA engineering school, I realised that I had to make a choice. Work on big aircraft under semi-factory conditions, or on small planes, in closer contact with flying.

Having a Commercial Pilot's Licence I started looking for a flying job, hoping my engineering experience would help. The airlines were out because of my age and lack of experience. I heard that Arthur Schutt, who ran a light aircraft maintenance business at Moorabbin Airfield, was starting a crop spraying company and might need pilots.

9

The Art of Crop Spraying

Next time I was at Moorabbin Airfield I went to see Arthur Schutt and asked him if it was true that he was starting a crop spraying company and did he need pilots?

"Yes," he said, "true on both counts. We hope to be in operation in about a month." He asked me a few questions and was very interested in my engineer's licences. "You'd better meet Johnny Considine, the Chief Pilot."

He called Johnny in from the hangar. He was much younger than me, wearing overalls and had obviously been working on an aircraft. Arthur introduced me and Johnny asked me some more questions. "I've only got about 250 flying hours and I know nothing about crop spraying," I told him.

"That's all right," he said, "I'd rather have someone with no previous experience, you won't have acquired any bad habits and we can train you how we want you to operate."

To my delight and surprise, I was offered a job.

When I told some of the pilots I knew, they were horrified. One senior airline pilot said, "You wouldn't get me crop spraying for all the tea in China. It's bloody dangerous." Far from putting me off, it made me feel very adventurous and maybe a little superior!

As the Tiger Moths were still being converted to crop sprayers I helped in the hangar alongside the engineers. The conversion was designed by Johnny Considine and the Chief Engineer, John Pennington. Many of the parts were made in the company workshops.

All the controls, instruments and seat were removed from the front cockpit and a tank installed. A pump driven by the airstream was mounted under the front fuselage, connected by pipes to the tank and the spraybooms, which were mounted on brackets at the trailing edge of the wing. The spraybooms were metal pipes extending almost to the wing tips and had spray nozzles at regular intervals, to atomise the liquid to a fine mist.

An ON/OFF valve was fitted into the system operated by the pilot. There was also a brake on the pump, to stop it turning when not spraying, such as on ferry flights. A plate fitted to the bottom of the tank, or hopper as it was called, was replaced by a door when spreading granular fertiliser. While I was helping to install this equipment, Johnny explained how it worked and some of the techniques of crop spraying.

After work we usually went to the pub for a few beers and talked about the job. Many engineers, pilots and staff from the airfield used the pub and asked Johnny about the new venture. "What's this crop spraying lark, then, Johnny?" they asked.

"We spray chemicals on the crops to kill weeds and insects," he said.

"Poor little insects," someone muttered. "What harm do they do?"

"They can ruin a farmer's crop," replied Johnny.

"This fertiliser you spread, is it like manure?" another asked.

"Something like that," said Johnny. "But it doesn't smell so awful."

"Have you got a name for the company?" asked another.

"Not yet; we are thinking about it."

"As Arthur Schutt is spreading manure, what about calling the company 'Schutt Shit Shooters'?" asked a wag.

"That sounds good," Johnny grinned.

"Yes," piped up a chap at the back, "then your advertising slogan could be 'Have your shit shot by Schutt'."

The bar collapsed into laughter. Needless to say Arthur did not take this up and the company was called Schutt Airfarmers.

It was very unusual for a commercial pilot not to have a Tiger Moth on his licence, as all the clubs used them for training. As I had trained on the Wacket, I had to get it on my licence. I went to a small club on the airfield run by Gertie McKenzie, who was quite a character, and one of a small band of active women pilots.

Having gone solo on the Tiger Moth in England, I soon became familiar with it again.

Now began some crop spraying training under Johnny Considine. Most flying is done from fields or farm roads. Fields can be small, the landing surface rough, the approaches and exits may have obstructions, such as trees, buildings or wires. It is essential that a pilot is competent at short field and cross wind landings.

On a corner of the airfield at Moorabbin, Johnny demonstrated to me what were really precautionary landings, which I had already done in the Wacket Trainer. He laid a white sheet on the ground, and I had to aim to touch down beside it and stop in the shortest possible distance. My first attempts were not too good, but as time went on I improved and eventually satisfied him that I had reasonable control.

By this time the first two Tiger Moths were ready, and calibration of the spray output had to be checked. Using a formula incorporating airspeed, and swath width, with an output of two gallons per acre, it was possible to find out how long it would take to spray a known quantity of liquid at a desired pressure.

A combination of pressure and jet size gave the correct droplet size of the spray. Too coarse, it would not wet all the crop. Too fine then the droplets would drift and evaporate. After several flights, timing the output of a known quantity of liquid, and adjusting pressure and jet size, it was known that if you flew at a certain airspeed, with a certain spray pressure, then the output would be two gallons per acre. This took quite a number of short flights, which also gave me further practice of short landings.

After this we took the two aircraft and went round Victoria visiting farms and agents to arrange spraying contracts. This gave me experience of landing in strange fields.

When landing in an unknown field, it would first be surveyed from the air for suitability and any obstructions, such as fences or wires. Having decided on the landing area a low pass would be made to inspect the surface and look for rabbit holes, ditches and boulders and similar hazards. Only after this inspection was a landing made. Before take off an inspection on foot would be made, to ensure that a hazard was not missed.

Even then it could be deceptive. Following Johnny into a large smooth field, the aircraft vibrated so much on the landing run, that it made my teeth chatter. On examining the surface, we found lots of little ridges about six inches apart and the surface was rock hard. From the air it looked ideal, but it would have been impossible to operate from it.

On one flight Johnny said: "We'll fly this at low level; it's all open countryside." We set off in formation, bowling along at about 10 feet, hopping over fences and hedges. I was keeping fairly tight formation, which meant I had to concentrate on my position in relation to the other aircraft.

A line of trees showed up across our path, about 40 feet high, with a gap just wide enough to take one aircraft. Johnny altered course slightly and headed for the gap. As we got closer I realised there was not room for the two of us, so I broke formation and climbed over the trees, while Johnny went through the gap. When I formated on him again, he looked back with a wicked look on his face as much as to say, "Nearly tricked you that time!"

This tour resulted in orders for spraying and a week later we went off again. Johnny did the spraying and I watched all the phases of the operation, and gained knowledge that could not be acquired in books, but only by practical experience. This covered selection of landing strips, weather limitations, mixing and loading the chemical, deciding how to spray a field in relation to obstacles and wind speed, briefing of human markers and many little practices to ensure a safe, quick and accurate operation.

From that first day until my last spraying day, thirty years later, I never stopped learning. Every day was different. The weather, the chemical, the crop, the obstacles. However experienced and watchful you were, there was always a little gremlin waiting to catch you out. Complacency could kill!

To ensure that all the field was covered by the spray, human markers stood in the field to guide the pilot. He lined up and flew over the marker, who then stepped out the swath width and the pilot lined up on him again for the next run. This went on until the whole field was covered.

I went into the field with the markers to see Johnny spraying and also to appreciate the marker's work. I came to the conclusion that maybe the marker's job was the most dangerous. To have an aircraft flying towards and over you six feet above the ground could be quite frightening. There was an occasion where a marker tied his flag to a pitchfork. The pilot flew over him very low, the marker threw himself to the ground, but left the pitchfork sticking up. It dug into the bottom of the aircraft, tearing the fabric and buckling a fuselage tube. It did not do the pitchfork much good either! This procedure was later altered and markers were instructed to move on to the next swath as soon as the pilot had lined up. In this way the pilot always had the marker in sight as he passed beside and not over him.

A few days later Johnny said: "It's time you tried your hand at spraying a field. I'll mark for you and see how you go." I climbed into the cockpit and set off to spray my first field. It was like doing circuits and bumps all over again, not enough time to do everything. Line up with the marker, cross the fence at the correct height and airspeed, switch the spray on and off at the correct time, look out for obstacles. It called for great concentration. After spraying a few hundred acres, the sequence slowed down and became more automatic as I relaxed.

At last the final run was made, followed by a run across each headland and back to the strip to land. I got out of the cockpit. "Phew, this is hard work."

Johnny came back to the strip. "Not bad for a first try, at least you didn't hit anything, not even the marker," he grinned.

Soon after this the season started in earnest and I spent many weeks flying in parts of Victoria, New South Wales and South Australia. I worked off many different strips, some rough, some narrow and some very marginal, but in my ignorance and enthusiasm, I happily roared off strips, clearing the fence with only a few feet to spare. Someone must have been looking after me, because although I had a few accidents, I never hurt myself.

On my second season, a now wiser and more experienced pilot, I went back to farms where I had sprayed the previous year. A farmer drove me round, showing me the fields to be treated and took me to the landing strip. "This won't do, we'll have to find something better than this," I said.

"Why?" asked the farmer. "You used it last year."

"I couldn't have used this strip," I exclaimed. "It's far to rough and short, and look at those trees!"

"Honestly, you sprayed 500 acres for me off this strip," he said, "and 200 acres for my neighbour."

"I must have been mad, I certainly can't use this strip, we'll have to find something better." This situation arose on several occasions.

I'm sure Arthur Schutt used to worry at times over the antics of his young pilots. He was never happy when he saw us operating out of marginal strips. Keith Goodheer and I were using a strip that had a wind-break of tall trees across our take-off path. There was not enough room to turn a fully laden aircraft after take-off, so it meant a straight climb to clear them. Take-offs had to be timed just right. Take-off too soon at low airspeed, or start the climb too late, and the clearance was very small. We settled down to a take-off technique whereby we cleared the trees by 20-30 feet. If an engine had spluttered in the climb we would have been in trouble.

Arthur arrived on the strip and after watching us for a while, disappeared. Soon after we saw him at the trees with two men from the farm. They cut down trees in the path of our flight, wide enough for an aircraft to pass through. It made the operation much more comfortable, but took away a little of the thrill.

My first accident, (yes, I had several), occurred when operating out of a good but short field. I had done several take-offs, clearing the fence nicely. On the next take-off the airspeed was slow to build up; something was wrong and it looked as if I would not get airborne before the fence.

If I abandoned the take-off I would surely run into the fence and damage the aircraft. There was a chance that if I carried on I might just make it. With my hand firmly on the throttle, holding the tail up, I kept the aircraft on the ground to the last minute, hauled the stick back and lifted over the fence. The wheels cleared, but the tailplane hit a fence-post. I was only just flying and this slowed me down. The aircraft sank into the high wheat crop, the tail lifted and the aircraft turned slowly on to its back.

Remembering that pilots in this situation had released the harness, fallen out of the cockpit on their head and broken their neck, I put one hand on the ground, while I undid the straps and crawled out from under the aircraft. I looked around; what on earth had happened? Then I felt the wind on my face. It had swung right round and I had a tail wind as I took off.

I found that this is a feature of winds in southern Australia; they can switch through 180 degrees in a few seconds. As I became more familiar with the elements in which I was flying, I was able to sense changes in the wind while airborne. Great changes in wind direction were often accompanied with a drop in temperature. Of course, flying in an open cockpit helped; these changes would not have been so obvious in a cabin aircraft.

In my next accident I was operating from a large grass field, big enough to land a DC3. The water tank, on a trailer, was parked at one end of the field, and our agent at St. Arnaud, Frank Griffith, was loading me. He had parked his car in line with the trailer.

The view over the nose of the Tiger Moth is very poor, and as I turned towards the trailer I could see the car over the side of the cockpit and adjust my turn to run parallel beside it.

I had been doing this all morning and I suppose I was lulled by the routine. I landed and taxied towards the trailer, which was now hidden by the nose of the aircraft; as I turned I saw the car and adjusted my turn to run parallel to it as usual.

Unfortunately, while I was away Frank had slipped up to the farm in his car and on returning had parked it several feet nearer the fence, consequently I was heading straight for the end of the trailer. Suddenly there was a jolt and a splintering sound as the propeller shattered. I looked over the side to see Frank standing 15 feet away, still with the loading hose in his hand, and a surprised look on his face. "What the hell are you doing?" he shouted. I was not quite sure myself, as I was stunned with surprise. The one thing in an enormous field and I had to hit it! It brought home to me that if you relax your attention for only a minute, something can happen.

But I was learning. After this incident whenever possible I arranged the trailer in a position where I taxied round it, so it was in sight all the time.

I landed on a farm one afternoon and taxied up to the gate, going quite slowly and the engine idling. The tail must have gone over a tree stump, because it lifted, the propeller struck the ground, and the engine stopped with the propeller vertical. I got out and found the propeller had dug into the ground, and broken the tip. "Oh, no!" I thought. "Not another accident."

When the farmer arrived I asked him for a saw. He came back with a hacksaw and I cut off the damaged tip, laid it against the other blade and sawed off an equal amount. On starting the engine, it ran smoothly, with no vibration, so I took off and did a quick flight.

Everything seemed all right, no vibration, and the performance did not seem to suffer. The farmer looked on in amazement! I got a message to Moorabbin for another propeller, which was being sent by rail. I went spraying the next day, and everything was fine, so I moved on to other jobs, and continued working. It was a week before I was able to collect the new propeller.

One Sunday morning I was on a landing strip at Bordertown, about 300 miles from Melbourne, in South Australia. I took off with the first spray load at about 6.30 am, flew to the field, opened the spray valve, but no spray came out. Then I realised the brake on the spray pump had been sticking and I had forgotten to check if it was free.

I landed back on the field, well away from the trailer, switched off the engine, got out and freed the pump brake. I switched on and swung the propeller. The engine started with a roar, the aircraft moved forward and I could not reach the switches to stop the engine. I managed to get hold of the wing tip, but this meant we were going round in a big circle.

I let go and made a dash for the cockpit, hoping that if I missed the cockpit, I might grab the tail. But as the aircraft was moving in a circle, the tail swung away and I missed everything. The aircraft straightened up and went roaring across the field, while I stood helpless. The tail lifted and the aircraft went over on to its back. There was a deadly silence as the engine stopped. In my haste, I had not checked the position of the throttle before swinging the propeller and it was fully open instead of shut. What a bloody fool!

With the help of the farmer and various onlookers, I got the aircraft back on to its wheels and parked beside the trailer. I now had to ring the boss and tell him the sad news. I thought Arthur would definitely not be pleased to be awoken early on a Sunday morning and told that one of his aircraft had been wrecked 300 miles away. Still, it had to be done.

After I had told him the whole sad story, there was a pause, then he said, “As a commercial pilot, a flying instructor and a licensed engineer, aren’t you ashamed of yourself?” I could only reply in the affirmative. “Right,” he said, “let me have a list of the damaged parts. I’ll go to the airfield and get the trailer out. Ring me at Moorabbin with the list, I’ll load up and be with you this evening. Book me into the hotel.”

DC3 departing on charter, Jersey. Watched by author.

Author at Rhodes grave, S. Rhodesia (Zimbabwe).

Our Rondavel home in Rhodesia.

The house built by Bob and the author in Australia.

Refuelling Tiger Moth in Sudan.

Tiger Moth over Sudan.

Loading a Tiger Moth with chemical in the Sudan.
'Hotel' in background.

Low pass by author in a Tiger Moth - Cameroons.

I went back and checked on the spares needed, a port upper wing, interplane strut, rudder, propeller, nose cowl. I rang Arthur back with the list. "Right," he said, "I'll be with you tonight. Start removing the damaged parts as far as you can." I spent the rest of the day stripping off the broken parts and then went back to the hotel.

Arthur arrived in the evening. After dinner we organised some food to take with us in the morning, as we were starting at first light.

We spent all morning changing the damaged parts and rigging the aircraft, and by 2 o'clock it was ready for me to take up on test flight. It flew well, so Arthur loaded the trailer with broken parts and the farmer came to mix the chemical for me to start spraying.

From the time he arrived, until he left, Arthur made no mention of the accident. We worked together just like a couple of engineers repairing an aircraft. He did not complain or harp on the mistake I had made. He had said his piece over the telephone and said no more. I certainly admired him for that. Many bosses would have kept on about it.

I did not advertise my horrible mistake, but, of course, in such a small industry, it got around. Two experienced crop spraying pilots, whom I looked up to, quietly said to me on two different occasions, "Sorry to hear about your accident. As a matter of fact, I have done the same thing myself, so don't feel too bad about it." It made me feel better.

I had two more accidents during my stay with Schutt Airfarmers. I put the wheels into a high wheat crop and once again ended up on my back. It was right in the middle of the field, so by the time we righted the aircraft and got it out, much of the crop was flattened. I apologised to the farmer, "We recommend aerial application because it does not damage the crop, like a tractor, but we seem not to have succeeded in this case."

"Aw, don't worry," he replied. "As long as you are OK, that's the main thing."

Then I skidded into a fence while turning on a sloping wet field and damaged a couple of wings. None of the other pilots, with no more experience than me, had so many accidents. Two of them, Colin Stephens and Keith Goodheer never damaged their aircraft.

A sequel to all these accidents was that my aircraft was

referred to as 'The Whore'. "Why 'The Whore'?" I asked in all innocence. "Because it always ends up on it's back." I was told!

The company was expanding and now had five pilots. I was sent to Sydney to collect another Tiger Moth. I set off after lunch on the trip back to Melbourne. My first refuelling stop was at Goulburn, high in the hills of eastern New South Wales, then I was due to go on to Wagga Wagga (yes, there is actually such a town!), but the weather was not good so I decided to stay the night.

Goulburn is high in the hills and it was winter, bitterly cold. There was no heating in the pub and only cold beer to drink. I decided the warmest place would be the cinema, but with only twenty people attending, it was not much warmer. When I came out I was so cold that my teeth were chattering and I could not stop them. I found a place where I could get a hot milk shake, had dinner and went to bed. I have never been so cold before or since.

When I filed a flight plan to Wagga Wagga next morning, the controller told me, "I'm sorry, but Wagga will not accept you."

I asked, "Why is that?"

"I don't know, they just say they can't accept you," he replied. "I suggest you fly to Canberra, which is not far out of your way. They have good communication with the area control at Sydney."

I flew to Canberra, went to the control tower and filed a flight plan for Wagga. "It appears that Wagga will not accept you," said the controller.

"Yes, I had this trouble at Goulburn, what's the problem?"

He said, "Hang on, I'll try and find out." After 10 minutes he came back: "Apparently they have had a lot of rain and the grass area is unsuitable for landing."

"That's all right," I replied, "I'll land on the runway."

More chat to Wagga. "They say that as you're flying a Tiger Moth with a tail skid, you can't use the runway," said the controller.

"What a lot of nonsense!" I exclaimed. "The tail skid won't harm the runway. I can't stay here until the grass dries out, it might be weeks. I'm on my way to Melbourne, I have to refuel and Wagga is the only place."

"I'll get on to Area Control in Sydney," said the controller. Another 10 minutes and he came back. "Area Control will agree to you landing on the runway at Wagga, but the landing will be at your own risk."

"When is it otherwise?" I commented. "Anyway, thanks for your help. I'll be off before they think of something else!"

I landed at Wagga with no problems, refuelled and delivered the aircraft to our hangar at Moorabbin. "I was nearly stuck in Goulburn for the winter," I told Arthur, relating the problems I had with flying control.

Australian aviation has an excellent safety record, but they can be bureaucratic. Filing a flight plan at Moorabbin control tower late one afternoon the controller said, "I may have to close the airport soon."

I looked out at the clear, sunlit sky. "Why, what's the matter?" I asked.

"There is a storm to the North and I think it is moving this way. If it comes within three miles of the airfield boundary I have to close the airfield."

I looked to the North and the sky was dark and threatening and obviously raining. "Well, I'm going South, so it won't affect me," I said.

"It's getting closer," declared the controller, studying the approaching weather.

"If you're going to close the airport," I said, "hang on a few minutes and let me get away. I'm going South and it won't catch me up."

"No," said the controller, "I shall have to close the airport."

He started to recall the aircraft in the air, and put out the 'closed' signal.

"Oh, hell," I exclaimed, "now I shan't get away tonight."

Having made up his mind and closed the airport he seemed very satisfied with his decision. It was 15 minutes before the storm arrived and after half an hour it had passed through and the sun was shining again, but it was too late to reach my destination before dark.

Before any flight over 50 miles it was necessary to obtain a favourable weather report and file a flight plan. We used to file a flight plan to our first refuelling point, which was a non-controlled country airfield. Closing the flight plan on arrival, we would then carry on without a flight plan. Coming back into the Melbourne control area we would do the same in reverse.

Returning to Moorabbin after working in South Australia, I

stopped at Ararat, about 100 miles from Melbourne and rang for a weather forecast. “Oh,” said the weatherman, “there is a bad front with rain and low cloud at Ararat.” I looked out at the sunlit sky.

“I’m at Ararat now, and there’s not a cloud in the sky.”

“Maybe it hasn’t arrived yet,” said the weatherman, “but it’s coming from the west.”

“I’ve just come from 100 miles west and it’s been sunshine and clear skies all the way.”

There was a long silence over the telephone.

“It’ll be all right, then, if I carry on to Moorabbin?” I asked.

“If you are satisfied that the weather is fine, I suppose so,” he answered. I think he must have been looking at a different chart!

10

Caterpillar Crisis

Once a caterpillar infestation struck the barley crop. When the barley was nearly ripe, it had a small, milky nodule at the top of the stalk, below the ripening ear. The caterpillar climbed up the stalk and fed off the nodule; the ear then fell to the ground and was lost. A heavy infestation of caterpillars could go through a field of barley in a night, completely ruining it.

Panic calls went out from the farmers for their crops to be sprayed with insecticide and saved from the ravages of the caterpillar. We, and several other companies, were working all the hours of daylight for several weeks. Flying from farm to farm, farmers could be seen standing by the tractor and trailer, with water and chemical ready, waiting for the arrival of the spray aircraft - any spray aircraft. When they heard the noise of an approaching aircraft, they rushed out to the middle of the field waving their arms to attract attention as we passed over. If they were not one of our customers, we had to ignore them.

Starting early in the morning before the hotel served breakfast, and flying from farm to farm all day, food and drink became a problem. We would finish at one farm before lunch, arriving at the next one after lunch, so missing a meal. Farmers were normally hospitable with refreshments, but there was such rush and urgency, that they probably never realised that we had had no food.

Most hotels served an evening meal between 6 and 7 o'clock; if we arrived after that time the dining-room would be closed.

Sometimes working all day we did not know where we would end up, so after a hard day's flying we had to hunt for a bed in the nearest town. Some towns would have a café, but not all, so much of the time we lived off pies, sandwiches and bars of chocolate, with an occasional proper meal if we were lucky.

After about two weeks of this we were tired and hungry. Johnny Considine came to see us, and after listening to our moans, we stopped flying early and he drove us to a hotel he knew in a nearby town. It was very comfortable and served meals all the evening. After a leisurely shower and a few cold beers, we went in to dinner. The food was very good and served at an unhurried pace, allowing time to chat and smoke between courses. A few glasses of wine mellowed us and life took on a rosier hue.

At about 10 o'clock, the landlord put a plate of cheese and biscuits on the table, with a large jug of coffee, and announced that he was going to bed, but we could carry on as long as we liked. It was a relaxed and enjoyable evening, the first for a long time, and the next morning we were fully refreshed to restart the war against the caterpillar.

There were three different types of farm and farmer. On the big sheep stations, which were owned by a farming company, with a manager, you were treated as a contractor. You were housed in the shearers' quarters and ate with the stockmen, usually on mutton, which was in plentiful supply. It was very impersonal and if you had any problems with the aircraft or loader, that was your concern.

On the sheep stations and wheat farms, run by the owner, you were almost welcomed as a guest. Many of the farms were fairly isolated and the owners were glad to see a fresh face. They put you up in the house and you ate with the family. On one farm, which bordered on the Murray river, a lunch hamper arrived on the strip, consisting of Murray cod, freshly caught, fruit salad and cream, cake and a large pot of tea. In the afternoon came another hamper of sandwiches, cake and tea. At the end of the day, after a shower, they would offer a drink and chat. If the weather made spraying impossible, the farmer would take you shooting or into the local market or take you round the farm. All very interesting and enjoyable.

On one occasion when I could not spray, I was with the farmer, watching a large flock of sheep being brought into the yard. They were either going to be sheared or dipped or crotched or treated for foot rot; I'm not sure which, as the poor sheep were always being subjected to some treatment or other.

The farmer suddenly went into the flock and dragged out a ram, sat it on its haunches between his legs, took a sharp knife which he put into the eye of the ram's penis and cut down its length. Then he dabbed some black tarry disinfectant over the cut and pushed it back into the flock. "What on earth was that for?" I asked, quite horrified. He explained that some of the grasses the sheep grazed on were long, with sharp barbs like an arrow. When the ram was grazing, a blade of this grass could enter the penis, which would fester, and if left the ram would be unable to urinate, and would die. Rams, of course, are very valuable for breeding. Due to the barbs it was not possible to pull the blade of grass out, so it had to be treated in this way. Flying around during the next few days, I would remember the scene, and my loins would flinch!

On another farm, I walked into a barn with the farmer. "I must kill a sheep for the house," he said. Going into a stall, he brought out a sheep. Taking it over to a drain, he put it on its back and cut its throat. He chatted to me, rolling a cigarette while the sheep pumped out its life blood and quickly expired. I don't know what the 'animal rights' body would have thought of this!

The other type was the mean farmer. Some, of course, were farming poor land and had quite a struggle, but others, small farmers on rich land, could also be mean. Roughly, those who had large farms were big and generous in character, those who farmed small tended to have little mean characters.

Spreading fertiliser in the hills of the upper Murray river valley, one of the farmers was a real hillbilly type and as mean as they come. "I don't want any of my fertiliser to go on my neighbour's land," he told me. "I'd rather you left the edges untreated than any go over my boundary." Another farmer, who was also having his land fertilised, and was helping to load, winked at me.

When loading the aircraft, some fertiliser unavoidably gets spilt onto the ground. When this happened the farmer sent his son to get a pan and brush, swept it up, all half pound of it, and put it back into the loading bucket. Sometimes we had to move the aircraft so he could sweep underneath!

After lunch we started working for the other farmer, who was a very nice person, and was getting as exasperated as me. When we went for lunch, I had left the hopper door on the aircraft open, so the first load went right through and ended up in a neat heap between the wheels. We had to move the aircraft and shovel it back into the loader. "Sorry about that," I said to him, "but I'm glad it happened to you and not the other farmer." He nodded and smiled.

Landing on another farm I found the agent had not yet arrived with the chemical. An hour passed and the farmer started complaining. Another hour passed. I had not been invited into the house or offered a coffee. I went to the house and said, "I think I had better ring up and see what's happened."

"And who's going to pay for this call?" demanded his grim wife.

"I shall pay, of course," I replied. I found that the agent had been delayed, but was on his way. I suggested to the farmer that while we were waiting he showed me the fields he wanted sprayed.

There were no complete fields to spray. He wanted two runs on one field, only the headlands on another, half of another field and so on. It was difficult to calculate the acreage of such work, but as the aircraft was calibrated to put out two gallons per acre, we agreed that he would be charged on the basis of chemical used.

When the chemical arrived I suggested that the farmer marked for me as only he knew accurately what parts he wanted sprayed. It was time consuming work, but I got it finished and made out the bill. It was usual for the farmer to give a cheque to the pilot when the work was finished.

I handed him the bill. "Will you let me have a cheque for this?" I asked.

"Well," he said, in a moaning voice, "how do I know it's going to work?"

"I've sprayed hundreds of acres with no problems, so I see no reason why it should not work for you," I replied. "In any case, if there are any problems the company will come back and put it right."

"Well," he whinged, "I'm not sure I can pay until I see the result."

"When you ordered this work you were told that payment was expected on completion," I said firmly. He still complained in a mumbled voice. I had had a frustrating and difficult morning and I was getting fed up. "All right," I said. "I have to account for payment for the work I do, so I will pay for your damned spraying myself."

I put my paperwork away and started to load the aircraft. I turned it round and went to swing the propeller. He then sidled up to me. "Hang on a minute," he said. He disappeared into the house, probably to discuss it with his dragonish wife. He came back and handed me a cheque. I gave him a receipt.

"I hope I never have to work for you again," I said. I started the engine and took off. I was pleased to leave that farm.

Many amusing incidents occurred. Colin Stephens landed on a farm. "I wasn't expecting you so early," said the farmer. "I'll drive into town and get the chemical. I'll be about an hour, so make yourself at home. Play some records if you like," pointing to a radiogram. Colin was very fond of music and thought he could amuse himself for an hour. When he looked at the records, he found they were all a horse-racing commentary of the Melbourne Cup over the years!

Spraying at St. Arnaud for our agent, Frank Griffith, with Bob Hamdon we had a tragedy. Frank had a lovely Labrador dog of whom he was very fond. Frank was a bachelor and his dog meant a lot to him. The dog went off to the field with the marker, and when Bob flew by, low, it jumped up and was hit and killed by the aircraft wheel. I really felt sorry for Frank. Bob remarked later in the pub, "There aren't many dogs that have tried to retrieve an aircraft."

In the Murray valley near Corryong, the landing strip was next to the river. Fertilising was dusty work and at the end of the day a shower was most welcome. The Murray was quite shallow at this point, crystal clear and cool. Instead of going to the hotel at the end of the day we stripped off and bathed in the river. Much better than a shower cubicle.

Another time working with Bob, we were held up for lack of fertiliser. While waiting we decided to clean out our cockpits, which collected spillage when loading. We got most of it out, but a lot of dust remained. We really needed a vacuum cleaner. "I know," said Bob, "let's go up and turn the aircraft upside down, then all the dust will fall out."

I agreed, "What a good idea."

We both took off and I climbed to 2,000 feet and turned the aircraft on its back.

My goggles slipped down over my forehead and the dust went into my eyes, stinging them and making them water, so that I could hardly see. I dare not wipe them with my hand or sleeve, as they were covered in dust too and it would only aggravate. By repeated blinking I managed to wash my eyes, so that I could see well enough to land. "That was a bloody stupid idea," I said to Bob.

"It sounded a good idea at the time," he answered.

Spraying with Johnny in north Victoria, it started to rain. We took shelter in the cab of the loading lorry, and watched the rain pelting down. Soon the wind got up and started to rock the aircraft.

"We should tie the aircraft down," remarked Johnny.

"We'll get soaked," I said.

"If we took our clothes off," said Johnny, "at least we would have something dry to get back into."

If anyone had been passing by, they would have seen two naked men rushing round the aircraft driving tie down stakes into the ground!

On a cold winter's day I had to fly to Swan Hill in northern Victoria. It was bitterly cold and I was well wrapped up; underpants, trousers, overalls and a flying suit. There had been a lot of rain and most of Victoria was flooded. Australia seemed to suffer from flooding or bush fires, sometimes at the same time, but not in the same place.

About half an hour from Echuca, my refuelling stop, I wanted to pee. I looked around for a field to land in, but they were all under water, so I had to fly on. It got very pressing. I jumped up and down in the cockpit, flew with my legs crossed, hummed a tune and thought of other things. When I got to Echuca, I threw the aircraft on to the ground, undid the straps before the aircraft had stopped, then jumped out. I unzipped the flying suit, then the overalls, then the trousers. My whole body was so cold I could not feel anything.

But what a relief! Then I felt my legs getting warm and wet: I had not got my penis clear of all my layers of clothing! I had an uncomfortable journey to Swan Hill, where I showered and changed, got warm and felt better.

The oddest incident was not real, it was a dream! Several times I dreamt that I was flying along the streets of Melbourne, trapped underneath the overhead tram wires. I was not worried, but wandered along Flinders Street, up Bourke Street and down Collins Street looking for the tram terminus, so I could escape!

The chemicals we sprayed had strong, lingering smells. The aircraft always smelt, and after a day's flying the pilot and ground crew also smelt. Entering a bar for a beer before we showered, the customers would exclaim: "Phew! what an awful smell," and move away. We never had trouble reaching the bar in a crowded pub.

When spraying, the aircraft was loaded by a small pump, with suction and delivery hoses. These were normally transported from job to job by van. Sometimes, however, the gear had to be carried in the aircraft. Although the aircraft hopper was empty, the loading door was too small to take the pump and hoses. So the hoses were wound round the lower wing root and tied to the fuselage. The pump was put in the rear locker, which left nowhere for the pilot's overnight bag, so this had to be tied to the flying wires on the other lower wing root.

The pump in the rear locker made the aircraft tail heavy. Even with the trim lever right forward, you still had to put forward pressure on the stick to fly level. It could become tiring after a time, but most of the ferry flights were short. Although the aircraft was far out of its centre of gravity limits, I never had any problems flying the aircraft this way. But then aerodynamically the bumble bee should not be able to fly!

A large contract came up to spread fertiliser on a 5,000 acre sheep station on the Murrumbidgee river in New South Wales. At 2 cwt to the acre and with the 4 cwt load of the Tiger Moth this involved about 2,500 flights!

The station was on a hill in a loop of the river which surrounded it on three sides. The landing strip was at the highest point. On arrival the first thing that registered was a large barn with six bays, full to the roof with bags of fertiliser. "This job will take months!" exclaimed one of the pilots, and it nearly did.

We started off with three Tiger Moths, but later one of these was replaced by a twin-engined DH 84, which carried half a ton.

The whole station had to be treated, so we divided it into areas, in order not to interfere with each other. Flights could be made in a wide circuit, spreading soon after take-off and landing back for another load. It was very quick and after a few days very monotonous. To relieve the boredom, two aircraft would spread in formation, or race each other back to the strip for the next load. To keep the aircraft going there were six men moving the fertiliser and loading the aircraft, and they were kept working flat out.

The nearest town was fifteen miles away, along a dusty road, but we never saw it as we had no transport. The weather was hot and dry the whole time, and by the end of the day everyone was covered in dust, the loaders especially, with eyes staring out of white faces. The bath facilities were primitive; a large cauldron full of water, heated over a log fire, and a tin bath on a cement floor. Afterwards the bath was emptied through a drain in the corner, ready for the next man.

As nine people needed a bath, it was a slow process, but we sat round the fire drinking beer and chatting, awaiting our turn. Then supper and bed. There was nothing to do in the evening, but after flying all day, we were only fit for sleep.

Gradually we emptied the bays of fertiliser. We had cleared four and the end seemed in sight, when six big lorries arrived and filled them up again. Our hearts sank, would we never finish. At last, after about five weeks, we completed the job. It did not give me much satisfaction. We hardly saw the owner. He never offered us a beer, nor was he concerned or interested in our welfare; we were just contractors.

After two years' crop spraying, I thought it was time I moved on. I was deliberating between New Zealand and New Guinea or perhaps going back to England, before everyone forgot about me.

I heard that some DC3s had been sold to West African Airways. I located the man who was organising the delivery and asked if I could get a lift to Lagos. He agreed, providing I paid my own expenses. A few weeks later I left Sydney on one of the DC3s, the pilot was Brian Monkton, a well known flying boat pilot. Beverly Snook, who had been demonstrating an EP9 spraying aircraft in Australia, was also hitching a ride home.

Stopping overnight at the BOAC rest house at Darwin, I had my last experience of quaint Australian social rules. We all went down to a bar, next to the swimming pool. The bar had open sides covered in netting to keep out flies and mosquitos. I went for a swim, and the rest of the crew sat drinking beer inside the netting. Wearing swimming trunks - the temperature was in the 90s, with high humidity - I went in to join them and was told to wear a shirt. I took my beer and a chair, sat next to them, but outside, and chatted through the netting. In funny ways, Australia was quite puritan.

The trip to Lagos was uneventful. As long-range fuel tanks were carried in the fuselage, the legs were long and boring. I was surprised to see no one keeping a navigation plot. All the navigation was done on the radio compass and the only maps I saw were radio navigation charts. I do not think there was a topographical map on board: a change since I was on charter flights from England a few years ago.

I spent a few days at the airport hotel at Ikaga airport, arranging a flight home, and playing billiards with a lonely BOAC captain staying there. All his crew were in Lagos having a good time, but because of the airline's policy of crews staying in different hotels according to rank, the poor chap ended up on his own.

In many ways I was sorry to leave Australia. I liked the country and the Australians and made some good friends. I had extended my engineering qualifications, gained a commercial pilot's licence, built a house and learnt 'to give it a go, mate!'

My flying training was very good, thanks to Don Stewart and I am sure this contributed to my surviving thirty years of crop spraying. Arthur Schutt was one of the best bosses I worked for, and I gained much of my crop spraying experience at his expense, I'm afraid.

11

The Lure of Africa

Returning to England in the summer of 1957, after six years in Australia, I spent a few weeks visiting friends and relatives before deciding what to do next. I again met Colin Stephens, who left Australia a year before me, and was now flying for a charter company. When he first arrived in England he flew for an aerial crop spraying company called Crop Culture, which had several overseas contracts. He told me they were looking for pilots and were a pleasant company to work for.

I went along to meet their Chief Pilot, Jim McMahon, an Australian, at Stapleford airfield in Essex. At this time I had about 1,000 hours experience on Tiger Moths. We had a chat about mutual acquaintances in Australia and the work of the company. He asked if I would do a few circuits with him in a Tiger Moth.

Stapleford was a small but adequate airfield with two grass runways. I did a few circuits and a crosswind landing on the short runway without any problems. Walking back to the clubhouse, Jim remarked: "It's amazing the number of pilots who profess many hours on Tiger Moths, but show some resentment at being asked to display their skill, and some make a complete hash of it."

I can never understand this attitude. If you have skills and are confident of your ability, it should be no problem to demonstrate them. People who resent such a request immediately make me suspicious of their claims. As a result of this interview, I was offered a contract for the coming cotton-spraying season in the Sudan. This was to lead to a long association with the company.

Over the ensuing weeks I learnt something of the make-up of Crop Culture. Jim McMahon was an experienced crop-spraying pilot and a practical down-to-earth person. Desmond Norman, ex-De Havilland student, Auxiliary Air Force pilot, was an engaging extrovert, with a flare for salesmanship and administration. John Britten, also an ex-De Havilland student was a quiet boffin type and a clever designer. Frank Mann, who ran a large fruit importing company in the west country, had business experience. These four very different people brought their respective skills by various roads and circumstances to form Crop Culture. Desmond and John were later responsible for the design and manufacture of the successful Britten-Norman 'Islander' aircraft.

Through a separate company, Micronair, they developed an alternative spraying system to the conventional one. In place of the boom and nozzle, a rotary atomiser is fitted to each wing. It consists of a gauze covered drum, revolving at high speed by a wind-driven propeller. Spray liquid is fed into the centre of the drum, and centrifugal force throws it out to the inner side of the drum, where the gauze breaks it up into droplets forming the spray. The advantage is that the spray droplets are of more uniform size. The droplet size is altered by adjusting the pitch of the propeller driving the drum. The faster the speed of the drum, the smaller thc droplet size. The system is used on all Crop Culture aircraft and sold world-wide to other operators. Over the years it was refined and improved.

I went down to the company base at Bembridge airfield in the Isle of Wight, where the aircraft were being prepared for the ferry flight to the Sudan. Two Tiger Moths were to be flown by Jim and myself and an Auster by another Australian, John Freeman. The Auster was fitted with a long-range fuel tank, and the spray tanks of the Tiger Moths had rubber liners fitted to hold extra fuel. The fuel was pumped up to the main centre section tank by a hand pump fitted in the cockpit.

The Gipsy engines are notorious for high oil consumption, so the oil tanks were enlarged to hold four gallons, and a plastic pipe was taken from the filler to the cockpit. Two one-gallon cans of oil were stowed each side of the pilot's seat. By removing the screw cap from the can and screwing on a similar cap fitted to the end of the pipe, the can was held up and oil flowed to the tank by gravity. A simple form of flight re-oiling. This was necessary, as with full fuel we had a duration of 12 hours, and on some legs we flew 8 hours without landing.

I was told that the previous year, after spraying in the Sudan, the aircraft could not return through Egypt because of the Suez war, so they were flown back via West Africa. This meant flying west from Khartoum across the southern Sudan, a bleak route with few airfields.

The first refuelling stop was El Fasher, but passing El Obeid, Jim indicated to Desmond, who was flying the other Tiger Moth, that he was going to land there. On landing, Desmond went across to Jim's aircraft to find out what was the matter. While attempting to re-oil in flight, the cap had come of the can, covering Jim and the cockpit in oil. When Jim got out, dripping oil, Desmond exclaimed, "Is that all, I thought it was something serious!"

The rotary atomisers were not fitted for the ferry flight, as the drag would seriously reduce our cruising speed. They were stowed in the aircraft with other equipment and spares. Every nook and cranny in the aircraft was filled with spares. Space in the cockpit was cramped, with two oil cans, the petrol pump, thermos flask, sandwiches and maps for the route.

After a favourable weather report we set off on the 27th, September 1957 for the 10-day flight to the Sudan. Clearing customs at Lympne, we flew to Marseilles, via Lyon, where we stopped the night after 7½ hours flying. Then to Rome, Palermo and across the sea to Bone, in Algeria, where Jim had some business.

Over the sea, as soon as land disappears from sight, the engine always seems to run rougher! We saw no shipping and were relieved to see the African coast appear. The next day we started on the long flight along the North African coast to Cairo. We flew low most of the time, seeing debris from the desert war and harbours still full of sunken boats. At Benghazi I met a Singhalese engineer who had been training with Australian National Airways when I was there. At the RAF staging post at El Adem, gin in the NAAFI was 10/- (50p) a bottle!

We carried no radio, which would never be allowed today. Flying control at the airports had been informed of our intended arrival and signalled with an Aldis lamp. We landed at the new Cairo International Airport, which had a runway about two miles long. Receiving a 'green' from the control tower, I passed high over the runway threshold, slowly getting lower. As I descended the runway seemed to get much shorter, so I put the wheels on the concrete and taxied fast with the tail up. This seemed to go on for a long time, so I slowed up and dropped the tail. If I ran off the end of this runway I would never live it down! Even then I had to taxi a long way before I could turn off.

Every aircraft landing in Egypt had to be fumigated before the passengers could disembark. A little man would open the door and place inside a lighted fumigation 'bomb'. When it had ceased to burn, he would open the door and the passengers could leave. When he came up to the Tiger Moths with open cockpits he was very puzzled. Eventually he lit the 'bomb' and placed it on the pilot's seat! It fumigated most of the apron, where it probably did the most good!

Leaving Cairo the next morning there was a strong crosswind on the taxiway leading to the runway. It is very difficult to taxi a Tiger Moth in these conditions. Having no brakes and a tailskid instead of a tailwheel, the aircraft tends to weathercock into wind. Proceeding down the taxiway could only be done in short bursts, then the aircraft had to be manhandled back to a position to resume taxying. This meant getting out of the aircraft frequently to realign it with the taxiway, so progress was slow and in a series of arcs.

While struggling to reach the runway, a Hermes airliner followed me out. There was this huge aircraft, towering over me, its four engines thumping away. I could see the crew in the cockpit and imagined the captain drumming his fingers on the control pedestal with impatience and saying to his first officer, "When this idiot gets out of the way, we can get airborne." But, maybe, in my embarrassment I unjustly attributed these unpleasant thoughts to the captain. He could have been sympathetic, remembering his own early flying days.

Recently, recounting this incident, Denys Howard, who I worked with many years later in Norfolk, exclaimed, "I remember that, I was one of the pilots."

We set off for Wadi Halfa on the Egyptian-Sudanese border, following the Nile at about 300 feet. It was fascinating to watch life drift by in this narrow fertile strip, either side of the river. Farmers were hoeing their crops; small boys herding goats; fish hung on lines to dry in the sun; water wheels turned by oxen, walking in a never ending circle, to irrigate crops. All very peaceful and rural, but probably hard work to get a modest living.

After an eight-hour non-stop flight we landed at Wadi Halfa an hour before sunset, and spent the night in a houseboat on the river bank, attached to the only hotel.

The next day we had another long flight to Khartoum, so tried for an early start. The controller informed us that we could not take off until official daylight, which was in half an hour. It was light enough to read a newspaper, and the nearest aircraft was either miles away or passing over at 30,000 feet, but he would not let us go.

He sat in the control tower directing a red light at us and checking his watch. As soon as it showed that official daylight had arrived, he gave us a green and we could go. If it had been a British controller, under the old colonial administration, he would probably have said: "Hurry up and go, then I can go and get my breakfast."

Thirty years later an airliner en route from London to Aberdeen called up and gave its ETA as 20.32. Due to noise abatement regulations the airport closed at 20.30, and the controller would not accept the aircraft. It had to divert to another airport. This caused inconvenience to the passengers, who had to be bussed to their destination, and put the aircraft in the wrong place to start operations in the morning. All for two minutes! African bloody mindedness had found its way to Europe!

South of Wadi Halfa the Nile swings west in a big loop, so we followed the railway line across the Nubian desert. It was the most desolate country I had ever seen, just like the face of the moon. Absolutely barren, no life, no colour, no movement, dead. We stayed very close to the railway line! It made you realise what the troops of Kitchener's army went through trying to relieve Gordon in Khartoum. We rejoined the Nile north of Atbara and followed it to Khartoum where we landed after a 7½ hour flight.

Desmond and an engineer (I think it was Ted Cheale) were there to meet us and we stayed at the Sudan Club, which was the remaining symbol of colonialism. Set in large grounds, surrounded by a high wall, it was getting rather shabby. Reduced membership since many of the British administrators had left, meant that finances to maintain the building were limited and this showed in lack of paint and repair. It still upheld the old traditions and the Ambassador held his party there for the Queen's Birthday.

Every morning we left for the airfield, armed with large thermos flasks of iced water and sandwiches. We worked all day removing the long range fuel systems and fitting the spray gear and came back dirty and sweaty, looking forward to a shower, a cold beer and a good meal.

We used to enter the grounds through a side door and walk to the club. One evening we returned after dark and walked along, chatting to each other. Suddenly we realised the grounds were full of people, the men in dinner jackets, the ladies in long dresses, all standing in groups sipping drinks. We had intruded into a smart official party in our sandals and dirty shorts, carrying lunch boxes. It was too late to turn back, so we carried on, the conversation dying out as people turned to stare at us.

We went to the cinema that night and on returning we found the party was over, but the bar was full of members, who previously had been showing decorous behaviour, sipping their gin and tonics with the ladies. Now they were red and sweaty-faced, dinner jackets discarded, bow ties undone, rowdily singing rude verses of *Nellie Dean*! "Well," I thought, "the colonel's lady and Judy O'Grady?"

Soon we left Khartoum to live a semi-nomadic life, wandering up and down the Blue and White Niles, spraying cotton schemes irrigated by the rivers. With the Sudan being so flat, it was easy to find landing strips near the work. Accommodation was primitive, sometimes in rest houses on the cotton scheme or in Sennar and Kosti.

A hired lorry and a Land-Rover followed us around, carrying petrol, tinned rations and our gear. We had an old Sudanese cook, who considering he only had two primus stoves, served reasonable meals. In one region where we had a lot of work, we hired two straw huts from the village headman. The village was on a large open space, with little vegetation nearby, and the nearest water was in a canal about a mile away. The village women fetched it in four-gallon petrol drums, balanced on their heads.

All our petrol was supplied in these drums, and when emptied, they were in great demand to carry water and for making native beer. Water was precious and there was only enough for cooking, tea, and shaving. As I had a beard, I did not wash for days. In a hot and dusty climate it got a bit uncomfortable.

Two Sudanese agricultural officers paid us a visit and kindly invited us to their house nearby for a beer and a shower. We all jumped into the Land-Rover that evening and I had visions of standing in a tile-clad shower while hot water cascaded over me.

After a chat and a cold beer, it was my turn. The servant took me out to the back yard where there was a concrete slab, with a two-gallon bucket of warm water beside it. What a disappointment! How can you have a decent shower out of a two-gallon bucket! No good moaning; have to make the best of it.

I soaped myself all over and began to feel better. Then I splashed myself with clean water and emptied the last pint over my head. A smart rub down with a towel and I felt marvellous. It was the best shower I had in my life. It made me realise that the enjoyable things in life are brought about by contrasts. You may enjoy your pint of beer in the local pub most evenings, but it does not compare to a cold beer, when you come in hot and tired from a day's flying.

In October and November the Sudan is on the migratory route for birds that summer in Europe. Cranes, ibis, storks, pelicans and many other birds I did not recognise used to feed in the cotton, especially after it had been irrigated. They were in large flocks and could be a menace to a spraying aircraft.

They flew up as you approached them, and then settled down again further into the field. Some of these birds were very big and you had to keep an eye on their movement, because if you hit one it could badly damage the aircraft.

All three aircraft were operating from a strip at Birket El Agab, south of Kosti. We had a base strip a few miles away, next to the rest-house where we were staying. Around midday we all decided to take one more load and then fly to the base strip for lunch.

I set off with my last load. The field I had to spray was covered in birds. I managed to herd them further into the cotton, giving me a clear area to spray, but there must have been a laggard amongst them. As I was spraying he flew up under the aircraft, hit the propeller and shattered one of the blades. I pulled up and turned towards the landing strip, but the engine was vibrating badly and I could not maintain height.

I put it down on the nearest piece of clear ground, but it was very rough and the aircraft tipped up on its nose, my own nose hitting the padding above the instrument panel, causing it to bleed. I got out and could see the other aircraft spraying, but they were too far away to attract their attention.

In due course they flew off to the base strip. Ah! I thought, when I don't turn up for lunch they will come and look for me. I saw them land and heard the engines switch off. Nothing happened; it was all very still and quiet. After about fifteen minutes I began to feel sorry for myself, sitting beside the aircraft with a bleeding nose. The lousy bastards, I thought, sitting there, eating lunch. They don't care if I bleed to death!

Then I heard a Tiger Moth start up. It took off and flew towards me. Jim spotted me and flew low; I waved to let him know that I was all right. Half an hour later they all came out to rescue me in the Land-Rover. That afternoon we got the aircraft back to the base strip and assessed the damage. It needed two wings and a propeller.

Jim and I went back to Khartoum, where Crop Culture had a store of spare parts. We found two serviceable wings and a propeller, and hired a 'souk' lorry to take them to Birket El Agab. The lorry owner was given strict instructions not to pick up passengers or goods on the way.

The lorry crew consisted of the owner, a driver and a small boy. I was going back with the lorry to look after the wings, which were quite fragile if not handled properly. I took a supply of Coca-Cola, biscuits, cheese and fruit to last the two day journey.

We left Khartoum early in the morning for the long drive south. We passed many people on the roadside wanting a lift, but the owner refused them. At one stop, a young man and woman asked for a lift. The owner looked at me questioningly. "All right," I said, "let them up." I felt a bit sorry for them, and as there was room, it seemed a nice gesture.

But I had opened the floodgates! A little later we stopped by another small group, who in spite of my protests, scrambled on board. Then I saw money being put into the owner's hand. In my naivity I thought we were giving these people a free lift! From then on, I rode in the back, making sure no one put a foot through a wing or dumped one of their numerous parcels on them.

We stopped in a village for a break and a cup of tea. Suddenly all the customers, including the lorry crew got down on their knees and went through their prayer ritual. I felt a little uncomfortable, sitting drinking tea, while all around me people were praying. However, they seemed to find it quite normal, which put me at ease.

Then I thought; how great, it was time to pray, so with no embarrassment or inhibitions, they prayed. If someone went on their knees and prayed in an English high street, everyone would be embarrassed and think him mad.

When it got dark, we stopped and the lorry crew brewed tea and made an evening meal. I drank Coke and ate biscuits and cheese. They curled up in blankets and slept under the lorry, while I slept on the bench seat in the lorry cab, though I did not sleep too well. Wearing shorts, the mosquitos bit my ankles, in spite of wrapping a blanket round my legs, and I smoked my pipe to keep them away from my face.

By the second night I had finished my supply of Coca-Cola, so I drank tea with the crew, who looked after me very well in their way. They carried drinking water in animal skin bags which they refilled from the Nile. There is a Sudanese saying that if you drink water of the Nile, you will return to the Sudan. It was true in my case as I returned nine more times!

While the engineer and I repaired the aircraft, Jim and John Freeman went off spraying in other areas. We changed the wings and the propeller and repaired other minor damage. Not having any instruments to check the rigging we had to do it by eye. Our eyes must have been accurate, because when I took it up for a test flight, the aircraft flew straight and level 'hands off'. I rejoined the others and continued spraying.

We were in Kosti on Sudan Independence Day, which was a public holiday and the town was crowded, people coming from miles away to celebrate. A group of horsemen rode in from the desert region of Kordofan. Mounted on sturdy horses, wearing breeches and tunics, rifles in holsters, bandoliers across their chests, they rode proudly into town. Heads held high, they glanced down scornfully at the town-folk dressed in their white djellabas.

There were camel and horse races and a band playing. Jim had decided that our contribution was to fly over the town in formation spraying water dyed with the colours of the Sudanese flag, which were red, green and black. We lined up in Vee formation, John leading in the Auster. Flying over the town at about 200 feet we made our gesture. Later, walking in the town a man came up to me and pointed to his djellaba covered in red spots. "No, no!" I exclaimed, "I was spraying green." When another man came up, showing his djellaba covered in green spots, I exclaimed, "No, no, I was spraying red!"

As Jim said later: "It seemed a good idea at the time!"

End of November saw the end of the spraying season. At this time the cotton was only sprayed once or occasionally twice. In later years it was sprayed four or five times.

I flew back to Khartoum, where I found a strong crosswind on the main runway. A second runway ran about 30 degrees to the main runway, and was slightly less crosswind, but it was narrower and the ground either side was rough.

I decided it was better to use the main runway, landing on the downwind side, so if I ground looped, there was plenty of room. When I taxied up to the apron a car drove up and the driver said I was wanted in the control tower. He dropped me off at the terminal building and I climbed the stairs to the control tower. "Ah, Captain," greeted the controller. "Why did you land on the main runway, the other runway was more into wind?"

I explained my reason to him.

"But Captain," he said, "didn't you see the landing 'T'?" (A 'T' in the signal area indicates to the pilot which way to land.) I had seen the 'T', but it was positioned at right angles to the runway.

"Yes," I answered, "I saw the 'T' but there was no runway in that direction."

"Ah, but Captain," insisted the controller, "we put the 'T' in that direction to show you which way the wind was blowing."

There were two windsocks on the airfield to show wind direction, but I could see it was no good arguing if he interpreted international signals his own way.

In subsequent years, crop-spraying pilots were frequently summoned to the tower for alleged contravention of airport rules.

I think they got at us because we were an easy target on whom to exert their authority. If two or three airliners were approaching Khartoum, they would discuss their ETA's amongst themselves and decide what order they would land, so the controllers instructions regarding landing sequence were a mere formality.

The Chief Engineer of the company's operations in the Cameroons was leaving and I was asked to fill the gap until a new one was appointed. Just before Christmas I left Khartoum in the weekly DC4, operated by a local airline, for Lagos.

It followed the route over the southern Sudan to West Africa which early traders had followed with camel caravans. The passengers were the modern equivalent of these traders. They climbed aboard, laden with cases, bags and parcels that filled the luggage racks and every space between and under the seats. The only thing they did not have was livestock! It was a long, cramped, and not very comfortable flight.

I spent the night at the airport hotel at Ikaga, where I had stopped on my way to England from Australia. Next day I flew to Tiko in the British Cameroons to take over from the departing engineer.

12

Bananas and Jungle

Before the First World War, the Cameroons had been a German colony. After the war, it was split, the west part under British mandate, and the east under French mandate. Later, the two parts amalgamated as the Cameroon Republic.

Crop Culture was first based at Penja on the French side, but this was taken over by a French company, Ardic, and Crop Culture moved to the British side, basing themselves at Ekona. The company was under contract to spray bananas for the Commonwealth Development Corporation.

Ekona was several miles inland and much higher than the coast, so it was cooler and less humid. The mess for the pilots and engineers was a large, airy house, built by the Germans. It was situated on a hill, across a small river from the main township, and made of local timber, with beautiful timber floors. The airstrip was a mile away, with a hangar made from local materials.

One of the first people I met was Dave Brent, a young Australian, whom I last saw as an ANA engineer in Sydney, several years previously. He was now a pilot. Tragically he was later killed in an air crash in India, on his way to join Aden Airways.

Two engineers, Ted Cheale and Maurice Jackson, made up the engineering staff, with two local men, Paul and Victor, who were good lads. Paul was still with the company when I returned to the Cameroons in 1966.

The aircraft were a mixed fleet of Tiger Moths and Austers. I had hardly settled in when we had trouble. One Auster was unserviceable with a cracked crankcase, then we had Tiger Moths suffering engine failure and landing in the bananas. Luckily banana tree trunks are fibrous and not like the hard unyielding trunks of ordinary trees. Although the aircraft were damaged, the forced landings in the bananas were softened and none of the pilots was hurt.

Ian Taylor was spraying a plantation next to the French border near Tombel. While turning, the engine cut, and he crash-landed on the French side, near a customs point. As he scrambled out of the aircraft, the customs officers drove up. "You can't land here, Captain," they cried. "You have to go to Douala and clear customs."

Ian had great trouble convincing them that he was not attempting to enter illegally, but had been forced to land because the engine stopped! When he got back to the landing strip at Tombel, Paul commiserated with him, "So sorry your bird fall out of sky."

A few days later Dave Brent appeared on the strip at Ekona, having taken off a couple of hours earlier to spray in an Auster. "What have you done with your aeroplane?" asked one of the engineers.

"It's in the bananas, down the road, the engine cut out," was his reply. Things were getting a bit serious, two Tiger Moths and an Auster crashed with engine failure, another Auster with a cracked crankcase - we were running out of aircraft!

When the house falls about your ears, you can either laugh or cry. Crying does no good so you may as well laugh. We worked hard to keep the remaining aircraft flying and salvage the wrecks from the bananas, but we did not go round with glum faces.

The manager, Jack Akers, was on leave, and the acting manager was a South African, and South Africans are not noted for their sense of humour. We could not do much immediately to rectify the situation as we were waiting for spares from England, so I tended to be flippant, just to wind him up. It wasn't really fair, as he had responsibilities to keep the contract going.

Although the engine failures stopped, Desmond arranged for a De Havilland engineer to come out to investigate. Gipsy Major engines were not really De Havilland's scene in the jet age, but together we went through all the fuel systems with a fine tooth comb, from tank to carburettor, but found nothing. As far as I know the trouble was never located. A few years later, flying from Kenya to the Sudan in a Piper Pawnee, I had carburettor icing at 3,000 feet over the southern Sudan. The temperature was quite high, with a lot of rain about, but it was the last thing I expected under those conditions. It did make me wonder if it was icing in the Cameroons.

One of our local drivers came down from up country, where he was working, to renew his driving licence. He asked me, "Would you come to the police station with me, as you know how the African treats the African." At the police station I explained to the constable that the driver was needed by us up country, and would he renew his licence so that he could return to work.

The constable looked at the licence and then at us. "Wait," he said. This is a standard reply from junior officials, just to impress on you their authority. We sat down for about half an hour, then the constable called the driver to the counter. "Why do you come bothering us today?" I heard him say. I was amazed; the chap only wanted to renew his driving licence and it was the constables job to do it. After more waiting, the driver got his licence. As we drove back to Ekona I remarked, "I see what you mean."

Our transport was a left-hand drive Land-Rover imported from the French side. Several of us were going to a party one night when we were stopped by the police at a checkpoint. The policeman came to the right hand side, which in this case was the passenger side and asked to see his driving licence. The driver passed his licence to the passenger, who handed it to the policeman.

The policeman examined it by his torch, shone the light on the passengers face, then back to the licence. He seemed a little puzzled, but signed for us to proceed. The passenger said, "Excuse me officer, but have you seen a steering wheel anywhere, I have lost mine?" The policeman looked in the window, just as the driver let in the clutch and roared away! I bet he thought it was white man's magic!

The Land-Rover came to grief in a spectacular way. The parking area in front of the mess was on a slope, which ended in a drop down to the river. The Land-Rover had a weak hand-brake, so it was always parked in gear.

I came back to the mess for lunch a little late and everyone was already eating. I parked the Land-Rover on the slope, put it in gear, jumped out and ran up the steps to the mess. A noise made me look round and I saw it slowly going backwards towards the edge. I had no chance to get to it in time, and realising what was going to happen called out, "Quick, chaps, come and see this, quick."

Everyone rushed out in time to see the Land-Rover run over the edge, rolling, turning and twisting, until it ended upside down in the river bed. It was just like a scene from an American gangster film. Everyone cheered and someone said, "I didn't quite see that, Pete, would you do it again."

On the way to the airstrip was a house occupied by three Scotsmen, employed by a timber company. They worked hard extracting trees from the jungle, and they also played hard; many a lively party we had with them. Some mornings, when we passed their house, they would be drinking their breakfast from a bottle of Amstel beer. They would wave a bottle invitingly and the driver would turn into the drive, where we all piled out to drink an ice-cold beer.

On my birthday we held a party in the mess and invited the Scotsmen. It got very lively, and someone suggested we formed a pyramid, three people at the base, two on their shoulders, and I was elected to complete it at the top. When I got to the top, I saw in front of me a four-armed light fitting. "I've always wanted to swing from a chandelier," I cried, as I launched myself forward to grab it. My weight pulled it from the ceiling, the lights went out and I landed on my back on the hard wooden floor, clutching the light fitting to my chest.

I heard Dave Brent say, "Are you all right, Pete?" as he bent over me. As I did not reply he sounded worried, but I could not speak for laughing. If I had been sober I would probably have broken something.

Between the banana plantations was dense jungle, a canopy of tree tops covering trunks 150 feet high. If you crashed in the jungle, I doubt if you would ever be found. The weather could be tricky. At times low cloud would settle over the jungle, with heavy rain pouring down, visibility almost nil and the air very turbulent. Many times pilots crept back from outlying airstrips by flying west of Mount Cameroon to the coast where the cloud base was higher, following the coast to

Victoria, then up the road to Ekona.

At one end of Ekona airstrip jungle fell away to a deep river valley. Early one morning I took off in an Auster, with Dave Brent on board. Due to the humid atmosphere, on a cool morning the inside of the windscreen sometimes misted up. Taking off towards the jungle, I reached about 50 feet, when all forward visibility went. I hastily wiped the inside of the windscreen, but it was still all white - we were in cloud! Dave was shouting, "Get down! Get down!" There were 150 feet trees sticking up out of the bananas, so I was not going down!

A gentle climbing turn brought us out into sunshine. I saw the river valley was full of cloud which was spilling over the top and racing towards the airstrip. It was only about 100 feet high, but right down to the ground and had already reached the edge of the airstrip. I did the fastest, tightest circuit ever and touched down just before the whole airstrip was covered. With difficulty I found my way back to the hangar. That made the adrenaline flow!

In due course a replacement Chief Engineer arrived, along with several other engineers and pilots and I started to do more spraying. Ian Taylor and I took two Tiger Moths over to the French side to help Ardic, the French company flying from Penja. Ardic operated Piper Cubs and I was envious. With an enclosed cockpit, better performance, and wheel brakes they were better than the Tiger Moths.

The strip at Penja was tarmac and this made landing and manoeuvring the Tiger Moth, with only a tailskid and no brakes, quite exciting. Trying to keep straight with rudder and bursts of throttle increased the speed, so you arrived at the end of the strip travelling fast. We had to station an engineer there to grab the wing tip and help the pilot steer to the loading bay.

On one landing I passed Ian's aircraft at right angles to the strip with its wheels sitting in the drainage ditch that ran alongside. Luckily he switched off the engine when he lost control and the propeller stopped horizontally, and no damage was done.

One banana plantation was on a hillside beside the landing strip. The slope was so steep that it could only be sprayed downhill. This meant circling and climbing a heavily laden Tiger Moth over the strip until enough height had been gained to commence the spray run, which only lasted about 20 seconds. Then a 10-minute climb back up to spraying height. Very boring and tiring.

We all lived in a mess similar to that on the British side. The pilot/manager was a Frenchman called Pierre Dulac, whose wife was with him. There were also several French pilots and ground staff.

Amongst these was a man called Francois Lesieur. He had been a deep sea fisherman until the flying bug got him. Crop Culture offered him a job if he obtained his commercial pilot's licence and agreed to help him. He came to England and worked at their base at Bembridge, while he studied and learnt to fly powered aircraft, as opposed to gliders.

To take a technical examination in your own language is bad enough, but in a foreign language it is twice as difficult. Francois built up his hours ferrying aircraft to parts of England during the spraying season; eventually he got his licence and went to Jamaica, spraying bananas. We met again over the years, in Cameroon, and England and became good friends. Later we were partners in a spraying company in Norfolk.

The French pilots in the mess were an exuberant lot, and drank champagne at the drop of a hat. Every morning at breakfast they went round the table shaking hands. Ian Taylor, an undemonstrative New Zealander, who was not good in the mornings anyway, thought this a lot of Gallic nonsense.

I received a telegram from Desmond Norman, which ran something like this: "Are you interested in spraying 10,000 acres of bananas every two weeks for new company in South America. New Piper Cubs. Good salary. Lovely climate and beautiful girls?"

This sounded interesting, so soon I left the Cameroons for Ecuador via England.

13

South American Venture

Two months later I found myself sitting in a DC7 en route to Ecuador, via New York, a journey that took about 20 hours, with only a brief stopover to change planes.

Twenty hours sitting in an aeroplane was going to be very boring, so I gently anaesthetised myself with a steady intake of gin and tonic. This put me in a benign mood to tolerate the frustrations of air travel, such as delays, customs and immigration.

I was met at Guayaquil airport by Lucho Estrada, a large imposing man, with a black goatee beard, who was the Ecuadorean director of the company. Arriving in the early hours of the morning he took me to the Humbolt Hotel to sleep off the effects of the long journey.

Later in the day I walked to Lucho's office, dressed in white shorts, shirt and socks, the usual non-working dress of West Africa. People stared at me, and while talking to Lucho, the girls in the office were sneaking looks at me and giggling amongst themselves. Lucho smiled at me. "It's the way you are dressed," he said, "We don't wear shorts in Ecuador." I paid particular attention to what people wore, and in spite of the hot climate, went back to wearing slacks. During the next three months I learnt much about life in Ecuador.

To start with, thieving was endemic. Every house had metal grills over the windows, everything was locked, and many people had large bunches of keys hooked to their belts, making them look like prison warders. No one would slip round to the corner shop for a packet of cigarettes without double locking the front door.

Anything on the outside of a car which was detachable would be stolen. Hub caps, mirrors, spare wheels, were all taken off before the driver ventured on the road. Even windscreen wiper blades were kept in the glove box until it rained, and then put back afterwards. Someone leaving Guayaquil on a rainy night, wrote back to say his last view of the city was of his friends waving good-bye from the airport balcony with wiper blades in their hands.

There were two police forces. The regular police looked like a broken down army. Ill-fitting uniforms, unshaven, small and generally scruffy. The traffic police, however, were tall, well-built and smart. They wore blue trousers, light blue shirts with breast pockets and epaulettes and a white sun helmet.

The smartest place was the cemetery; very clean, with bright white walls, black wrought iron gates, full of elaborate tombs and headstones, all well kept. Another smart organisation were the 'Bombardiers' - the firemen. They earned great affection in the eyes of the public.

Ecuador is divided into three areas. The coastal plain is forest and grassland. Much of the forest had been cut down and planted with bananas. The climate is hot and humid and the sky is often covered in cloud, caused, I understand by the cold Humbolt current that swept up the coast from the south.

The mountain spine of the Andes runs through the middle of the country and is inhabited mainly by Indians, descendants of the Incas, engaged in agriculture and sheep rearing. From the wool they wove cloth, and made superb rugs, many with traditional Inca patterns. Mountains, such as Cotopaxi and Chimborazo, rise to 18,000 feet and are snow covered all the year round.

East of the Andes, the ground falls away to the headwaters of the Amazon basin. It is primitive rain forest and largely unexplored.

Two brand new Piper Cubs had arrived fitted with external belly tanks for the spray chemical. The Ecuadorean Chief Pilot, Carlos de la Paz, and I carried out calibration trials and visited parts of the country both by air and ground. All the work would be on the coastal plain around Guayaquil. I was lucky to visit Quito briefly on two occasions with Carlos, by air and by road.

The journey by road was most impressive. We set off in daylight and drove through the mountains at night. The sky was absolutely clear and thousands of stars shone brightly; they seemed so close that you felt you could reach out and touch them. Many of the stars were not visible from lower altitudes or in more polluted atmosphere, so it was a surprise to me how crowded the sky was.

When daylight came, the whole wonder of the Andes was revealed. We drove up mountain sides and plunged into valleys, and on reaching the bottom climbed up the other side. The valleys were full of small fields, creeping up the side of the mountains to the line where the fertile soil finished and the tundra began. The line was quite distinct and in the morning sun it looked as if someone had laid a colourful patchwork quilt in the valley.

Approaching Quito, the scenery was rugged and barren, and Carlos told me it was llama country, but we did not see any. At the time I was not very knowledgeable about the history of Ecuador and the Inca civilisation so I did not take full advantage of my visits to Quito, nor the opportunity to see other towns in the mountains.

Many male Ecuadoreans had a shocking habit of spitting. With great ceremony and respiratory rumblings they would bring up the sputum and expectorate it with great force; it seemed to give them great satisfaction.

Lucho had some business in a small town and took me along. We were having lunch in a rather primitive eating house when we were joined by a large Ecuadorean who knew Lucho. While we were eating he sat at our table and at regular intervals went through the whole ceremony and spat between his legs. It was with great difficulty that I managed to eat a not very appetising meal.

Lucho looked at me on several occasions, raising his eyebrows, and I could see that although he found it as distasteful as me, he was too polite to say anything.

Soon after I arrived I was hailed by a man from across the road. He came over to me. He was neatly, but a little shabbily dressed, wore a tie and his shoes were polished. "How are you?" he beamed. "How do you like Guayaquil?" He seemed to know me, but I could not remember where I had met him.

"I'm sorry," I said, "but I can't remember where we met; was it the airport?"

He nodded, "Yes, yes, the airport. Everything well with you?"

We chatted for a minute or so, and then he said, "I have a problem. My wife is ill and I have a prescription for some medicine, but at the moment I have not enough money to get it. Could you help me with a loan?"

I said, "I'm sorry, I have no money on me at all."

"Never mind," he beamed. "I will go and find another friend. So pleased to have met you again." He shook me by the hand and went off down the street.

I thought it all a bit odd as I could not remember meeting this man anywhere before. Later in the day I mentioned the meeting to Carlos. "Ah," he said, "you have met Emilio, our con man. Whenever he sees someone who is obviously new to the town, he tries his con trick, that's how he makes his living. You didn't give him anything, did you?"

I shook my head, "Luckily I had no money on me, because he almost conned me!"

There was always a crowd of poor-looking people outside the entrance to the hospital. When I asked someone why, I was told they were blood donors. Apparently if a patient needed a blood transfusion the relatives had to supply the blood. These people sold their blood and made a sort of living out of it. And we complain about the NHS!

There were many Americans in Guayaquil. As they were used to having their food double-sealed, sanitised, pasteurised and made hygienically tasteless, they would not eat local food. Neither would they drink tap water, which was perfectly safe, but drank Guitig water - the local Perrier, and even cleaned their teeth with it! They bought imported tinned and frozen food from an American-type supermarket opened by an enterprising Ecuadorean.

As their bodies never had a chance to build up an immune system, if they had a cup of tea or a meal away from home, they got stomach problems, which, of course, confirmed their view that local food was unhealthy.

I think I was immunised early in life, probably with landlady's food during the war, because in spite of eating local food and drinking local water, in many countries, including water from the Nile, I rarely had any stomach problems.

After a few weeks in Guayaquil, driving through town to the airport, one of the traffic police stopped me at a crossroads. My Spanish was non-existent, but I gathered he wanted to see my driving licence. I showed him my International Driving Licence, which he studied intently, then got into the Land-Rover and directed me to the police station.

In we went to the office of a Captain, who looked at my licence and said to the policeman, "It's OK, he can drive." I took the policeman back to the crossroads where he resumed directing the traffic, which seemed to have managed quite well in his absence. I did wonder if he was really necessary.

Off I set to resume my journey to the airport. At the next cross-roads there was another policeman directing traffic. When he saw me he came over and wanted to see my driving licence, which he studied carefully, then got in the Land-Rover and directed me back to the police station.

Out we got and once again I was taken to the Captain's office. When he looked up and saw me again with a different policeman he waved his hand, "He can drive," and went back to his paperwork. A rather crestfallen policeman was driven back to his station, and I was, at last, able to resume my journey.

Another amusing incident occurred with the traffic police. Outside Lucho's office was a small lay-by where he parked his car. One day notices appeared prohibiting parking. The next day he drove up, parked his car and as he was locking the door, a policeman came up. "Senor, you cannot park here." Lucho locked his car, went to the boot, took out his brief-case. "Senor, you cannot park here," repeated the policeman.

Lucho locked the boot and walked into his office, trailed by the policeman exclaiming; "Senor, you cannot park here." Lucho sat at his desk, opened his mail, talked to his staff and completely ignored the policeman. The officer kept repeating his warning, but his tone became less assertive and less confident until he finally turned and slunk away. As far as I know Lucho continued to park as usual.

After three months in Ecuador, I returned to England for a short time, and then went back to start operations in earnest. On the flight back I did my gin and tonic routine and all went well until we left New York. I sat next to a Canadian, who had the same idea, so we talked and sipped our gin and tonics, until the hostess told us they had no more gin. "Not to worry," I thought, "we are stopping at Miami soon, so they will stock up again."

At Miami I bought some duty-free gin and we all got on board for the last leg to Guayaquil. When the flight settled down and the 'No Smoking' sign was extinguished, we called the hostess for two gin and tonics. "I told you," she said in a brusque way, "we are out of gin."

"But we've just stopped at Miami," I protested, "didn't you replace your stock?"

"No," answered the hostess, "we have no gin."

My anaesthetic must have worn off as this annoyed me.

"Oh, well," I declared, "I got gin in Miami; will you bring some tonic and two glasses." I got my bottle from my case and the Canadian and I drank on for an hour or two, until we fell asleep.

I was awakened by the hostess shaking my shoulder. "We are at Guayaquil, sir," she said. I awoke mussy-headed from a deep sleep, not too sober, got up and walked off the aircraft into the terminal building. Soon after a hostess came up with my jacket and then another one with my brief-case.

Luckily someone had been sent to meet me, and realised the situation. He took me in hand, found my passport, collected my bag, shepherded me through customs and immigration and took me to the hotel, where I climbed into bed and slept for most of the day.

More Piper Cubs had been delivered, and soon more pilots arrived. Ian Taylor from the Cameroons, Bob Pairman from Jamaica and Hans, a German ex-Luftwaffe bomber pilot from Colombia. We all lived in a house in Guayaquil, and had a daily cook/housekeeper to look after us.

We settled into the routine of spraying bananas. The weather was generally good, so there were few hold-ups in the programme.

Bob Pairman and I used to go frequently to Quevedo, a hick sort of town. Each spray cycle involved two or three nights away. Quevedo consisted of a wide unpaved street, which turned to mud when it rained. The sidewalks were wooden verandas in front of the shops.

Every other shop was a café or a bar, with a juke box and flashing neon lights. As every juke box played a different tune at full volume, the cacophony was terrific. As this went on until the early hours and the flashing lights flickered in front of the uncurtained windows of the hotel bedrooms, sleep was sometimes difficult.

14

Landing Problems

Landing strips were hard to find as most of the land was either forest or banana plantations. In some areas we were allowed to use roads. Ian operated from a road which had a quarry at the end. Lorries coming out would turn and continue to drive down the road, even if an aircraft was taking off. Whether the drivers were stupid or ignorant, I don't know, but at times Ian's heart rate increased. Under normal circumstances there was plenty of room, but if an engine had failed, or the take-off prolonged for some reason, it could have been dangerous. Ian would come back in the evening and declare over a beer, "I have been playing chicken with the quarry lorries all day."

Bob and I operated from another road, which was long and straight but narrow, with drainage ditches on each side, so there was nowhere to go except forwards. At the end was a small lay-by, where the aircraft could turn round and load, and then take off in the opposite direction. There was just enough room to take the aircraft off the road to refuel. Two aircraft on the road at the same time could cause problems, so we staggered our sorties to avoid this. If one aircraft returned before the other aircraft had finished loading, the airborne aircraft waited until the other had taken off before landing. A man was stationed on the approach holding a placard saying, "Beware, aircraft landing and taking off."

I came back while Bob was still on the ground, so I orbited over the approach until he had taken off, then lined up for landing. As I started to hold off, three or four feet off the ground,

I felt a bump. I thought, "Bob's slipstream is hanging around a long time." I eased back on the stick and landed.

As the aircraft sank to the ground I saw to my horror a car in front of me; it was slowing down and then stopped. I jammed on the brakes, which were not good on the Cub, stopped the engine and came to rest two yards from the car. The driver got out and said, "Why did you land like that?"

I replied, "Didn't you see the man with the warning down the road?"

He said, "Yes, I saw that, but when I saw you take off I thought all was clear. Why did you come back and land?"

I explained that two aircraft were operating and it was the other aircraft he saw take off. As I was descending over the road, he was underneath me and we were both travelling at about the same speed, so neither saw each other. One of the aircraft wheels had made a large dent in the roof of his car and the radio aerial had been broken by the propeller!

He could see that I was rather shaken, so he took me up the road to a café and bought me a brandy, while we exchanged names and addresses. Thank goodness it was a car, if it had been a lorry it could have been very serious for me and the lorry occupants. It gave me a good story to dine out on. Not many pilots have landed on top of a car on the highway!

Ian had a new customer in his area. As the owner had no a map of his plantation, he suggested that he would go up with Ian and show him the boundaries. "Then," he said, "you can drop me off at my house, I have a landing strip nearby."

They took off and mapped the area, and the owner directed Ian to the strip. When Ian saw the strip he turned to the owner and said, "It looks a bit small; has anyone else landed here?"

The owner replied, "Oh, yes. My good friends, John and Joe always land here when they visit me."

Ian thought, "If John and Joe can get in, so can I."

He made a slow approach over the bananas, with full flap, but was too high, so he went round again. On the third attempt he got in and stopped a few yards from the end of the strip.

"Thank you very much," said the owner as he climbed out.

"As a matter of interest," asked Ian, "what sort of aeroplanes do your friends fly?"

The owner circled his hand over his head, "Oh, you know,

what do they call them? Ah, helicopters."

Ian was not amused and only managed to get out again because there was a gap in the bananas.

While operating at Quevedo a man came up to me and said his tractor had broken down and he needed a spare part urgently. Could I take him to Guayaquil when I returned that night? Only too willing to help anyone in trouble, I agreed and told him when I expected to leave.

While the aircraft was being refuelled for the flight back, I saw him standing by his truck. "All set?" I asked. "We'll be off in about five minutes."

He went back to his truck and appeared with an enormous suitcase in one hand, as if he was going on a month's holiday, and a little boy about six years old, in the other. "You are not taking the boy with you?" I asked.

"Why, yes," he said, "I want to take him too."

"I'm sorry," I replied, "but there is only a seat for one, I can only take you."

"He can sit in the luggage space at the back," he replied.

"No," I said, "that won't do. It is illegal to carry a passenger without a seat for him."

He looked upset and said, "It will be all right, I'm a great friend of the Director of Civil Aviation."

"And where is that enormous suitcase going?" I asked.

"I'll carry it on my lap," he replied.

I could see that it was all getting out of hand. "No, no, this won't do at all," I said. "I can take you and the case, but not the boy. Anyway, I thought you were only going to get a spare part for your tractor."

"The lad wants to see his grandmother in Guayaquil," he replied.

"You didn't mention that when you asked for a lift," I said. We argued for a few minutes, and I could see that I was being imposed on so I left without him.

All the pilots got on well together. We had worked in many countries and had similar experiences and mutual friends. Hans, the German pilot was a very good companion, and we agreed how silly it was, that if we had met a few years earlier, we would have tried to kill each other. Hans was asked if he had ever been to England. He hesitated a minute, then said, "Yes, I went to

Coventry in 1940!"

When we were not flying we would drink a beer or a coffee, sitting outside one of the cafés in the main street. Young 'urchins' about seven or eight years of age would crawl under the tables trying to clean shoes or tug your shirt, trying to sell you imitation Parker pens, or cigarettes.

Dark-skinned Indians, wearing ponchos, wide brimmed hats and pigtails, moved quietly from table to table, offering hand-knitted ties, slippers and leather goods. They never pestered you like the 'urchins'. They were rather despised by the townspeople, but I always found them gentle and polite - consequently I found myself with ties I did not want!

Sometimes we were joined by pilots from Petroleum Helicopters, an American company also spraying in Ecuador. They only had a three months visa, which had to be renewed after that time. They could not renew it in Ecuador, but had to leave the country and apply at an Ecuadorean Embassy. Every three months they flew to Lima, went to the Embassy, where it had been previously arranged, handed over the fee, got their passports stamped and caught the next plane back. It all seemed very odd to me, but talking to both the American and British consuls, they told me the same rule applied in their countries. Good business for the airlines, though! We had to go to the immigration office for the issue of Resident Permits. I found it a humiliating experience. After producing my passport and filling in forms, I was put against a white screen and while holding a placard against my chest with a number written on it, I was photographed. Going to another room a large silent policeman seized my hand, forced my fingers into an ink pad, then held them on a sheet of white paper, to take my finger prints. It made me feel like a criminal

The senior helicopter pilot was a Texan, called Hank, who wore tooled, high-heeled, cowboy boots. One of the younger pilots had recently married. Hank turned to him "Son," he said, "as an old married man let me give you some advice. If you have been out with the boys, drinking and playing poker, and get home late, don't creep in quietly, taking off your shoes and try and get into bed without waking your wife. She will be waiting for you and give you hell. Come in making a lot of noise. Slam the front door, clump up the stairs, throw open the bedroom door, switch on the light and cry. 'Are you ready for me love'. You will find your wife sound asleep." At the end of the working day, all the office girls were going home. They were young and attractive and we viewed them with appreciation. A young girl, with a well-formed bottom, that waggled and undulated provocatively, walked past. Hank watched for a few seconds, then exclaimed, "Gee, that broad's got more movement in her arse than a shovel full of Swiss watches!"

At a travel agent and bureau de change in Guayaquil it was possible to buy an airline ticket to any part of the world; buy or change travellers cheques and transmit money overseas.

One Monday morning the staff arrived and found the office locked. The owner had done a bunk. I had to admire his cheek. The previous week he sent his wife and family, it was believed, to Argentina. He issued them with airline tickets and a handful of traveller's cheques. Then, over the week-end he issued himself with an airline ticket and more traveller's cheques and left the country. As far as I am aware, never to be seen again!

There was talk of sending an aircraft to Esmeraldas, a region in North-West Ecuador, to spray bananas. We knew nothing of the area, but the Ecuadorean pilots were horrified. "It's the end of the world," they exclaimed. "Primitive, hot, swampy and full of mosquitos."

Desmond Norman arrived soon after this was suggested, and decided to fly up with an Ecuadorean pilot to investigate. He went to the American-style supermarket to stock up with emergency rations for the trip, such as gin, smoked salmon, paté, tinned ham, butter and oysters and similar basic commodities. After three days they returned with faces so swollen with mosquito bites that their eyes had almost disappeared. Esmeraldas was not mentioned again!

Two interesting events occurred; an invasion of beetles and a revolution. Suddenly swarms of black, armour-plated, flying beetles, about two inches long invaded Guayaquil. They got everywhere, into air-conditioned buildings, into top rooms of high buildings and covered the streets. If they flew into your face it was quite painful, as they were large and hard. Squashed by car wheels, they made a sound like nuts being crushed and left a bloody blob on the tarmac.

At night they hovered around the street lights and piles of dead and dying beetles accumulated at the base of the lamp standards.

Sweepers heaped them into in the gutters, shovelled them into carts and took them away to be burnt. It went on for two days, and then, as suddenly as they arrived, they departed.

True to South American form Ecuador put on a revolution for us, though it was only a mini-revolution. A junior officer had seized one of the barracks with some of his men. As South American governments are rather nervous of this sort of thing, they reacted quickly.

Lucho rang in the evening to say there was trouble about and a total curfew had been proclaimed. He told us to stay at home or we might get shot.

That night we heard a few shots, but I think it was a nervous or trigger-happy soldier, rather than any real action. In the morning we looked out on to the street from the upper balcony; it was empty and quiet. A tank sat on a corner, dark, still and ominous, its gun pointing down the road. There was no sign of the crew. "I expect they are inside playing cards," remarked Ian, "and we may as well do the same." Ian was a skilled and ruthless player, so the revolution cost me a lot of money!

The next day a few lorries drove down the street at intervals, full of armed soldiers, as if on patrol. Then a column of twenty soldiers marched past in single file, with a sergeant calling out, "Left, right; left, right; left, right."

"That's odd," I said, "he's drilling them in English."

Ian remarked, "How would you like to call out, 'Izquierda, derecha; izquierda, derecha; izquierda, derecha." He had a point.

It was all over the next day. The tank had gone, the town back to normal, and everyone going about their business. I suppose the rebels were languishing in jail.

The control tower at Guayaquil was very odd. After my experiences with airfield control in Africa, I kept well away, but some strange things happened. Taxying out in the morning I would be stopped at the runway entrance by a red light directed from the tower, which could be pointed at you for as long as ten minutes. You assumed that an aircraft was approaching to land, but there was nothing in sight. Sometimes the delay was so long that I got out and smoked a cigarette. Then suddenly, the light would turn to green and off I would go.

On one occasion, just as I was airborne, I saw an aircraft in the distance approaching to land; on another, just as I opened the throttle to take off a DC3 taxied across the runway in front of me. I wondered if the Aldis lamp was wrongly calibrated and when the controller gave me a red, he thought he was giving me a green, and vice versa.

I never went to the tower to find out, but just kept my eyes open at take-off. The controller never complained that I was disobeying his signals.

On one trip to Quevedo Bob and I had continued flying as long as possible to finish the spraying and avoid another night there. We had left it rather late, and before we reached Guayaquil it was starting to get dark. When we arrived it was quite dark; we had no radio and control were not expecting us.

I circled round trying to think of a safe way to land, when I saw an airliner approaching, its landing lights on and the windows lit up.

I thought, “With that airliner on the runway there will not be another coming in until it is clear.” The airliner stopped at the end of the runway and started to turn round to taxi back. I immediately shut the throttle, put down full flap, did a steep descent, landed short and turned off at the first taxiway, taxied to the hangar and switched off the engine. As I got out of the aircraft, Bob taxied in from the other direction. He had landed at the other end of the runway. So at one time there were three aircraft on the runway - the airliner in the middle and a Cub landing at each end! We put the aircraft away and went home. We heard nothing about it from flying control, so I can only assume they were unaware of the situation.

Ecuadorean pilots were now taking over. Hans had gone back to Colombia, Ian and Bob had left for England. Soon I too, went. A few months later I married. As well as a lovely wife, I acquired four super step-children, what you might call a package deal.

My youngest stepson was only eight and the others were in their teens, just starting off into the world, so my wife did not want to leave England. I could not stay with Crop Culture and refuse to go overseas on long contracts if they required me to, so I decided to freelance, taking short seasonal contracts.

Financially it was a little precarious. After a contract the bank balance would be very healthy, but if contracts fell through for any reason, it could be several months before the next one, and the bank balance decreased alarmingly. When things started to look bad, luckily something always turned up in the nick of time.

I flew in England for some summers and went to the Sudan in the autumn for the cotton spraying season. I took short contracts in West Africa and Austria, but slowly the overseas work died out and I operated in England full-time.

15

Some Pigeon!

Aerial crop spraying in England is very different from overseas contracts, which are usually one crop and one chemical. Crops in England are of a wide variety, attacked by different diseases or insects, and have to be treated with many types of chemical. Treatment is with liquid spray or granules. Cereal crops are treated with nitrogen fertiliser in granular form to encourage growth and sometimes seeds are sown by air.

The capricious weather conditions can make work difficult; we had to hang about for hours on desolate airstrips waiting for suitable weather, which may only last an hour or two. Some crops can only be treated when the leaves are dry, some fields can be sprayed only in light winds or if winds are in a certain direction, because of drift.

After the open wheat plains of Australia, large cotton schemes in the Sudan and banana plantations in West Africa, English fields are small. Numerous houses, villages and sensitive areas, together with hazards such as overhead cables, pylons and trees make flying difficult and call for more concentration from the pilot.

Aerial fertilising, applying granular nitrogen, calls for accurate calibration and accurate flying. If the wrong swath width is used, or the aircraft flown at the wrong height (normally 40-50 feet), or the flight path is inaccurate, then some of the crop is overdosed and other parts under-dosed. This shows up as strips of different shades of green as the crop grows and is almost impossible to correct after application.

Different companies formulate the granules in different ways. Some are bulkier than others, some flow faster or slower. All absorb moisture from the air, so humidity can affect the flow rate and so alter the calibration. It is therefore important to keep a close check on the calibration settings as the fertiliser is applied and constant minor adjustments are necessary during application.

Fertiliser can be applied in most weather conditions, providing the winds are not too strong and the visibility is good enough to fly. After flying for several weeks in windy and turbulent conditions, I wondered why I began to feel excessively tired. Talking to other pilots I found they felt the same. We concluded that flying heavily-loaded aircraft every day in such conditions called for much physical effort and could become very tiring.

Most liquid spraying is carried out in the summer, when the weather is warmer and calmer. Although flying only about six feet over the crop, everything was steadier and tight, smooth turns could be made at the end of the spray run. On a cool, calm morning, smooth, accurate flying could be achieved in a relaxed and enjoyable way.

Early in 1960 I was back flying Tiger Moths for Crop Culture, fertilising crops in Lincolnshire. I flew up from the Isle of Wight and landed in a field near Boston to meet the agent. It was very windy and the forecast over the week-end was bad. I tied the aircraft down, driving pegs into the ground and securing the wings with chains. The tail I tied to a concrete fence post, locked the controls and chocked the wheels back and front. As there were sheep in the field we obtained an electric fence from the farmer to put round the aircraft.

The weather being unsuitable for working, I borrowed a car and went to see some friends in Nottingham. It was a blustery week-end and on the Sunday night the agent rang to say that my aircraft had blown away and was wrecked. I could not understand this as it was well secured and the winds were not gale force. When I got back, I went to look at the damage.

The Tiger Moth was wrapped up in a ball, about 30 yards from where it had been tied down. The wing tie-down brackets had broken and the chains were on the ground by the stakes. The rope holding the tail was broken, the chocks still in place and the electric fence in position, undamaged.

A strong gust of wind, probably a wurly-wurly, had lifted the aircraft straight up several feet and carried it over the electric fence and dumped it back on the ground. I was glad I had secured the aircraft in the approved way before I left, so my conscience was clear.

Two days later, when the weather improved another aircraft was sent from Bembridge and the engineers came to collect the wreck. I travelled all over Lincolnshire, spreading fertiliser whenever the weather allowed, and stayed in local pubs.

Lincolnshire is a miserable county in winter, cold and bleak and some of the towns are grim. Probably the worst was Brigg. The pub where I stayed was quite good, with a jolly landlord, but they did not do an evening meal. There were no cafés open at night and the only hotel stopped serving dinner at 6.30, shades of Australia! Rarely was I back in time and the only food available was in the foyer of the local cinema, so I lived on bars of chocolate!

I went back to Lincolnshire for the spraying season in the summer. The manager of the agricultural merchant I was attached to was an active, unrelaxed sort of chap, always worrying. He expected you to be out from early morning until late at night, even when the weather was bad, just in case it should improve. This can be tiring and unproductive. Hanging around on an airstrip, doing nothing all day, can be more tiring than a hard day's flying. When the weather does improve the pilot is worn out.

We had been spraying potatoes when the weather became wet and windy for several days. Wet warm weather is ideal for potato blight, and more orders came in, causing a large backlog of work. Twisting in his chair and drumming the desk with his fingers, the manager exclaimed, "What are we going to do? We are behind with the work and more is coming in everyday. What can we do?"

I looked outside; the wind was lashing the treetops around and driving rain against the window. "I don't know about you," I said, "but I'm going for a beer." He was quite annoyed by my attitude, but it is no good getting your knickers in a twist about things that are beyond your control.

Soon after I was sent to Somerset. Peter Ayles, who had been operating there, hit some cables and wrecked the aircraft. The wings had folded back over the cockpit, which you could just see

Courtesy Maurice Jackson

A landing strip in the banana plantation. British Cameroons.

Courtesy of Maurice Jackson

The Land-Rover that ended up in the river bed.
British Cameroons.

Courtesy of Maurice Jackson

Repairing the crashed Tiger Moth at Birket El Ageb.
Rest house in background.

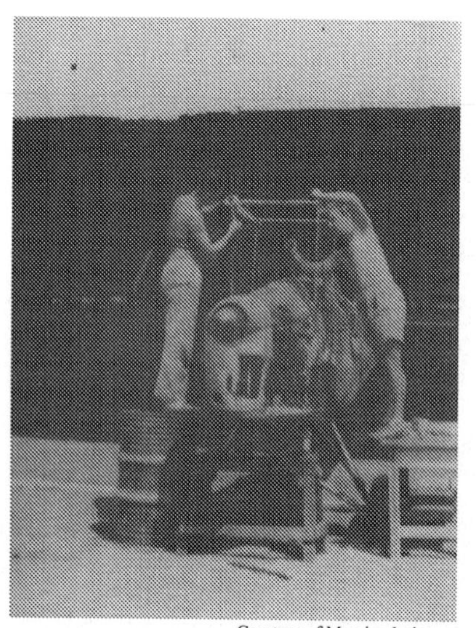

Courtesy of Maurice Jackson

Maurice Jackson and Ted Cheale assembling
a Tiger Moth at Ekona, British Cameroons.

The 'morning after' my birthday party - we seem to have had fun with the fire-extinguishers. Maurice Jackson and Peter Wickstead having breakfast. Author taking photograph of someone taking a photograph of him. British Cameroons.

Author in Piper Cub. Ecuador.

Francois Lesieur landing.

through the tangled wreckage. He was in hospital, but not badly hurt. Although the Tiger Moth was prone to accidents, because it was often flown overloaded and was underpowered, rarely was the pilot badly hurt. I went to see Peter, who was quite cheerful, enjoying being pampered by the nurses, one he subsequently married. Crop spraying has many hazards!

Operating from Yeovil aerodrome, I had taken the last load before lunch. As I dived rather sharply into a field of potatoes I heard a loud bang. It was not the engine and I could not place it; everything seemed to be working correctly. Back at the airfield I decided I must have left something in the rear locker, which lifted up and thumped down again when I dived into the field, but the locker was empty.

Walking round the aircraft, I noticed small holes in the starboard mainplanes. "Looks like holes made by shotgun pellets," said one of the ground crew.

"Yes; that's it," I exclaimed. "As I went into the field I heard a bang, some idiot has shot at me."

After lunch we continued work. While spraying a nearby field, I heard two bangs and felt pellets hit me. "Good lord, the chap's shooting at me again!" I pulled up and flew around looking for him. I saw a man standing on the edge of the field with a shotgun. I throttled back and flew towards him at about 30 feet, looking over the side of the cockpit. As I approached he raised the gun and emptied both barrels at me. Momentarily I was shocked, then angry. As I passed over him I pulled the dump lever and emptied yellow dyed spray on him.

The markers had seen and heard this and were running up. The man pointed the gun at them and told them to get off his land, which they wisely did. When we met back at the airfield, they told me my dump had been on target, which pleased me.

This was now getting beyond a joke, so I went to the police station and reported it. The rest of the day was spent with me and the markers making statements. The next day I went to the police station to find out if it was safe for me to continue working; they assured me the man had been warned and would be charged.

The case came up at Chard magistrates court two months later. The man was charged under one of the Air Navigation Acts of 'unlawfully shooting at an aircraft'. He engaged a London lawyer, who maintained his client was shooting pigeons and the aircraft got in the way. Some pigeon! I wonder what I would have been charged with if I fired six shots at a passing car? It transpired that the farmer had been in a mental home at one time, so I was not quite so angry with him. But I did wonder how in these circumstances he was allowed a gun. He was fined £20.

The case got into the popular papers and even in the *Daily Telegraph*, where my brother who was a sub-editor, saw it. A few weeks later a telegram arrived from the Scots timber men in the Cameroons. 'Fly over here and we will shoot you down, too.' it said.

The next year, spraying in Yorkshire in a Piper Cub, I nearly had a serious accident. After spraying the field, I did a run alongside some electric cables which passed over the field on 30 foot poles. Perhaps the cross-wind was stronger than I thought or I was not paying enough attention, but I found myself getting too close. I pulled up and banked away to the left. Suddenly the right wing dropped and I found myself in a steep bank to the right. I applied full opposite aileron and then suddenly I was straight and level.

I looked around and saw the right boom had gone and the electricity poles were oscillating backwards and forwards; then several of them toppled over. As I pulled up one of the spray nozzles caught under a wire and pulled me round. Luckily the boom broke away, but the stretched wire had whipped back and forwards with great force, causing the poles to oscillate and fall down. I had cut off the electricity to a part of Yorkshire. It was all over so quickly, there was no time to be scared, but after I landed, I realised what a near thing it had been!

In the spring of 1962 I flew a Boeing Stearman, applying granular fertiliser in several English counties. The Stearman was the American elementary trainer, the equivalent of the Tiger Moth, but bigger and more sturdily built. It was the basic crop spraying aircraft in America for many years, until special aircraft were manufactured. This was the only Stearman flying in England. It had been re-engined with a 450 hp Pratt and Whitney engine, and was capable of lifting a large load. However, in accordance with the thinking of the aviation authorities it was licensed to carry a smaller load than a Tiger Moth.

There was no starter, so it had to be hand swung. It started easily from cold, but could be difficult if the engine was hot. As it was nose heavy, application of the brakes had to be made with care, or it could end up on its nose. It should have had a weight in the tail to balance the larger engine.

The aircraft was flown from the rear cockpit, which was very spacious with the rudder pedals so widely spaced that it seemed to have been designed for a bandy-legged cowboy. The cockpit being so far back, with a large engine in front, the view forward was restricted. The cockpit was also very wide and it was not easy to look forward over the side. But in spite of these drawbacks the aircraft was pleasant and responsive to fly, and I was soon carrying large loads.

Taking delivery of the aircraft at Northampton, I had to fly it to Beccles on the Norfolk-Suffolk border. The compass had not been adjusted and was so far out as to be useless, which meant I had to map read over unfamiliar country and got hopelessly lost. I saw a grass aerodrome and landed to find out where I was. It was RAF Swanton Morley, way off track. I was not happy on this flight, in a strange aircraft, with no compass and not sure of the engine fuel consumption. However, I did arrive at Beccles without mishap.

On one occasion I nearly lost the aircraft on the ground. We parked it on a disused airfield where the ground surrounding the runways was rough, full of potholes and rubble. We left the aircraft and the marker's van overnight.

The next morning was cold, but clear, with a heavy frost. On arriving I swung the engine to start and as it was very cold I left it ticking over to warm up. When we tried to start the marker's van, the battery was flat. We had no tow-rope, so we pushed it on to the taxiway, which had a slope. It was reluctant to start and we had to push it a long way. When it did start we were out of breath, gulping lungfuls of freezing air.

I looked back at the Stearman and saw it slowly moving forward. While we had been trying to start the van, the oil had warmed up, and the speed of the engine increased enough to set it in motion. Everyone was exhausted and out of breath, but the aircraft was moving slowly and surely towards a pit full of stones and bricks.

Gasping for breath and the freezing air searing my lungs, I ran back to the aircraft. I managed to grab the throttle just as it got to the edge of the pit. I switched off the engine and collapsed on the ground, completely exhausted. It was ten minutes before I recovered enough to stand up. It was a near thing and not a good start to the day.

As the sun warmed the ground, mist rose over the airfield. We went off to the nearest transport café for a good breakfast. After about two hours a gusty wind blew the mist away and late in the morning it started to rain. We had now been up for eight hours, so I decided the Gods were against us, and it was better to pack up for the day and start afresh on the morrow.

The company also operated two Tiger Moths. I took over from one of the pilots for a week-end. After flying the Stearman, a bigger aircraft, with a powerful engine giving a throaty roar, it was like flying a sewing machine!

The company manager was an energetic, hardworking man, leaving home early in the morning and after driving hundreds of miles, visiting the units, agents and customers, returning late at night. He would work out complicated moves for his units and often good working time was lost. I used to think that if he sat down over a cup of coffee for half an hour before he set off, and gave some thought to the day's programme it might save him a lot of work and increase productivity.

Telephoning him early one morning he told me to meet him at a farmer's field and gave me a map reference. It was only three miles from Northampton aerodrome, so I suggested I met him there. At least we could communicate if either was delayed. He was not agreeable to this and assured me it was a big field. I had some premonition and insisted on the aerodrome. I looked at the field on the way to the aerodrome. He was quite right, it was a lovely big field, but as the farmer had ploughed half of it, it was now a small field!

It was fun flying the Stearman, but I would not have liked to spray with it in England, due to the poor visibility from the cockpit, so I looked for another contract for the summer.

16

Return to the Sudan

The Sudanese proverb that says those who drink the water of the Nile will return proved true in my case. I returned to the Sudan for the 1960 cotton spraying season, and every season after, until 1968.

The growing of cotton was developed when the Sudan was administered by the British. As well as private schemes along both banks of the Blue and White Niles, south of Khartoum, a large Government scheme was started in the Gezira, the area of land formed by a triangle between Khartoum, Kosti and Sennar. A dam was built across the Blue Nile at Sennar and a canal to take irrigation water to the scheme. The land being so flat, most of the cotton is irrigated by gravity.

The area is divided into cotton schemes of about 5,000 acres each, under a manager. These again are divided into blocks of 90 acres, and a three-year crop rotation is worked, cotton, doura, and fallow, the total area of the scheme being about 15,000 acres. Doura is a form of millet and is part of the staple diet of the villagers. Each tenant works his five acres of cotton, doura and fallow and the government supplies the seed, chemicals, irrigation and management. A form of share farming.

Before the monoculture of cotton all the pests and insects had a hard time scratching a living in the scrub. Then these luscious, succulent crops appeared and their standard of living rose to great heights. They prospered and multiplied, but started to damage the crops, affecting the yields and quality of the cotton.

The only way to control the pests was by spraying the crops with insecticides. Initially this was done by tractor, but the areas were so big and the tractors were slow and tended to damage the crop, so aircraft were employed. In the early days of aircraft, in the mid-fifties, it was only necessary to spray the crop once, but as the insects prospered on these lovely crops, they started to reproduce faster. By the time I last flew in the Sudan, the crops needed spraying four or five times to control the insects.

Two companies, Crop Culture and Fisons had local companies in the Sudan. Both operated their own aircraft and Fisons also contracted in companies from England, Holland and East Africa. Other companies from Sweden, England and Bulgaria competed for government contracts on the Gezira schemes.

The season in the Sudan was from September to December, which coincided with the end of the European season, so pilots and ground staff of many European nationalities took contracts there. Pilots and engineers came from England, Holland, Denmark, Sweden, Finland, Germany, East Africa and France. A very cosmopolitan set-up.

Spraying was easy, as there were few obstacles. No trees, wires, houses or roads. The weather, except for occasional rain and haboob (desert dust storm), in the early part of the season, was fine and hot. The most trying part of the work was the heat. Someone remarked that it was more an endurance test.

The crews to load the aircraft with chemical regularly migrated from their villages to seek seasonal employment. They arrived with their string beds and a bag containing all their possessions. Walking in Khartoum I would be greeted by a smiling Sudanese calling, "Abu Digin." (Mr Beard) "How are you?" Their English was limited, but their greeting was full of warmth.

In the field they were a semi-nomadic community. Moving from strip to strip they loaded all their possessions, beds, tents and cooking materials on to the tractors and wagons, and then set up a little camp on arrival. They allocated duties between themselves, one cooked, some mixed the chemical, others loaded the aircraft or filled the mixing tanks with water from the nearest canal. They worked hard and were always cheerful, but woe betide you if you upset them. They would become sullen, slow and unco-operative.

They loved to be involved. If you got out of the aircraft for a smoke and a drink and pointed to the mark on the aircraft tank where you wanted it filled, they would stand on the wing, and with great concentration watch the liquid rise and shout "Abaase" (enough) at the exact point. They always had tea brewing and brought the pilot glasses of hot, sweet tea during the day. Working with a regular crew, when shopping in a nearby town, I would bring them packets of tea and sugar.

The crews used to suffer from cuts and sores, which tended to fester. Seeing a young lad with a nasty sore on his leg, I got the aircraft first aid kit, put some antiseptic on the sore and covered it with a bandage. After that most mornings someone came up for medical treatment. Eventually I found I was running a morning surgery and had to buy more supplies!

The crews had great loyalty to their pilot. Near Ed Duem a pilot hit the only tree for miles. The aircraft caught fire and he was badly burnt. Taken to Ed Duem hospital, the doctor said he had to be flown back to England. Sudan Airways would fly him out of Ed Duem in a Dove if the strip was lengthened. The loading crew worked all day and most of the night removing bushes and boulders and filling holes so the Dove could land.

My first trip back to the Sudan was with ADS, a Southend company run by Ladi Marmol. He flew an EP9 and I flew a Piper Cub. It was a much more comfortable trip than my previous flight in a Tiger Moth. The Cub was faster, had brakes and a radio.

It was without incident, except for two things that I remember. Stopping the night at Tripoli in Libya, we asked the hotel for lunch boxes. Next morning we were each given two boxes tied together with string. After being airborne a few hours, Ladi called up on the radio: "Have you opened the lunch box yet?"

"No," I replied, "are they any good?"

"Not bad at all," he said, "Chicken leg, lamb chop, tomato and salad. Quite good."

I opened one of my boxes. A banana, an apple, a piece of fruit cake, some biscuits and cheese. Ah, that's the dessert, I opened the other box. A banana, an apple, a piece of fruit cake, some biscuits and cheese. I had both dessert boxes and Ladi had both main course boxes! Only in Africa could this happen.

At Cairo in transit to Luxor, I suggested to Ladi that we could clear ourselves through as we were not stopping. We took all the aircraft papers to customs and asked them to clear us while we had lunch. Returning we found nothing had been done. "The man to do this is not here," said the official.

"When will he be back?" asked Ladi. "We want to get to Luxor tonight."

The official shrugged his shoulders. "If you are in a hurry, see if Misr Airways can clear you."

We went to Misr, who for a fee cleared us quite quickly. We should have realised that in Africa everyone has to have his percentage and you cannot by-pass the system.

The next year I flew to the Sudan again, with Ladi Marmol. We had two EP9s, one flown by Ladi and the other by Ken Rutter, a Piper Pawnee flown by Peter Greensmith and I flew the Piper Cub.

It was a routine flight until we left Tripoli in Libya. Soon after take-off Ladi called on the radio, "If we fly direct to Benghazi instead of following the coast we shall save time." This took us across the Bay of Sirtes and I was not too happy about this, as I dislike flying over water in a single-engined aircraft unless it is absolutely necessary. However, the others agreed, so we altered course and set out over the sea, and soon the North African coast disappeared.

About an hour after leaving the coast, Peter called up to say his oil pressure was dropping. Immediately we all turned towards the coast. Ken called up saying that there was an emergency landing strip marked on the map due south of us, and he would fly ahead and locate it. Peter reported that his oil pressure was not getting any lower, but Ladi and I stayed with him. The coast came in sight and Ken called up to say he had found the landing field. It was just a level area in the desert, with no buildings and nothing around for miles.

On landing we found that the copper pipe taking oil to the pressure gauge had a small crack and was leaking. Little oil had been lost, but this accounted for the fall in pressure. We cut the pipe and bent the end over to seal it. It meant the pressure gauge would not be working; otherwise it was safe to continue.

While we were putting the engine cowls back on to the engine, a large cloud of dust appeared on the horizon, and revealed several vehicles approaching at high speed; a jeep leading three army lorries.

The jeep drove up and an army officer got out. The lorries

swung round and took up stations around the landing ground. The tail boards dropped and ten soldiers jumped down from each lorry, lined up and pointed their guns at us. We could hear the rifle bolts click!

Libya and Tunisia at that time were having border squabbles, so the officer was suspicious. We explained to him why we had landed and that we were en route to Benghazi, and then on to the Sudan to spray cotton. He examined the aircraft and was suspicious of the spray booms in the fuselage of the EP9s, thinking they might be some sort of weapon.

Eventually he said he would have to take all the aircraft papers to be examined by his commanding officer. Rather than us all going, Ken said he would take the papers in the jeep with the officer. We settled down to await his return under the scrutiny of the soldiers who remained in an alert attitude, pointing their guns at us. Two hours later Ken returned and said we were not allowed to continue and we all had to go to the town. It was now too late to continue anyway, so we secured the aircraft, took our overnight bags and piled into the jeep.

We were taken to the barracks and shown into the office of the commanding officer. He had all our documents on his desk, and was very polite, but explained that he could not let us continue until he had clearance from his superiors in Tripoli. We were put into a hotel, accompanied all the time by an officer as our minder. Although treated courteously, we were obviously under house arrest. We had dinner with our minder and went to bed with two armed soldiers stationed in the corridor.

Our minder appeared at breakfast. They had no reply from Tripoli, so he suggested we all went to the beach for a swim. We spent the morning there, then after lunch were told that we could continue our journey. It was too late to leave that day, so we had another night in the hotel, but with no guards. Next morning we took off, stopping at Benghazi to refuel and then to continue to El Adem to stay the night.

When we got to the entrance of the runway at Benghazi, flying control recalled us to the apron. Ladi went to the control tower to find out the problem. El Adem was an RAF staging post in Libya, near the Egyptian border and you could only land there with prior permission. Ladi had arranged all this before we left England, but no one at El Adem knew anything about it and would not accept us.

The controller was most helpful and signals went off to El Adem and Tripoli, and finally London. Being a week-end it was difficult to find any officials, so we had to stay the night. What went wrong we never knew. Whether someone at El Adem had lost the bit of paper, or if it was the side effects of our unscheduled landing was not clear. However, by the morning it had been sorted out. We took off for El Adem and Cairo, where we stopped the night, then on to Wadi Halfa and Khartoum with no further problems.

At about this time, Ian Taylor, who had started a spraying company, Airspray (Cyprus) Ltd, with another ex-Crop Culture pilot, Jack Akers, was taking four Piper Cubs to the Sudan. One of the spray pilots was not available to ferry an aircraft, and was coming out later by airline. An airline pilot, one of Ian's friends, agreed to ferry the fourth aircraft during his leave.

Spray pilots rarely use radio and dislike it; they prefer to go quietly on their way with as little control as possible. The airline pilot, well versed in radio procedures was elected to lead the flight. They proceeded over Europe to the Mediterranean, with the airline pilot talking to all the control zones and areas on the way.

They left Sicily, to cross to Tunisia by the short over-water route, and then turn east for Tripoli. Fully loaded with fuel in the long-range tanks, they climbed slowly to 3,000 feet. Entering Tunisian air space, the leader called Tunis control, giving position, height and ETA at Tripoli.

Tunisia was as touchy as Libya about aircraft near their border. Tunis control came back. "Climb immediately to 20,000 feet." Fully laden they could not get much higher than 3,000 feet, let alone 20,000 feet. This order left the airline pilot speechless.

As no reply was forthcoming from the lead aircraft, Ian picked up his microphone, "Climbing immediately to 20,000 feet," he stated.

"Call at 20,000 feet," replied Tunis control.

"Roger, will do," replied Ian.

They trundled along at 3,000 feet, altering course a little to give Tunisia a wide berth. After about 20 minutes, Ian called up. "Levelling out at 20,000 feet."

Tunis control replied, "Maintain this height to the Libyan

border." When they passed into Libya, Ian handed back communications to the airline pilot.

The EP9 needed careful maintenance as the engine cooling system was not very good in the hot Sudan climate. Ladi had a good engineer, Charlie Grund, who was kept busy keeping the aircraft serviceable. Charlie was a German who had been a parachutist in the war. He was taken prisoner, and spent some of his time in a prisoner of war camp in North America.

He told us one evening that, along with other prisoners, he was put to work packing boots for the American army. Some were destined for Europe and some for the Pacific. As part of their war effort, they packed all the left boots for Europe and the right boots for the Pacific!

Birds were still a menace over the cotton. Peter Greensmith once landed back with a broken windshield. As he opened the door of the Pawnee we saw his face covered in blood. It looked as if he had been seriously hurt, but when his face was washed, he only had a small cut on his forehead. All the blood was from a large bird which had become a squashed mass in the back of the cockpit.

On another occasion while approaching the cotton, I heard a loud bang and caught a glimpse of a large bird as it struck a glancing blow on the wing root next to the cockpit. It did no damage and after I had sprayed my load I saw it lying on a piece of open ground. It looked like a stork, and two other large birds were standing near. I thought I had killed it, but returning with another load, I saw it moving its head and now surrounded by seven or eight other birds.

They stood round in solicitous attitudes and seemed to be saying, "Come on, storkie, you've had a bad shock, but you can't just lie there. Move a wing or a leg and see if you can fly." Every time I returned it seemed to be recovering more, until at last it was standing up, moving its wings, but looking rather ruffled. Next time I returned they had all gone. It was intriguing to watch its slow recovery and the antics of its sympathetic friends and I was pleased that it came to no harm.

In 1962 I went to the Sudan with several other pilots to fly a 'Snow' aircraft for Crop Culture. We were leaving England on an evening flight and the company had arranged with the Sudanese embassy for us to pick up our visas that morning.

We all went to the embassy, presented our passports to the clerk and explained that it had all been arranged. "I don't know anything about this," said the clerk, "come back tomorrow."

"We are booked out on a flight tonight."

The clerk shrugged his shoulders and looked uninterested.

"Anyway tomorrow is Friday, aren't you shut then?"

"Yes," answered the clerk. We could see that we were being fobbed off by a lazy official, and after strong words he disappeared into the depth of the embassy and came back with the man who knew all about it. Our passports were stamped and we left for the airport.

On arriving in the Sudan, the first thing was to familiarise myself with flying a new aircraft. The Snow was a large aircraft, carrying 200 gallons and powered by a Pratt and Whitney 450 hp engine.

It was a simple, rugged aircraft, with the cockpit a long way back, but the sloping nose gave good visibility in the flying attitude. I first flew it light and found it viceless and easy to handle. Progressively taking heavier loads, I eventually flew it at maximum weight and found it easy to fly.

However, although normally docile, the aircraft had one trick up its sleeve for the unwary. Fully loaded it normally needed a long runway. In the heat of the day its performance deteriorated alarmingly.

About midday I took off with a full load of chemical and full fuel tanks. The take-off run was longer than usual, and when I eased the aircraft into the air at the end of the strip, I only just had flying speed. Continuing straight and level, 10 feet above the ground with the throttle fully open, I waited for the speed to build up, but it did not. The ground clearance was not enough to lower the nose to gain airspeed and if I raised the nose the airspeed dropped to near the stall. I could only fly straight out into the desert, striving to keep the aircraft airborne.

After several miles, gently juggling the stick and with the help of a few mild up-currents, I began to gain a little height. Eventually I had enough height and airspeed to start a wide, shallow turn, but the cylinder head temperature was very high as I was still on full throttle. Slowly I was able to turn some of my height into airspeed and ease back on the throttle. The cotton was now miles away and it seemed ages before the plot I was to spray came in sight. I lined up a long way off and slowly descended, building up airspeed on the way. Arriving at spraying height, I opened the spray valve for my first run. After three runs, with very gentle turns at the end, the aircraft weight had been reduced and it performed normally. Back at the strip after an hour and a half, I found everyone was starting to get worried. After that episode, I was careful to reduce my load as the day warmed up.

In subsequent years, until 1968, I flew for either Crop Culture or Airspray (EA), from Kenya, who were one of Fison's sub-contractors. I enjoyed my early years in the Sudan; desert countries can have a fascination and I got to know and like many Sudanese. Pilots and engineers, like me, returned for many seasons and we would meet every year in Khartoum at the Metro bar or the Grand Hotel.

Two Danish pilots, Sven Neilson and Kristian Kjaer, were regulars. Sven, small, dark and thin, spent all his free time lying in the sun, until he turned a mahogany colour, and with a towel round his waist he looked like an Indian fakir. Kristian, small and round, full of energy, reminded me of Charlie Drake, the comedian. Entomologists Peter Whitworth, Alan Bond and Arthur Toms, together with managers, Les Hewitt and Ted Jenkins were there most seasons.

Pilots came from England. Digby Goss, Peter Greensmith, Bob Milson, John Keats, Bill Bowker, Mike Pruden, Denys Howard, Francois Lesieur, Peter Ayles and Timber Wood from Kenya and many others. Some came only for one season, others for many. If you hadn't done a Sudan season, you were not really a proper crop spraying pilot!

Bill Trollope, a freelance engineer, who worked all over Africa, usually turned up with one of the companies. He was the engineer with Crop Culture in 1966, when I was flying an Auster Workmaster. I always disliked Austers as I could never land them properly. Trying to make three-point landings, the tailwheel would hit first, bouncing the aircraft on to the main wheels, which would bounce it back onto the tailwheel, so I would kangaroo all down the strip. I tried wheeling it on, with flap, with no flap, a little faster on the approach, but I always made an untidy landing.

While I was reloading Bill would stroll round the aircraft, inspecting it in an exaggerated fashion, implying that my landing may have damaged it and humming, "Hold me kangaroo down sport."

I shook my fist and shouted, "Bastard!" Bill went and sat on a barrel, laughing his head off.

Every season I met old friends. On several occasions I had dinner with Dave Savage. I flew many charters to the Middle East with him when I was in Jersey. He now flew Comets for Sudan Airways. Cyril Irbe, Chief Engineer with Island Air Charters in Jersey, was also now with Sudan Airways.

One day I met Mac Olde, walking to the terminal building, from an Avro York freighter that had just landed. Mac was flying for Ciro's Aviation, when I was with Westminster Airways back in 1949, and we did their maintenance. He pointed to a sheaf of papers he was carrying.

"This is what it's all about now," he remarked. "Flying the aeroplane is the easy part. Now you have to be a business manager and a diplomat when dealing with officials in African countries." A year later his fellow pilot from Ciro's, Joe Walton, flew me to England from Kenya in a British United Airways VC10. Stopping overnight at Entebbe, flying back to Kenya, I met Ernie Coombes, who had been with Westminster Airways. The aviation world was small and friendly in those days. Now jumbo jets fly vast distances non-stop and nobody meets anyone!

In those days you were likely to meet people you knew in all sorts of places and this sometimes resulted in some odd situations. Francois Lesieur was travelling in the airport bus between terminals at New York airport. Sitting opposite was a man whom he recognised and was sure he had met somewhere. He glanced at him several times, and the man could see from the expression on Francois' face what he was thinking. He leaned across and said in a low voice, "David Niven, old man."

Another time, Ted Cheale, a Crop Culture engineer was passing through Rome airport. One of the company's overseas managers, Jack Akers bore a close resemblance to Jack Hawkins, the actor. Ted had only met Jack Akers briefly, and going up to the bar, he saw who he thought was Jack Akers standing there. "Hello, Jack," he said, "what are you doing here?"

"I'm on my way to Athens. Where are you off to?" said Jack.

"I'm going back to England," replied Ted.

"Would you like a beer?" asked Jack.

"Thank you very much," said Ted.

Over their beers they got talking, but seemed to be on different tracks. Eventually Jack said, "I think you may be mistaking me for someone else. I'm Jack Hawkins, the actor." Poor Ted was most embarrassed.

Over the years I learnt enough Arabic to obtain basic needs, such as food, water and beer, and to instruct the tanker crews what load I wanted or how much fuel I needed. However, when talking to Arabs, it is useful to know the subtle meaning of some of their phrases.

If you enter an office, especially a government office, with a request or a query, you will be told. "Come back tomorrow," which means, 'I can't be bothered with you.' If you asked for something which has been ordered or previously arranged they will answer, "It will be here tomorrow," which means, 'I have done nothing about it yet.' Should you go to an office and ask to see someone by name, you will be greeted courteously, offered a chair, brought a coffee and be informed, "Wait, he is coming." After several fruitless waits, you realise this could mean he has just gone for a coffee, or he has gone to see his cousin in another town and will be back tomorrow!

Some of the owners and managers of the cotton schemes were very suspicious and seemed to think that the spraying company was out to cheat them. Others were crafty and tried to get a free spray. A spray treatment kept the cotton free of insects for about 14 days, after which reinfestation could occur, needing another application.

An owner would wait several days until he knew the entomologist was miles away, then send a message that the spray had not worked. By the time the entomologist returned on his inspections, natural reinfestation had occurred, but the owner tried to get a free spray and another 14 days protection.

One owner claimed the treatment had not worked because the chemical was not strong enough. Crop Culture's entomologist, Peter Whitworth, examined the crop and found all in order, but the owner insisted that the chemical was not strong enough. "Why do you think that?" asked Peter. "There are no insects in the cotton."

The owner waved his hand and said, "I tethered a donkey in the cotton while it was being sprayed and it did not die!"

Some owners believed the lower the aircraft flew, the better the spray treatment. If the aircraft flew with its wheels in the crop, they were delighted. But this is bad spraying as the lower the aircraft flew below the optimum of six to eight feet, the narrower the swath width, which could leave strips unsprayed.

This was explained to our Sudanese supervisor, and he was asked to impress this on the owners. "I know," he exclaimed, "I tell them, but these people are so ignorant!" This supervisor had a small cotton scheme of his own and a few days later it was due to be sprayed. As I walked out to the aircraft that morning, he came up to me. "You are spraying my cotton today, Captain?" he queried.

"That's right," I replied, "it's here on my list."

"Captain," he said, confidentially, putting his hand on my shoulder, "you will fly low, won't you?"

"Of course I will. I will fly with my wheels in the crop!"

"Thank you, Captain, thank you," he beamed.

There is also a widespread belief that aerial spraying should not be carried out in winds in excess of 10 mph. I have no idea how this arbitrary figure was arrived at, because I have sprayed satisfactorily in winds higher than this, and on the other hand have, under certain circumstances, refused to spray a particular field in light winds.

One of the scheme owners must have got hold of some articles or papers on aerial spraying. When I arrived on the scheme, there was a little boy armed with an anemometer, a hand-held instrument that indicated wind speed. I had been spraying for about three hours and the spray was settling beautifully into the crop. Landing to take on another load, the crew would not load me and pointed to the little boy.

He was standing on top of a tractor, with the indicator about 10 feet above the ground. It was indicating about 8 mph with occasional readings of 10 mph, so on the instructions of the owner had stopped the spraying. No way could I persuade the tanker crew to load me. Obviously they, too, had been given instructions by the owner and judging by their blank expressions, were embarrassed by the situation.

I was very annoyed and was not going to hang around until this little boy allowed me to continue. (It was not really his fault, he was only obeying orders.) I flew back to base and told Les Hewitt, Crop Culture's manager, about this ridiculous situation and said I was not returning until the boy and his instrument had been removed.

The next day the boy had gone and I was able to continue with my work, but a day's spraying had been lost. I found over the years that for every person assisting us to spray the cotton, there were an increasing number who tried to obstruct us for various dubious reasons.

On a Government scheme in the Gezira, some of the blocks were in line, with only a road between them. This was most unusual and the pilot took advantage of it and combined the two blocks in one run spraying over the narrow dividing road. This eliminated 40 turns, which is non-productive flying.

The manager saw this and went back to his office and from the scheme map worked out the acreage of all the roads on the scheme. He wanted that acreage deducted from the bill, as he was not paying for his roads to be sprayed! If the blocks had been sprayed separately two headland runs would have to be done parallel to the road, using as much chemical.

On another Gezira scheme, the manager wanted all the blocks to be sprayed in the consecutive order in which they were numbered. Some blocks ran east-west, some north-south and some were small due to the canal layout. It is time consuming and tiring to spray a small area with a fully-loaded aircraft as tight turns are not possible, so the pilot sprayed part of a large block, then with a lighter aircraft, would spray the small block. Also it was not possible to spray the east-west blocks early in the morning or late evening because the low sun blinded the pilot. Pilots moved around the scheme, spraying blocks out of sequence but according to the conditions at that time of day, keeping a record on the scheme map they carried.

These problems were pointed out to the manager and the reasons why blocks were not always sprayed in consecutive order. He had to accept these reasons but was still very suspicious, in spite of the fact that the cotton was inspected by an entomologist after spraying.

He decided to check on our work by sending out 'watchers' to count that the correct number of runs were made on each block and that each block was sprayed. These 'watchers' were mounted on white donkeys and wore red turbans, so they were easily recognisable.

It was very easy to confuse the 'watchers'; as two aircraft were working the scheme and they were not sure which aircraft they were watching. The pilot would move round the scheme and by the time the 'watcher' had caught up with him he would already have sprayed a block and moved on to another. If he only sprayed half a block and then moved on to another, the 'watcher' jumped onto his donkey and trotted off to the office to report only half a block sprayed. In the meantime the pilot would return, finish the block and move on.

By the time the 'watcher' returned, he had completely lost track of the situation and eventually he tethered his donkey and went to sleep on the canal bank!

One year we had a German-Swiss entomologist attached to us, whom we called Fred. He was a likeable chap, fitted into the mess well, and was good at his job. However, he tended to be a bit Germanic. After lunch everyone tried to have a short doze before returning to work and it amused us all when Fred would don an eyeshade, lie on his bed at attention and declare, "I now sleep!"

When part of the scheme had been sprayed, the manager called to say one of his tenants had complained that his cotton had not been sprayed. As the tenant's cotton was in the middle of a 90 acre block that had been sprayed the previous day, it could not have been missed. Fred inspected the cotton and assured the manager that this man's cotton had been treated with the rest of the block. The manager, however, still backed his tenant and the wrangle went on for several days.

One morning Fred met the manager out on the scheme. They greeted each other and talked for a while, then Fred said to him, "How was Khartoum?"

"What do you mean, how was Khartoum?" asked the manager.

"I heard you had been in Khartoum for three days," answered Fred.

"I haven't been to Khartoum," exclaimed the manager. "Where did you get that idea?"

"I met one of your tenants, and he told me you had been to Khartoum."

"Oh, you don't want to take any notice of them, they are all liars."

"Do you think so?" said Fred. "It was the tenant who said his cotton hadn't been sprayed."

The manager jumped into his Land-Rover and shot off in a cloud of dust. That was the last we heard of that!

During the ten seasons in the Sudan, I worked along both Nile rivers, from Khartoum to Renk on the White Nile and to Sinjah on the Blue Nile. When working on the government schemes in the Gezira, we set up mess in what had been the club house when the British ran the schemes. In those days this was the social centre with a bar, dining-room, lounge, billiard room, garden and tennis court, and bedrooms for guests.

After the British left, the clubs were not used much by the Sudanese. The gardens and tennis courts were neglected and overgrown and in those that still had a billiard table, it had torn baize and broken cues. At other bases such as Kosti, Sennar and Ed Duem, a house would be rented for the season.

When working we flew from dawn to dusk, except for a midday break, so life consisted of work, food and sleep. Food played a prominent part in our lives and all the companies I worked for did their best to supply good meals.

One season we had a terrible cook. He was so bad that most of us refused to eat his food and loaded up with tinned food from the Greek store in Wad Medani. Tins of ham, fish, paté and butter were kept in the refrigerator, along with bottles of 'Camel' beer.

This was the only beer available, a local brew, which varied in quality from bottle to bottle. It was known as 'camel piss' and had the picture of a camel on the label. As someone remarked, "The only beer to have a picture of the brewery on the label!"

The next year, Les Hewett, Crop Culture's manager had great difficulty in finding a cook. The cooks who could provide European food were trained in British households and were now very old or had taken other jobs.

The only suitable candidate was a younger man, but he wanted more money than Les was prepared to pay. Reluctantly he was taken on, but he was worth every penny. He produced wonderful curries, roast joints, meat pies, fresh Nile perch, fresh fruit salad, all local produce. Everyone looked forward to meal times, and he must have saved the company far more than his extra salary, because no one went to the Greek store for expensive tinned food.

Kosti was the best town to be based. It was quite large, with a market, a cinema, bars and cafés. One day a Dinka and his wife approached the town. The Dinkas are a tribe from southern

Sudan, very tall and slim with long legs, and the males have an exceptionally long penis. None of them are clothes conscious. The man was dressed with a spear and his wife with a string of beads.

The Sudanese authorities did not take kindly to these primitive people walking around the town in this state and they were stopped on the outskirts. A dress was found for the woman and a pair of shorts for the man. But when the man put on the shorts, which were very short, he was still partly exposed. The police gave up and waved them on. They walked into town with puzzled expressions on their faces.

I had been operating on the White Nile south of Kosti for several days and had reached almost as far a Renk. Another pilot and an entomologist were with me. We had a few days work in the Renk area and when it was almost completed, the other aircraft and the entomologist set off back to Kosti, leaving me to finish off the work. As I went to bed that night, I realised that probably the nearest European was at least 100 miles away. It caused me no concern and I slept easy.

Returning to Kosti, I learnt that President Kennedy had been assassinated ten days earlier. I thought then, that for ten days I, along with many other people, had been going about our work totally oblivious of this world-shattering news. Blazing headlines in the newspapers, graphic scenes on television, and while all this was going on I had gone out and sprayed cotton as usual, had a beer at the end of the day, eaten my supper and gone peacefully, untroubled to bed.

It made no difference to my life, and if in the future it did, I could do nothing to alter it. In the days before modern communications it could be months before people heard about a great victory or terrible defeat. In the meantime their lives went on, they gathered the harvest, took their produce to market, married, buried their dead. Do these apparently earth shattering events really affect ordinary people going about their mundane daily tasks? And if they do, can they do anything about it? Maybe I should not read newspapers or listen to the news and live a trouble-free life.

Stationed at Sennar one year, Abdul, the Sudanese supervisor, asked me to come gazelle hunting with him and his friend. This appealed to me as a welcome break so I agreed. Abdul arrived with his friend in a Land-Rover carrying a gun; I think it was a 12-bore shot gun.

We set off into the scrub north of Sennar, towards the River Dindar. They asked me to drive and after about an hour we spotted a gazelle. It ran off and we followed, bumping over the rough terrain, until we were in range. I stopped the car and Abdul fired. The gazelle ran on for several yards, and then it's hindlegs collapsed and it fell to the ground. We drove up and stopped beside it. It was shot in the rear and was lying whimpering with pain and fright, looking at us with large liquid brown eyes. It was a beautiful animal.

Abdul jumped out. "Where's the camera?" he asked his friend. They started to rummage around in the car.

"Finish it off, Abdul," I cried.

"In a minute," he replied, as he put his foot on the back of the gazelle, with hand on hip and gun at the slope, taking up the stance of a big game hunter. The gazelle was still whimpering and looking at me with those large frightened eyes.

"Finish it off, finish it off," I cried in desperation. His friend then took up the same stance, while Abdul took his photograph. When they had finished photographing each other, they cut its throat and put it out of its misery. I was now right off gazelle hunting. My idea of hunting was a clean shot through the heart.

They slung the gazelle in the back and off we set again, me driving quite slowly. Soon we saw another gazelle. "After it!" shouted Abdul. I revved the motor in low gear, steered for the roughest ground and tried to give the impression that I was catching up with it. After a while it turned off into some thick scrub where we could not follow it and escaped.

17

Eating Humble Pie

On arriving in the Sudan, passports were taken by the immigration officer at the airport and a receipt given. After two or three days they could be retrieved. What the authorities did with them in the meantime I never found out.

Several of us went to collect our passports. Francois Lesieur, being a Frenchman, had a French passport which the officer could not find. "Come back tomorrow, Captain," he said. Francois returned the next day, but no passport. "Come back tomorrow, Captain," he was told.

The same thing happened again the next day and Francois was getting annoyed. Sitting down in a chair in front of the officer's desk he declared, "I am not leaving here until you find my passport." This brought about great activity, desks were searched, drawers opened, filing cabinets gone through, without success.

Idly watching all this activity, Francois looked down and saw something familiar under a leg of the desk. Removing it he found that it was his passport! It had been put there to stop the desk rocking on an uneven floor! "Ah! Captain, I am so sorry, what a stupid thing to do," exclaimed the officer, "I will find out who did this stupid thing and reprimand him severely." As Francois was leaving he looked back and saw the officer slip another passport under the wobbly leg!

One year I was almost deported from the Sudan a few days after my arrival. Although there was a Department of Civil Aviation, with a Director, they issued no licences of their own, but validated foreign ones. This was a slip of paper, typewritten, not printed. I used to attach it to my British licence, so it would not be lost.

The validation was only for the spraying season and had to be renewed each year. My licence had been sent in for validation, but the next day, Arthur Toms, Crop Culture's resident entomologist, came to me with a worried expression on his face. "You are in some sort of trouble," he said. "They are refusing to validate your licence."

I was puzzled. "I can't think what the problem can be," I said. "My British licence is valid."

"Well, they seem very serious about it," said Arthur, "so I have arranged for you to see the Director this afternoon."

That afternoon Arthur and I went to see the the Director. After we had sat down in front of his desk, he looked at me and said, "You have written on your validation form, defacing a government document."

"But," I said still puzzled, "I haven't got my validation yet."

"No, and you may not get it. Look at this," passing me a piece of paper, which I recognised as last year's validation form. "See," he said, "you have scrawled something on the back."

I turned the form over and recognised the name and phone number of one of our agents back in England. "That is one of our agents in England," I said. "I can't remember writing this, but I must have been in a phone box and needed to make a note and had nothing to write on. As this validation had expired I looked on it as a piece of scrap paper, and I forgot to throw it away afterwards."

"This is an official document," he reiterated, "and you have mutilated it. You have insulted the Sudanese government."

"I can assure you I had no intention of insulting the Sudanese government. As it had expired, I thought of it as a piece of scrap paper and I should have removed it from my licence and thrown it away."

"I take a very serious view of this," he went on, "and I shall want a written apology from you before I validate your licence."

"I'm most sorry," I replied. "It was not my intention to insult the Sudanese government and if you require an apology, I will write you one."

When we left the office I said to Arthur, "What a lot of

codswallop."

"I know," said Arthur, "but if you want your validation, you will have to write an apology."

I went back to the hotel, and with my tongue in my cheek, wrote a humble, creeping and fulsome apology and got my licence validated. The Director, no doubt, filed it with great satisfaction.

While spraying in the Gezira, I was detached to Sennar, to assist the the pilot stationed there, Martin Coates, who was flying a Piper Cub. On landing I was met by the entomologist, Peter Whitworth. Normally a cheery chap, he looked very serious. "Martin's crashed into the dam," he said.

One is never prepared for this sort of news and I was quite shocked. "When was this?" I asked.

"About two hours ago," replied Peter. After two hours there was no hope of him surviving, but even in hopeless situations you feel that something must be done, so I took off and flew over the dam, but I could see nothing.

Martin was a very pleasant New Zealander and a good pilot. Apparently he had taken up a visiting engineer who had been working on the dam's hydro-electric plant and wanted to take some aerial photographs. According to eye witnesses, while flying over the lower part of the dam, the aircraft suddenly turned and dived into the water and disappeared.

Les Hewitt spent four days being rowed over the lower part of the dam with a grappling iron, until he finally located the aircraft. A barge with a diver came down from Khartoum and the aircraft was retrieved. Martin and his passenger were buried in Khartoum. No reason for this tragic accident was found.

From 1965 to 1967 I flew a Pawnee in the Sudan for Airspray (EA) Ltd, based at Nairobi, who were contracted to Fisons. I flew to Nairobi with British United Airways, who had an interest in Airspray. The first year I had to sit an air law examination to obtain an East African licence.

Another pilot who joined the company had to take a technical examination on the Pawnee, as he had not got it on his licence. The Pawnee is a very simple aircraft, but he failed the examination. He sat it again a few days later and failed again. When he failed it the third time, Alec Noon, the managing director was getting a bit upset as he had work for the pilot. He went with the pilot to the Civil Aviation office to find out the problem. These exams were of the multiple choice format, and it transpired that the clerk checking the paper was using the answer sheet for a different aircraft. No wonder the poor pilot was always failing!

From Nairobi I would fly to the Sudan via Entebbe, Juba and Malakal, over some desolate country. The range of the Pawnee was not quite enough for some of the legs between these airports, so a small extra fuel tank was fitted into the spray tank. This only gave a small reserve of fuel, so it was important to check the weather over the route as there was nowhere to divert to, especially on the outward journey which was at the end of the rainy season.

The worst part of the journey was flying over the Sudd, a large swamp on the Nile, just south of Malakal. If you landed or crashed there it was very doubtful if you would ever be found. It was while flying this route through rain, when to my surprise, I encountered carburettor icing.

The Chief Pilot was 'Timber' Wood, the most laid back, relaxed spray pilot I ever met. He would catch little 'catnaps' while he was being reloaded. I was told a story that while he was being reloaded with chemical and fuel, the crew chief noticed that the 'captain' had dozed off. "Quiet!" he said to his men, "the captain sleeps." They tiptoed round, making no noise or rocking the aircraft while they reloaded. When they had finished they sat on their haunches, in a circle in front of the aircraft and waited. 'Timber' dozed on for some time and then woke with a start. When the crew saw this they all jumped up, waving their arms and laughing gleefully. They thought it a great joke!

I sometimes suspected that 'Timber' also took the odd nap on ferry flights. Flying in close formation with him while returning to Sennar at the end of a day's spraying, I had the feeling that he had dozed off. Arriving at Sennar, I went in and landed, but 'Timber' carried on in the direction of Kosti, and disappeared from sight. After I had been back at the mess about ten minutes, drinking my first beer, 'Timber' came in looking a bit sheepish.

The advantage of working for Fisons was they had been in the Sudan a long time and were well established and organised. Their Sudanese staff were well-trained and efficient. As well as the company office in Khartoum, where the Managing Director, Charles Rennie, presided, there was a permanent base at Sennar, with Sayid Meckie as manager and another one at Kosti, where Lars Pederson was manager. Lars, a Dane, had been in the Sudan for many years and spoke Arabic. He was calm and unflappable and very efficient. There was another base at Gos Caberro, near Wad Medani, with workshops and a hangar for their own Piper Cubs.

This was like a little oasis. A long-established compound with many trees, cool bungalows and a swimming pool. An ideal spot to rest between spraying programmes.

Lars told me that one year he was travelling to Kosti by train in the rainy season. Heavy rains flooded the countryside and washed away part of the railway track. The train was stuck in the desert for a week, surrounded by a lake of water, so no one could get to them and the passengers could not leave. He had nothing to read, the ice ran out after three days and then food and water got scarce. He declared it was the most frustrating time he had ever spent.

'Timber' Woods and I went to spray a large scheme where the landing strip was in the centre. The manager came out with only one map. 'Timber' tore the map in two. "You do that bit," he said, "I'll do this bit." We worked all day with no word passing between us. When we had finished 'Timber' refuelled and left. After I had refuelled I had trouble starting the engine. In hot climates you have to get the engine priming just right or the engine will not start.

After fruitless attempts to start the engine, the battery was flat, so I started to hand swing it. I primed it and swung it. I blew it out and swung it. It just would not start. About half an hour later I was dripping with sweat and my arm ached. I had visions of being stuck out for the night. After a rest I tried again with no success. Then another rest and it started. What a relief! I realised afterwards, that instead of wearing myself out and getting in a sweat, if I had sat down for an hour and allowed the engine to cool down, it would have started on the first swing!

All the transit flying was done at low level, sometimes following the river hoping to see a hippopotamus or a crocodile. Flying over the scrub you might come on a semi-nomadic village of straw huts. When the children heard the aeroplane they rushed out of the huts at the same time as the goats, frightened by the aeroplane rushed in. They met in the doorway and all disappeared under a confusion of dust, black bodies and white fur!

Standing by our aircraft, getting ready to go spraying, a Sudanese drove his Land-Rover towards the aircraft at high speed, jamming on the brakes at the last minute and stopping two feet away from a Pawnee, grinning all over his face.

The grin soon left his face when one of the pilots shouted, "You bloody idiot, what the hell do you think you are doing. If your brakes had failed you could have wrecked an aircraft."

That evening the Sudanese manager came into our mess. "One of my drivers has complained that one of the pilots swore at him." We told him what the driver had done. "Well, I don't think you should swear at a Sudanese," said the manager.

"He wasn't sworn at because he was a Sudanese," we emphasised. "The same thing would have been said to one of our pilots or engineers, if he had done such a foolish thing." The manager was partly mollified.

Over the years it was becoming more difficult to work in these Third World countries. There was a great deal of nepotism and if you upset someone he would have a cousin in immigration, an uncle in exchange control or a son in the foreign office, and although they might not be able to take any positive action against you, they could make things very awkward.

While spraying the cotton, at times chemical drifted into the irrigation canals alongside and killed the fish. Walking beside a canal with our entomologist, villagers were gleefully scooping the fish out for their supper. "Shouldn't you tell them," I asked the entomologist, "that these fish have been poisoned and are dangerous to eat?"

"Don't worry," he replied, "they would be ill from overeating fish, before they ingested enough poison to harm them."

We were troubled by flies and mosquitos. At the end of each day, pilots would leave a small amount of chemical in their tanks and spray the rest-house before landing. It was very effective, but what the Health and Safety authorities in more regulated countries would have had to say about it, I dread to think. No one was ill from this practice, though food contaminated by flies might have made them so. The manager even asked us to spray his house!

Fisons bought some government surplus loading pumps. They were ex-navy, and like all service equipment built to last. A diesel engine drove the pump, both mounted on a strong metal chassis, with two wheels nearly five feet in diameter. It needed a tractor to move it. Unfortunately they were very slow and took five minutes to load the aircraft. I mentioned this drawback to Fison's managing director. "Ah," he said, "I deliberately got slow pumps, so that the pilot had a little rest between loads."

It certainly did not rest the pilot. To sit in the cockpit for five minutes in that hot climate was both uncomfortable and frustrating. The pilot had to stop every two hours to refuel anyway, when he could get out, drink a glass of tea, have a cigarette and relax properly.

There were pumps on the market which would load the aircraft in under two minutes and could be carried in one hand. This man rarely saw the operations in the field, which was fair enough as his job was administration, but why do managers not consult the people who have to use the equipment and listen to their views? It was also bad business as up to 100 acres of treatment a day were lost.

I only spent a few days each year in Nairobi, but it was a pleasant town. Although on the Equator, being 8,000 feet high days were warm and nights cool. I was shocked, however, to find parking meters decorating the streets! I did not realise then that they would spread to even the remotest parts of the world.

As I was paid by a Kenyan company, though working in the Sudan, I had to pay income tax in Kenya. As I only spent a week each year in Kenya, I reckoned, pro-rata, I was one of the most highly taxed people in the country! There was no way of avoiding taxation, as a tax clearance certificate had to be produced before it was possible to leave the country.

My last year in the Sudan was 1988 and I flew for Crop Culture again. By this time it was becoming increasingly difficult to operate. As I mentioned previously there seemed to be more people trying to hinder than to help. I swear that some owners were more interested in suing the operator for some minor or imagined infringement of the contract, than earning money from marketing their cotton.

The economy was not healthy and many goods were scarce or unobtainable. It reminded me of a frontier region. One year you could buy hacksaw blades, but no hacksaw frames. The next year you could buy the frames but no blades.

Again I had a paperwork problem, though this time not with the Sudanese. British pilot licences now had a Certificate of Experience attached to them, that had to be signed every six months by a pilot authorised by the Civil Aviation Authority, usually a company chief pilot or an instructor. Previously the pilot certified on the form at his medical examination that he had current experience. If this new certificate was not signed, then the licence was not valid.

A British pilot sent his licence to be validated by the Sudanese and it was rejected because his Certificate of Experience had not been currently signed. When I heard this, I checked on mine and found it was a month out of date. To send it back to England to get it signed by my usual man would probably have taken several weeks, providing he had not gone overseas himself. I looked at the certificate which he had signed several times previously and taking a pencil doodled with his signature. Then taking a pen I wrote his signature in the column and added his licence number. I had no qualms of conscience about this as my experience was current. When I got back to England, I told him what I had done. He smiled, shrugged his shoulders and said, “I can’t say I blame you.”

A crop-spraying pilot running a one man operation in the Cameroons encountered the same problem. He wrote to CAA in England asking what he should do. He was sent the names of three pilots with Nigerian Airways who were authorised to sign the Certificate. One pilot he knew had left to join Fiji Airways, another was on leave and the third he did not know. No one would risk their licence and log book to the vagaries of the African postal system anyway. How he solved it, I never heard.

CAA rules and regulations are usually drawn up with the airlines in mind, who have staff and organisation to deal with this sort of paperwork. Bureaucratic organisations have little time for people, such as crop spraying pilots, who do not fit into their neat pigeon holes.

The yearly season in the Sudan supplied me with a bread and butter income, but if I wanted jam, I had to find work for the rest of the year. Luckily there were short term contracts in other parts of the world to supply it.

18

Africa Wins Again

In 1963 Crop Culture obtained a contract for Quelea bird control from the Nigerian government. The Quelea is a small bird about the size of a wren and flourishes in a belt right across Central Africa. They eat crops and are almost as prolific and as destructive as locusts.

I had seen these birds returning to roost in the Sudan. Just before dusk, the sky from horizon to horizon would be covered with a weaving band of birds, just as if someone had flicked a black gossamer scarf across it. When roosting, hundreds crowd on to the branches, and although individually very light, their collective weight could sometimes break a branch.

The method used to control these birds was to locate their roosting and nesting sites, depending on the season, and place petrol drums in the woods. When they came in at night and settled on the branches, the petrol was detonated, eliminating the wood and the birds with a big 'whoosh'! Now a different method of control was to be tried, spraying the sites with a chemical to kill the birds.

The agricultural officer in charge of the control programme, Ray Hitchcock, showed me photographs of a site after it had been blown up. The dead birds were so thick on the ground that they almost came up to the knees of a man standing in the wood.

I flew by airline to Kano, where I was met by a European from the Ministry of Agriculture. I stayed the night there before going on to Maiduguri in northern Nigeria where I was to be based.

Over a beer that night the man from the Ministry chatted, in a light hearted way, of the problems and tribulations of working in Africa. He spoke of AWA. "What's AWA?" I asked him.

"Oh, you will come across AWA frequently," he replied. "It stands for 'Africa wins again'. Whatever you try to do and however carefully you plan it, the country will do its best to beat you. It is one big struggle and difficult to win."

He also told me that the Government had a small fleet of aircraft for the use of officials whose work involved travelling to various parts of the country. However, at the last minute the aircraft would be commandeered by a member of the Government, often for a frivolous journey. This happened so often, wrecking the officials' itinerary, that they rarely used the aircraft. Although this meant more time was spent, in less comfortable conditions, travelling in this large country, at least they had control of the situation.

The next morning I left for Maiduguri in a Piper Aztec flown by an Indian pilot. I was the only passenger. We arrived over the airfield at 3,000 feet, carried out a procedure circuit and landed about ten minutes later. As there are few aircraft movements at Maiduguri, and the pilot was in radio contact, I wondered why he did not make a straight-in approach. Maybe he was paid by flight time!

Maiduguri Airport, with two good runways, seemed out of place in such an isolated and sparsely populated part of the country. But I found out later that it had been built in the war as a staging post for aircraft flown or shipped into West Africa from America, and then ferried across to the Sudan and up to Egypt for the North African campaign.

Ray Hitchcock met me and took me out to his compound about 15 miles east of Maiduguri, where he lived in a luxurious, air-conditioned caravan. He had built a straw house for me and suggested, rather than stay in the rest-house in the town, I stayed with him.

The Piper Cub I was to fly had been previously flown over from the Sudan and was at the airport. I flew it to the airstrip Ray had made beside his compound. We could not do any spraying as all the safety equipment had not arrived. It was a dangerous chemical we had to spray, more dangerous than I realised at the time, and all the ground crew had to wear protective clothing from head to toe. Initially the programme was to try out night landings, check the portable radio I had brought out with me, and to survey the country for landing strips in the spraying areas.

First we checked the radio and night landing facilities. Ray had some kerosene gooseneck flares which were placed along the runway. We set up the radio in the back of a Land-Rover and assembled the aerial, which was about 20 feet high. Ray's headman, Abdullah, was delegated to hold it up while we were transmitting.

Just before dusk I took off and did some landings, to check both the the radio and thc flares. The radio worked satisfactorily, so I did some circuits and landings as it got darker. I had done little night flying, but as all operations would be near the landing strips, it did not seem too demanding.

I was getting used to flying and landing in the dark, and becoming more confident, when I lost radio contact with Ray. After what seemed a long time, but was probably only a few minutes, he came through again. "You'd better come in."

I landed and taxied up to the Land-Rover and switched off the engine. "Abdullah dropped the aerial and went off when it got dark," said Ray. "He's a Muslim and it's Ramadan, so he's gone to gorge himself, as he hasn't drunk or eaten all day. I had a job holding up the aerial and working the set!" I tied the aircraft down, while Ray collected the flares. Over a cool beer, back at the compound, Ray remarked, "That's the trouble with these people they have no sense of responsibility."

I murmured, "AWA!"

During the next few weeks we took the aircraft and inspected some of the strips that Ray had made, As the countryside was mainly flat savannah it was not difficult to make a usable strip for the Piper. Sometimes we spotted camps out in the bush, where people were repairing roads or boring for water. Ray knew most of them and if a suitable landing area was near, we would stop for a chat and a cup of tea.

One day a message came from Ray's brother, who worked for the Public Works Department, saying he had run out of cigarettes, and gave the location of his camp. It was about half an hour's flying away, so Ray went to the village and bought two cartons of cigarettes, placed them into a plastic bag and tied a long streamer to it. We located the camp, and I made a low, slow pass, while

Ray dropped the package, which landed spot on target. His brother waved his thanks as he retrieved his cigarettes. We had to log the flight as an airstrip inspection. Later when I saw Ray's brother I told him it had cost the government a lot of money to deliver his cigarettes!

As I would have to camp out on the strips when we started operating, some camping gear arrived. It was rubbish, District Commissioner's kit circa 1898!

The gear consisted of a large eight-man bell tent, that needed four men to erect it; a narrow bed that folded up like a concertina; even a canvas wash basin in a fold-up tripod. There was a selection of battered, black stained saucepans and an ancient kerosene cooking stove, "They don't expect me to use this lot," I exclaimed to Ray. "This is 1963, not the Boer War."

Ray had been trying to buy a lightweight tent, with built-in groundsheet, fly-cover and mosquito net, which could be erected by one man and was used by surveyors and water drillers when out in the bush, but he could not get authorisation. He was allowed to spend £50 a month without authorisation, but these tents cost £300. He was in the process of buying one piecemeal from the water drilling company, the groundsheet one month, the pegs another and so on.

The water drilling company operating in the area was run by Adrian Harman, whose family had owned Lundy, the island in the Bristol Channel. Visiting Lundy years later, where Adrian Harman is now buried, it brought back memories of Nigeria.

Ray did not get on well with the people from headquarters. He was a practical bushman, who had little time for paperwork and bureaucracy. He just wanted to be left alone to get on with his job.

A European official from the Ministry arrived on an inspection tour. "I would like to see your driver's log books," he said.

"I haven't any log books," said Ray.

"But you must have log books for each vehicle," said the inspector, "detailing the journeys, mileage, fuel uptake and so on."

"None of the tachometers work on my Land-Rovers," replied Ray, "and my drivers go into the bush to places that have no names; and anyway none of them can read or write."

"You shouldn't employ drivers if they can't read and write," said the inspector.

"My drivers have to go out into the bush and live rough," replied Ray. "If they could read and write they would get a job at headquarters, be supplied with a nice uniform to impress the girls and drive you to your club."

After he left, Ray raged, "They sit in their air-conditioned offices and haven't any idea what goes on."

Time was passing, and still we had not received all the safety equipment. Ray said, "Let's fly over to Fort Lamy (now N'Djamena) in Chad. I want to see someone there and the Airport Hotel serves very good food."

Next morning we set off and diverted to look at a fishery station on the shore of Lake Chad. There was no airstrip, but we flew around and the manager, a friend of Ray, came out and waved. Continuing to Fort Lamy we came across a large herd of elephants grazing in the swamp. We flew around them for about fifteen minutes. The big bulls were worried and getting angry, throwing their trunks up and no doubt trumpeting. The young elephants ran to their mothers for protection. It was a wonderful sight and I made the most of it. As it turned out they were the last wild elephants I was to see.

At Fort Lamy we went to the Airport Hotel, which was nowhere near the airport. It was surrounded by colourful tropical trees and shrubs and peacocks wandered over the green lawns. The dining-room was air-conditioned. Tables were covered with pristine white tablecloths and set with nice cutlery and glasses. And what a selection of food! Everything was flown in from France - fish, steaks, lamb, oysters, and this was in the middle of Africa!

When we ordered white wine, the bottle came in a large bucket, full of crushed ice, with the wine glasses up-ended in it, so the wine remained cool when poured into the glass. You have to hand it to the French. It made the rest-house at Maiduguri seem like Joe's café.

The beer in the rest-house was never cold at lunch-time, although it was in the evening. We commented on this to the manager, and it turned out that the barman, who was the last to leave at night, had been given instructions to turn off all electricity and lock up. He carried out his instructions most religiously and switched off the beer coolers, too. AWA!

This phase of the contract was coming to an end, and due to the non-arrival of the safety equipment, no spraying had been done. As it turned out this was just as well for me. Later in the year, when the second phase of the contract was due, the Piper Cub was damaged in a forced landing on the flight from the Cameroons. It was replaced with an Auster Workmaster. The Cub was fitted with an external spray tank and plumbing, but the Workmaster had an internal tank, fitted next to the pilot and internal plumbing. As the chemical was very toxic, this was not a good arrangement.

While spraying at night, the pilot hit an obstacle and crashed. He was not hurt badly, but the pipes ruptured and he was splashed with chemical. In spite of being injected with an antidote, it was many hours' travel to a hospital and he died.

Leaving Maiduguri to take the Cub back to the Cameroons, I stopped overnight at Jos, where I left Ray to visit friends. I then flew on to Calabar to clear customs out of Nigeria. Although I had no passengers or freight, I had to submit a cargo manifest to sundry officials. Even the sweeper put his hand out for one!

At Calabar, I found the left wheel brake was very weak, which made taxying difficult. I had no means of fixing it and anyway only had two more landings to make.

Flying to Tiko Airport in the Cameroons, I passed over country I remembered from my previous visit in 1958. I circled round Ekona, and saw that the German house, which had been our mess, was no more; only the foundations remained.

Calling Tiko tower on arrival, I got no reply. I circled the airfield, calling the tower to no avail. I saw a Fokker Friendship on the apron, but there were no other aircraft around and no sign of a visual signal from the tower, so I landed.

As I touched down, the Friendship taxied from the apron and started to backtrack down the runway. We passed each other going in opposite directions halfway down the runway. As we passed I exchanged greetings with the pilot.

I stopped on the apron and shut down the engine. The controller came up. "Why did you not call me on the radio?" he asked me by the way of a greeting.

"I've been calling you all the way in, but I got no reply," I answered.

"Your radio is defective." he said.

"Perhaps," I replied, "but it was working when I left Calabar; maybe your set is not working."

"My set is in perfect order," he said.

"Well, let's try both sets," I suggested. I called up but got no reply.

The controller came down from the tower.

"I heard nothing. Your radio is no good," he said in an unfriendly way. "And what do you mean by landing when an aircraft is departing."

I was getting rather annoyed at his attitude, and replied, "Why did you let an aircraft on to the runway when I was landing? You know landing aircraft have priority."

He turned and stumped off. I suspected that he was not listening out when I first called, but I had no way of proving it.

After hanging about for two hours waiting for customs and immigration, I got a message that I could fly to Crop Culture's base at Bota and report in the morning. I had to make a very careful departure, as now I had no left brake at all, and if I had had trouble taxying I am sure the controller would have tried to ground me. I flew to Bota and made a tricky landing in a crosswind, cutting the engine as I headed for the bananas, and had to be manhandled to the hangar.

I stayed two days at Bota with Crop Culture's manager, Jerry Fretz. I did not trouble to report to immigration; if they could not be bothered, why should I?

I met old friends, including Francois Lesieur, who now had his commercial pilot's licence and was working in the Cameroons. I had dinner with him and his wife, Jenny. Waiting to board an Air France Boeing 707 at Douala Airport, I met Pierre Dulak from the days at Penga.

I had not flown in a 707 before and it was a daylight departure. I was sitting in front of the wing. Air France are noted for their frisky flying. As soon as we took off, the pilot did a steep climbing turn. With a swept-back wing, the turn appeared steeper than it was and for one horrible minute, I thought we were going to roll right over! Little did I realise that I would be back in the Cameroons three years later.

I returned to the Cameroons for the third and last time in 1966. Crop Culture's operation had been decreased to one Workmaster spraying bananas. Flying an Auster again did not fill me with joy! The manager/pilot, Frank Sennett, an Australian, was taking his family to Australia for three months leave.

Ekona was a very different place from my time there in 1958. Frank was the only European living in the village and the club was no more. The only familiar face was Paul, who welcomed me with a big smile. It was a lonely posting as I knew no one and the other Europeans were at Buea, some way away.

The work was not arduous; there was flying only for three or four days a week, and spraying had to stop when the temperature got too high, usually about ten o'clock. I did not need a temperature gauge to tell me, because when it got to the critical level, the Workmaster started to fly like a brick!

The man I saw most frequently was Jim Wilkie, manager of a plantation some way up country. He used to drop in for a beer sometimes and always seemed to be late wherever he was going. I believe if he was invited anywhere, he was always given a time about two hours earlier, on the chance that he might arrive nearly on time. No one seemed to mind this failing, because he was such a nice chap and everyone accepted this little eccentricity.

A couple of times he invited me out to the plantation for the day with his wife and family. Wives on these plantations lived a lonely life, isolated from neighbours; no television, Women's Institutes, coffee shops or shops at all for that matter. But they seemed quite contented and fulfilled, looking after a husband and children, dress making, gardening and all the domestic chores involved in living in a relatively primitive environment.

I always experienced great hospitality in Africa, both from Europeans and Africans, genuine and unsophisticated. Due to uncertainty of supplies sometimes they had no beer or no meat, but what they had they shared with you and the hospitality was welcoming, warm and informal.

Most of the spraying was local, but there was one plantation at Tombel, up river from Ekona, that could have tricky weather. Just before the airstrip the valley widened out into a large bowl. Francois Lesieur, when working in the Cameroons, and flying up to Tombel found the cloud base getting lower and lower. When he almost got to the airstrip, the cloud lowered further and trapped him in the bowl, below the level of the strip. All he could do was circle in the clear space in the bowl. It was very tiring and the engineer he had as passenger was sick. After some time the cloud lifted enough for him to pop over the rim and land, rather shaken! I used to remember this and was always a bit apprehensive until the strip came in sight.

As well as taking over the Sennetts' house, I took over their steward, who cooked meals, did the washing and cleaned the house. Unfortunately he started to steal money, so I took his key and banned him from the house. As he was not my steward I could not sack him. I found this very disappointing, as during my previous visits to the Cameroons, I found everyone very honest. Money left in your room was never touched and if you left a camera or wallet in the Land-Rover, the driver would bring it to you.

Maybe dishonesty was creeping into country areas from the towns. Robbery in Lagos was a normal pattern of life. I generally found the poorer the people, the more honest they were. Prosperity seems to increase dishonesty, rather than reduce it and this seems to be born out in the Western world.

For the last month, an Australian engineer, Jim Gobert, together with his wife joined the company in Ekona. I knew Jim from the Sudan. They moved into a house a few doors away, so I had someone to visit for dinner.

Most of the houses had avocado trees in the gardens, in fact the noise of the pears dropping to the ground in the night used to keep me awake. At this time avocados were only obtainable in England from high class shops in London. We cooked them in place of potatoes, which were unobtainable at times!

As I now had to cater for myself, I asked Paul to come to the market with me to buy supplies. He told me that his wife was ill and the doctor had ordered a diet of eggs and milk. These items were too expensive on his income. I bought him two dozen eggs. It probably did not solve his problem but it made me feel better!

When Frank returned from leave, I was not sorry to leave the Cameroons.

19

Deep Flying in Austria

On returning from the Cameroons in 1963, I went to Austria, flying a Piper Cub for Airspray (Cyprus) Ltd, a company run by two former Crop Culture pilots, Ian Taylor and Jack Akers. Ian and I flew the aircraft to Vienna from Southend, via Stuttgart. This was the first of three summer seasons I spent in Austria.

The work was mainly north of Vienna, and we based ourselves at a small town called Laa, near the border with Czechoslovakia. Agriculture was based on the strip system, which was used in England several centuries ago. The fields were small, long and narrow, with no hedges or fences. Each field only needed two or three swath runs to cover it, and a field of ten acres was big.

The crops were a large variety of cereals and vegetables. With frequent changes of chemical and small fields, spraying productivity was not high, but lack of fences and obstructions made flying easier. Ian and I were amused to find that the Austrians called low flying 'deep' flying. It made us feel as if we were flying submarines!

Cherry trees were planted along the side of the roads by the local council. They were let to the villagers, who harvested and sold the crops. The trees were planted originally to mark the road when the featureless land was covered with snow, but using fruit trees made it productive.

Along the border with Czechoslovakia and Hungary ran the Iron Curtain, two rows of barbed wire with an open uncultivated space between. Every mile of so there was a high tower, manned by soldiers. A road out of Laa led to a town in Czechoslovakia, but the Iron Curtain barred the way, turning the road into a cul-de-sac.

If you stood on the road at the border it was possible to look across and see where the road started again, with people working in the fields. This curtain went all the way from East Germany to Hungary, hundreds of miles long.

Some of the spraying took us right up to the border and we could see the sentries watching us through binoculars. If we flew past the watchtower and waved to them, there was no response, other than a stare. Whether they were unfriendly or scared to respond, I don't know.

A field to be sprayed was situated in a corner of the border with Hungary, the curtain running round two sides. It was not possible to spray it without crossing the border to turn. To my surprise, permission was obtained from the border authorities to do this. I was a little apprehensive venturing into this forbidden land, even if I was at 100 feet, but no one shot at me. I did wonder what would have happened if I had engine failure and had to make a forced landing!

I found the food stodgy and uninteresting. Most meals consisted of pork or beef - no lamb for some reason - and potatoes and green salad. Rarely were there green vegetables such as peas, beans, cauliflower or cabbage, except sauerkraut. Driving to Laa from Vienna early one morning Ian said, "We'll stop at Mistelbach for breakfast." I had visions of bacon and eggs and hot coffee. All we could get was goulash and beer at 6 o'clock in the morning!

However, the beer and wine made up for the food. The draught beer was the best I have tasted. Cool, smooth, with just a tingle to it. Years later when driving to Austria for a skiing holiday with my daughter's family we stopped the night at a small hotel.

I was first down in the morning and while waiting for the rest of the family to come to breakfast, I saw some workmen at a table drinking long glasses of beer. I could not resist it and ordered a glass. When my young grandchildren saw me they cried, "What are you doing drinking beer for breakfast!" I think they thought I had really gone to the dogs!

In Austria I started to learn more about wine. The Austrians were up and about at 6 o'clock in the morning, the women to work and the men to the pub for the first glass of the day. The pubs did not shut again until 11 or 12 o'clock at night.

Ordinary drinking wine, which we would call 'plonk', but was much better, was served from two-litre bottles, the white wine kept cool in large ice-filled boxes. It was served like Coca-Cola, none of the pretentious sipping and tasting prevalent in England at that time. Better wine, however was treated with due reverence.

Most of the villagers had small plots of vines and made wine for their own consumption. There were rows of little cellars in the village. Inside were several barrels, a rough table and benches. The host, armed with a long glass tube sucked up wine from the barrel and put his thumb over the end, then went round filling glasses. Many a happy hour I spent at the end of a day's spraying, sampling the wines of the postman or butcher.

We soon discovered that the Austrians do not bath. The hotel at Laa had twenty bedrooms, but no bathroom for the guests. As the chemicals we used smelled quite strongly and permeated clothes and hair, we arranged with the landlady to use her private bathroom.

This was sometimes inconvenient and often I showered on the landing strip, using the water from the tanker. A pension where we sometimes stayed in Vienna had a bathroom, but no hot water. We went to the Sudbahnhof, a mainline railway station, which had showers for travellers.

When it was hot in the summer the odour in a crowded tram or cinema could be overpowering. It amazed me. In Africa all the tanker crews and the rest-house cook went to the river or canal to bathe every day.

Austria is one of the most bureaucratic European countries I have been in. Although I have fumed at the bureaucracy of some Asian and African countries, I sometimes think, maybe, we taught them! After getting a farmer's consent to use one of his fields for a landing strip, we still had to obtain permission from the local authority. This was only given for that particular field. If the farmer had a better field next door, you could not move over and use it without re-applying for a new permission from the local authority.

Taking the last load of the day, I thought I had enough daylight left to spray it out. The field was odd shaped and took longer to treat than I thought. When I set off back to the landing strip, only five or six minutes away, it was dusk and difficult to distinguish any features in the flat countryside. All the villages were now lit up and I could not locate the one next to the strip.

I flew around where I expected the strip to be. The ground crew put on car lights, but did not flash them, so they merged with all the other lights. When I found myself flying over some high tension cables, I decided it was time to find somewhere to land. I found a grass field and lobbed into it. After half an hour the ground crew found me.

A few weeks later I was taken by the agent to a government office, where we met an official. Neither the agent or the official spoke English and I spoke no German. The agent and the official talked for ten minutes, then we all shook hands and left.

I found out later that I had been fined £10 for landing in a field that night without permission. I was frustrated that I was unable to explain that it was an emergency, but it probably would not have made any difference.

While visiting farmers 50 miles from Vienna, the driver put the van in a ditch on a farm track. We dragged it out, but could not drive it as the wing had been pushed back and jammed the front wheel. I got a hammer and crow bar from the farm and bent the wing back, clear of the wheel.

We went into the village, and while I had a coffee, the driver was on the telephone. When he came back I said, "OK? Are we going back to Vienna now?"

"No," he replied, "we cannot drive the van."

"Why not?" I queried. "It's only got a crumpled wing and is quite driveable."

He replied, "The blinker is broken. It is illegal to drive with a broken blinker."

As it was the nearside blinker that was broken, I suggested that we drove it and left it on the outskirts of Vienna and went on by tram. But the driver was insistent that the van could not be driven and said, "You stay here for the night and I will come back in the morning with another car." It seemed a lot of fuss, just for the lack of a blinker, especially as I had struggled to fix the damage, so we could drive.

A few days later this driver picked me up from the pension in Vienna to take me to a strip west of the city. Instead of going west, he drove east. "Where are we going?" I asked. "This is not the way."

"I have to go back home," he replied. "I have left my driving licence in my other jacket, so I must go and get it."

So we lost two hours spraying because he would be in trouble if he was stopped and did not have his licence with him.

A week before the end of one season the agent told me that a spare part was in customs, but they would not release it as the paperwork was not correct. It was an inexpensive part and not essential to us, so we forgot about it. If this had been in Africa where the customs officer was poorly paid and less honest, a small bribe would have released it.

If a customs officer is strictly honest and works by the book it can cost the operator a lot of money if he has an aircraft on the ground for the need of a spare, and the paperwork is incorrect. In such a case an African 'dash' to the officer can save many pounds of lost revenue. Maybe bribery can help the world to go round!

One company, spraying in an African country, ran out of rubber diaphragms sealing the spray nozzles. They are small and cheap, but essential. A man was put on an airliner to England to collect some and bring them back in his pocket on the next flight. It sounded an expensive remedy, but really it was the quickest and the cheapest way, as the spray aircraft could work again and earn money.

After many years experience selecting airstrips I got caught out. There was difficulty in finding a strip in one area and I was taken to inspect one for suitability. It was a field that had been ploughed and harrowed ready for a crop to be sown. It was smooth and level though not very long, but it would do. Unfortunately I did not walk over it.

When I landed the aircraft stopped in a very short distance, which made me suspicious. I decided to try a take-off light, and found the aircraft was slow to accelerate. I got out and examined the ground and found there was a layer of fine tilth, two or three inches thick, which was acting as a drag. I was going to have difficulty getting out light!

I put the tail of the aircraft right against the hedge, lined up with the longest run, fully opened the throttle on the brakes, then let them off and started my run. I managed to get the aircraft airborne just before the end of the field. I was not very popular as all the bureaucratic procedures had to be gone through again.

It was pleasant to be working in a sophisticated part of the world for a change. Vienna, a nice city, was in easy reach, and when we were working in the area, we stayed in a pension there. The city was full of fine old buildings and had rather an old-fashioned feeling about it. Plenty of bars, cafés and old-fashioned coffee houses, full of gilt, chandeliers and red velvet.

People still spent several hours over a cup of coffee, playing chess or reading a newspaper. Afternoons brought middle-aged ladies to drink coffee and eat sachertorte, which probably accounted for many of them being overweight!

At first driving in Vienna was a nightmare. At junctions and squares, the traffic police stood in little huts, waving their arms and blowing whistles, which no doubt meant something if you knew the system.

As you felt your way across a big square with five or six roads entering it, suddenly there would be loud blasts on a whistle, which made you think you had done something wrong; but on looking around, you would see the policeman waving his hands in another direction. It was quite unnerving to start with, but after a while you ignored the whistle blasts. If you had done something wrong, the policeman could not do much about it, stuck in his little box.

On summer evenings we could spend an evening in Grenzig, a small village in the hills outside the city, full of bars and wine gardens, where we could drink the new wine, eat a meal, listen to music, and look out over the city lights below.

Before going to Austria for the 1984 season, Airspray asked me to go to Cyprus and carry out the annual Certificate of Airworthiness inspections of their four Piper Cubs.

I flew to Beirut, en route to Cyprus and introduced myself to the Air Registration Board surveyor for the area. He did not know me and was not too friendly, mainly I think because he was not very happy with the company's facilities in Nicosia.

Because the hangar rents at the airfield were very high, they had rented a large shop in Nicosia. Previously it had been a dairy, and when I saw it, I thought it was ideal. The floor and walls were tiled, which made it easy to keep clean, and the large shop windows in the front gave plenty of light. It was large enough to take two aircraft with the wings removed. The wings were taken off at the airfield and with the fuselage transported by truck to the workshop.

One of the company directors, Joe Lancaster, was living in a house in Nicosia and I stayed at a hotel. Joe was a well known test pilot who had flown for several companies. His last job was test flying the Blackburn Beverley. He did not look the part; with his large build, bucolic complexion, slow speech, he looked more like a farmer!

We got the first two aircraft into the workshop, opened up all the panels and started the inspection. The aircraft were not very old, so there was not much wear and tear. When all the working parts were exposed we sent for the surveyor.

He came, I think with rather a biased mind. Overhauling aircraft in an ex-dairy was not the conventional way of doing things. However, he was not able to find any faults with the arrangement and had to agree that it was satisfactory.

When the company started up, they had to produce a maintenance schedule for approval by the Air Registration Board. They were in a hurry, as they had an immediate contract, so they 'bought' a schedule from a consultant.

The consultant, to ensure that approval was given quickly and without any queries, had called for work and inspections to cover every possible eventuality. This led to problems later. One of the items called for 'trammelling' the mainplanes. The mainplanes are made up of several boxes between the front and rear spars. Adjustable bracing wires are fitted diagonally in each box to give rigidity and to square each box. If the wing had a major repair, the diagonals would be checked with a trammelling tool, ensuring that both diagonals measured the same.

"What are you going to do about trammelling the mainplanes?" the surveyor asked.

"As there is no sign of any movement, I don't think it is necessary," I replied. "As you can see the bracing wires are tight and there are no wrinkles in the fabric, which would indicate if anything had moved."

"It is called for in the schedule," the surveyor insisted, "so you will have to do it."

"But it will mean cutting lots of holes in the fabric," I argued, "which will make an awful mess in a perfectly good wing covering."

"You will have to do it," he insisted. "And I shall want to see the tool when I come next."

Obviously he was more influenced by the written word than sensible engineering practice. After he left I talked this over with Joe, and we contacted Jack Akers, another director in London, asking him to see ARB to get this and a few other items deleted from the schedule.

On his next visit the surveyor remarked, "I see you have got some items deleted from the schedule." I do not think he was very pleased that we had gone over his head, but his attitude became more co-operative. Joe, myself and a local Cypriot worked on the aircraft for two months. They were in good condition and no major work was necessary.

At this time the Greeks and Turks were having their quarrel and United Nations troops arrived. I neither saw nor heard any sign of the troubles except for the 'Green Line' that ran through the centre of Nicosia. We had the English national papers a day late and one of them reported firing all night in Nicosia along the 'Green Line'. I lived in a hotel in Nicosia, but heard nothing. Either I slept through it or the reporter exaggerated!

Joe and I took a day off and armed with our passports went to the north coast in the Turkish area. We had a look at Kyrenia, now cut off from the Greeks and had lunch at a restaurant in a lovely position overlooking the sea. We ate on the terrace, shaded by grape vines. It was so pleasant and peaceful, it was difficult to realise that people were killing each other.

The inspections completed, the aircraft were taken to the airfield, assembled and rigged and Joe did the test flights. The surveyor arrived to clear the aircraft and issue the Certificates of Airworthiness.

I was taking one of the aircraft to Austria. I had to stop off at Montpellier, in southern France, to meet Jack Akers and Ian Taylor and give a spraying demonstration. They were hoping to get a contract to spray vines in competition with French helicopter companies.

Not liking long over-water flights in a single engined aircraft, I flew north to the Turkish coast and followed it until I was abeam Rhodes, my first refuelling stop. This coast was very beautiful, steep mountains dropping down to a clear blue sea, with little fishing villages at the mouth of the valleys.

I wanted to avoid large airports, so I filled up the spray tank with fuel, which gave me ten hours' duration.

Climbing slowly out of Rhodes, bound for Corfu, a Cessna 210 which had taken off after me, zoomed by, retracting its undercarriage and disappeared ahead. I plodded on, passing Greece south of Athens, then up the coast to Corfu.

I had been at Corfu airport for almost an hour, sitting on the terrace, when the Cessna landed. Although faster, it had to refuel at Athens. My airspeed may have been slower, but having longer range and avoiding all the delay with formalities at Athens Airport, gave me a great advantage.

Next day I set off for Montpellier via Corsica. On arriving at Calvi, I did not like the look of the weather to the north. It was very hazy and there was no horizon as the haze merged with the sea. Flying in these conditions with no blind flying instruments can be dangerous. I had heard of experienced pilots becoming overcome with vertigo in such conditions and crashing.

Checking with the weather man and a pilot who had just landed it appeared that these conditions existed all the way to the French coast. This weather persisted and it was three days before it cleared and I was able to reach Montpellier.

Jack and Ian had flown from England in a hired Cessna and were waiting anxiously for my arrival. We got the aircraft ready for spraying and next day gave the demonstration. A difficult field had been selected with high tension cables at one end and a steep hill at the other. I think it had been selected purposely to see how we compared with a helicopter.

I was keen for the company to get the contract as a few weeks in the south of France greatly appealed to me. I flew the aircraft to its and my limits but to no avail. We did not get the contract.

The next day we all flew to Lyon, where after refuelling, we went in different directions. Jack and Ian back to England and myself to Austria. My next stop was Zurich. I was a little apprehensive as Zurich is a busy international airport and I only had a little Piper Cub and a weak radio. I need not have worried, Zurich control were calm, professional and treated me just like any other traffic. They did not get annoyed when I asked them to repeat an instruction, but re-phrased it in calm clear tones; unlike controllers in Africa who gabbled it again in a higher voice, distorting the reception, making it even more unintelligible. "You are number two to land," called the controller, "after the DC6 on short finals. Please land short and turn off at the first taxiway as we have a 707 on long finals."

It all seemed so easy, the way they slotted me in, with no fuss or drama.

After refuelling I took off for Innsbruck. Half an hour later the clouds started to build up on top of the mountains. Innsbruck lies at the bottom of a deep valley surrounded by mountains, not an airfield to approach in poor weather. I called Zurich for an actual weather report for Innsbruck, and as it did not seem very good, I informed Zurich I was returning. I could tell by the tone of the controller's voice that he thought I had made a wise decision. Back to Zurich and another calm and professional reception by the controller. I parked the aircraft and stayed the night. Next day I had an uneventful direct flight to Vienna.

Francois Lesieur in Piper Pawnee.

Ludham Airfield.

Loading Piper Pawnee with fertiliser.

Fertilising: Loading auger-type loader.
Author with back to camera.

Piper Pawnee - crop spraying.

The Author in one of his own Piper Pawnees.

20

Snowbound in Scotland

In 1966 I started to fly in England again during the spraying season for Westwick Distributors, based at Ludham Airfield in Norfolk. Westwick were agricultural merchants, who started in a small way and had been taken over, with other merchants in the area, by the frozen food company Ross Foods. Later Ross were in turn taken over by Imperial Foods.

The aerial crop-spraying section was managed by Denys Howard, who was also a crop spraying pilot. In spite of all the take-overs, this section was not affected a great deal. It did not fit in with the major business of canning beans and freezing peas, so was largely left alone to carry on as a small independent business within a large conglomerate.

Denys was a good manager, and being an active pilot himself, was aware of all the problems of aerial crop spraying. Free-lance pilots, some from Australia and New Zealand, as well as England were taken on for the season, which lasted about six months. After flying for three seasons with Westwick, I was employed full time. This suited me very well as overseas contracts were becoming fewer.

It was a happy company, run in a relaxed way. Everyone knew their job and got on with it, with the minimum of supervision. Such is the nature of the work that everyone was self motivated.

Westwick had one of the last Tiger Moths used for aerial spraying and I flew it frequently. On one occasion there were several small fields to be treated in a radius of Ludham, that could be done with one load of chemical. It was going to take some time and I tried to remember what the duration of the Tiger Moth was, with full tanks. I decided that the maximum safe duration was two-and-a-quarter hours.

When I had sprayed the last field, I set course for Ludham, having been airborne for two hours, which gave me, what I thought was a safe margin. I was approaching the airfield at about 500 feet, when two miles away, the engine spluttered and then picked up again. A few seconds later it spluttered again and only picked up when I closed the throttle slightly. I was running out of fuel in sight of the airfield! The engine spluttered and ran, spluttered again and ran, but the spluttering lasted longer each time. I rocked the aircraft from side to side to swirl the last drop of petrol over the tank outlet. The runway was getting nearer and it looked as if I should make it with luck. I just made it to the runway threshold, and as I eased the stick back to land, the engine finally stopped. We nearly didn't have a Tiger Moth!

Landing the Tiger Moth in a strong crosswind on the tarmac strip at Ludham had its problems. I developed a technique where I would land on the down-wind side, keeping the tail up as long as possible. When the tail dropped and I started to lose directional control, I would put on hard rudder and opposite aileron and execute a controlled ground loop.

I also did plenty of spraying in the Piper Cub, which I enjoyed flying. It was good at operating out of short strips and could also turn quicker than the Pawnee. The Cub had a weak rear fuselage and if you consistently turned one way with a loaded aircraft on a rough strip, the tail would twist slightly. Viewed from the back, the fin would be out of vertical. The remedy was to do all turns in the opposite direction until the fin was again vertical. Later, the manufacturers brought out a kit to strengthen the fuselage and that cured the problem.

For several seasons I had a young marker, Henry Labouchere, who was a keen pilot, but not very experienced at that time. Whenever the opportunity occurred, he would come up with me and do some practice from the rear seat. The Cub had a Sorenson spray system, with an external belly tank, which only gave about four inches ground clearance.

On a flight out of a good strip, Henry asked if he could land the plane. I monitored his approach ready to take over if he made a mess of it. He did very well until the round out, which was too high. I was slow to correct this and the aircraft dropped in hard from several feet. When we got out I saw that the belly tank had hit the ground and had a large split. I flew the aircraft back to Ludham for repair and on the flight I had to think up an excuse. I could not say that I let Henry land it, so I said that I made a heavy landing. As my untidy landings were well known, this excuse was accepted without question!

One job was to fertilise a forest in Suffolk. Due to the high trees it was not possible to mark it in the conventional way, so it was decided that the marker, who was Henry, would carry a balloon on a long piece of cord and mark along the fire break in the forest. The nearest strip was some distance away, so I was some time between trips. When the job was finished and Henry came back to the strip he was quite upset. "I did feel a fool," he exclaimed. "While you were away, a couple of horsemen rode down the fire break. There was I, standing all alone in the middle of the forest, holding a balloon on a piece of string. They didn't half give me a funny look!"

It was a funny thing, though the directors would authorise the purchase of a new aeroplane, costing many thousands, it was difficult to get the management to spend money on ground support equipment.

Denys would have a continual battle trying to get reliable vans for the markers and suitable lorries to load the aircraft. On some occasions an aeroplane capable of earning a great deal of money was grounded because an inexpensive piece of ground equipment had broken down. I can recall being grounded for the want of a spark plug for the loading pump.

One of the loading pumps gave continual trouble and was always being sent back for repair, only to break down again after a few days' work. This happened five or six times, until one of the loaders got fed up. He was Les Knights, a typical Norfolk man, slow to anger, but when he did get angry he spoke his mind in no uncertain manner. When the pump broke down again, he stood on the tray of the lorry, lifted the pump high above his head, and hurled it on to the concrete runway, where it shattered into a thousand pieces. Pushing his cap to the back of his head he declared, "They won't repair that bastard again!"

The busy spraying season coincided with vacation time from

colleges and universities, so students were taken on as markers. It suited them very well; they could earn good money, have a van to drive, and an open air life. On hot summer days they marked in a pair of shorts with a bottle of 'Ambre Solaire' and a flag as their essential equipment.

Being students, they were reasonably intelligent and a rapport was set up between the pilot and marker. Both carried a one-inch Ordnance Survey map and a work sheet with a sketch map of the field to be sprayed. The sketch map had features marked on it to identify the field, such as a haystack in the corner or a pit in the middle, and also warning of any hazards, such as electric wires. Most of the time the marker found the field without difficulty, but sometimes the pilot had to help him as, of course, he had a much better view of the countryside.

There was no communication between the marker and the pilot, so it was all done with signals. Sometimes the marker was unable to find a track to the field, or he drove up a track barred by a stream or a deep ditch. The pilot, being able to see the correct track guided the marker by flying along, waggling his wings in a 'follow me' signal.

Only a few simple signals were necessary. If something was wrong, such as a blocked spreader, so that fertiliser was only coming out of one side, or a spray pump or hose was leaking badly, the marker waved the pilot off and returned to the landing strip. If the pilot wanted the marker to return to the landing strip, he would 'blip' the throttle. If the pilot was able to finish the field without a marker, he waggled his wings, and the marker would move off to the next field. This speeded up the operation as the pilot did not have to wait, while the marker got into position.

A good, reliable marker could make a great difference to the smooth running of the operation. One agent remarked, "Markers? I can get any number from the labour exchange." He could get bodies but were they any good? I once had a marker who read a book while marking. When the aircraft passed him he walked the next swath width without even looking up. I could have flown past him with the aircraft on fire and he would not have noticed!

One season a retired Birmingham grocer named Sid was taken on as a marker. He was a nice chap and tried hard, but the East Anglian countryside was very different from the streets of Birmingham. He had great difficulty in orientating himself and drew the most amazing sketch maps.

All maps are drawn with north at the top of the page. In spite of having an Ordnance Survey map to refer to Sid would get the orientation wrong. Both the marker and the pilot were frustrated in their efforts to locate the field, until something clicked, and on turning the map upside down, everything fell into place! To help locate the area quickly, reference to a town or village would be made on the map, such as, 'Beccles, 5 miles', with an arrow pointing to the west. Sid would see a signpost, 'Beccles, 5 miles', which would be pointing to the east and he would mark this on the map, not realising that the road to Beccles wound round and eventually headed west. In desperation he got himself a small hand compass. Unfortunately when drawing his map he placed the compass on the bonnet of the van, not realising that the metal of the van was affecting the compass and giving an incorrect reading! When we understood his problems we turned his maps in all directions until they fitted into the Ordnance Survey map and then all became clear.

The Forestry Commission in Scotland asked for tenders to fertilise the forests from the air in the spring of 1969. Peter Greensmith was sent up to Innerleithen to find a landing strip near the work. The area was wild and hilly and the best he could find was a pasture field on the side of a valley north of the town. Although not very long, it was on a good slope, which would help on the take-off run. The start of the contract was delayed for several weeks, because of snow on the ground. Eventually the thaw set in and Francois and I took two Pawnees and set off for Scotland. Carrying extra fuel in jerry cans placed in the hopper we refuelled at a disused airfield in north Lincolnshire, then at Teeside Airport, where permission had been arranged for us to land and refuel, as we had no radio. Flying up the Northumbrian coast, we turned left at Berwick and crept up the Tweed valley.

There was still snow on the high ground, and as we flew up the valley, cloud began to form ominously on the hill tops. Eventually we reached Innerleithen and located the landing strip in a valley running north. It was not possible to make a direct approach due to the narrow valley.

Flying north up the valley I did a 180 degree turn and went back to make a right hand turn onto the strip. At about 500 feet, I encountered the most violent turbulence and had to abandon the approach. I made two more attempts and each time the turbulence was wicked, throwing me about in the cockpit. All this time Francois was circling above, watching my discomfort.

After the third attempt I flew back into the main valley of the Tweed, looking for a place to land, Francois following me. There was a pasture field beside the river, about three miles east of the town, where we landed and secured the aircraft.

We got a lift to the hotel with a friendly farmer and shortly after the local agent arrived. We explained the problem, which did not please him very much as landing areas were few and far between. Bill Bailey arrived that night, having driven the loader all the way from Norfolk. After a meal and a few beers, we went to bed.

Next morning we awoke to six inches of snow. It snowed and froze for two weeks before the sky cleared, but the snow was still on the ground making work impossible. We spent two weeks trapped in Innerleithen, unable to work or leave and were all fed up. We rang Denys Howard at Ludham, and he suggested that if we could get out, we should return to Ludham until the snow thawed. The hotel bills were mounting to no purpose.

The next day, which was bright and sunny, Francois and I scraped all the snow off the wings and ran a car up and down the strip to flatten the snow and make a take-off path. We put our bags in the aircraft and fled up the valley towards Berwick.

Escaping from the Tweed valley, we turned south for home, but had not gone far when the sky darkened and we ran into a heavy snow storm, reducing visibility to a mile or so. The map showed a disused airfield nearby, where we landed in worsening visibility.

Once more we tied the aircraft down and managed to find shelter in a village pub. We rang Denys, who told us to leave the aircraft there and catch the train back. When the weather improved Denys and Francois went north and retrieved the aircraft. The snow thawed a few weeks later and Francois returned to Innerleithen and managed to use the strip. However, the application rate was high and with a marginal strip, he could only carry enough fertiliser for three acres at a time and had to climb 1,000 feet to the site. The income was hardly paying for the petrol used, so Westwick gave the contract to a helicopter firm, operating in the area. The helicopter was able to operate from clearings next to the forest, and it was a more economic operation for them.

These contracts can look tempting from a distance as many hundreds of acres are involved, but the expenses of operating so far from base in difficult terrain can be high. There is no point in treating hundreds of acres and losing money, even if it is only a penny an acre.

21

Some Unorthodox Landings

Peter Greensmith had a tragi-comic experience while operating in Lincolnshire. At the end of the landing strip was the canal that took shipping from the coast to Boston docks.

Taking off with a load of fungicide to spray potatoes, the engine cut just as he was airborne and he flopped into the canal. The spray system was damaged and the yellow coloured fungicide leaked from the aircraft and stained the water. The aircraft was floating with Peter standing up in the cockpit, appraising the situation. Along the bank several men were quietly fishing. One man laid down his rod and walked towards Peter. Taking his pipe out of his mouth he called out, "Will that stuff hurt the fish?"

"No. No, no, I don't think so," answered Peter.

"That's all right, then," said the fisherman. Putting his pipe back in his mouth, he strolled back and picked up his rod.

The aircraft was settling in the water and slowly sinking. Peter had to step out and swim to the bank. It was only after he had got into dry clothes and had a warm drink that he was able to appreciate the funny side of this incident.

Aerial crop spraying did not fit into normal civil aviation. We never used airports as our activities would not conform to their procedures: we carried no radio, and the landing fees would have been prohibitive. Eastern England was covered in disused airfields left over from the war which had been returned to farmers, so it was usually possible to find one near the work. Over the years the concrete runways have been slowly broken up to provide foundations for motorways, which latterly made operations more difficult.

Our work at times was in fields bordering on civil and military airfields and the reactions of the controllers and commanding officers varied from co-operation to horror! The American Air Force were very helpful, probably because they were used to aerial spraying in their own country, and because they felt as guests in this country, they should try and accommodate us. Ringing flying control to tell them you had some fields to spray nearby, the controller would say, "Ha, crop dusting are you? Sure, don't fly over the airfield boundary. Have a good day." And that was that.

In contrast, I rang the controller at Norwich Airport to say I had a field to treat on the approach to their secondary runway. The controller told me to contact him on the radio, and was very worried when I told him I had none. "You can't do that with no radio," he said. "We might have some movements."

"What movements have you got?" I asked, "I will fit in with them."

"We have no movements at the moment," he answered, "but we might have."

"I'll be along in fifteen minutes," I replied, "and will not be more than half an hour. I shall not be near your main runway, and if you do have an aircraft coming in you can warn him that I am in the area, so the pilot will not be worried."

I did the job and rang him to say I had finished. I always found the least busy airfields put up the most difficulties.

Another time I had some fields to spray right in line with the main runway at RAF Wyton, in fact one field was on the airfield boundary. The controller said he only had six movements that day and we arranged that I would keep an eye on the tower, and if an aircraft was due he would give me a red light with an Aldis lamp, and I would move out of the way until the aircraft had landed.

I operated all day and never saw another aircraft; they must have arrived when I was away reloading. I rang the controller to say I had finished and to thank him for his help. "No problem," he answered.

In Lincolnshire, an RAF airfield was next to a large number of fields we had to treat. It was a rocket site and had no aircraft stationed there other than the Commanding officer's Tiger Moth. I went to see the adjutant and asked him if I could operate from the airfield. He agreed immediately, saying, "It will be nice to see a real aeroplane instead of these bloody rockets!" He allocated a part of the airfield to us and we brought in the loading lorry and started work. Twice a day the NAAFI wagon came up with tea and buns, and when we left the aircraft there overnight, the CO gave instructions that it was to be included in the guards' rounds.

At the other extreme, when I asked to use another dormant RAF airfield, the CO said I had to apply to the Ministry of Defence in writing. I told him by the time we got a reply the crop would be in the supermarkets as Mother's Pride bread.

I do not think the CO of RAF Coltishall at that time was very sympathetic to crop sprayers. The airfield lay directly in the flight path from the west to Ludham, so we had to fly round it. I used to pass the airfield at 300 or 400 feet and about four miles to the north. After one flight the controller rang up to say the CO had complained that I had interfered with his practice instrument approach. I told the controller my position and height when I passed the airfield and added, "I don't know much about instrument approaches, but what sort of approach was your CO making if I interfered with it?"

The controller chuckled. "I was asked to pass on the complaint," he said.

We did a good deal of spraying around RAF Coltishall and had a good liaison with the controllers. We did all our spraying after the RAF had ceased flying for the day or at week-ends. I went to spray a field next to the married quarters, but separated from them by a public road. To avoid flying over the buildings I did all my turns over open country.

The next day the Wing Commander flying, rang me at Ludham to say that the CO had come out of the officer's mess and seen me flying low over the married quarters and had raised a signal to the Ministry of Defence lodging a complaint against the pilot. "Before I send it off, I thought I ought to talk to you," he said.

"I did not fly over the married quarters," I protested. "I have the maps and work sheets and can show you how I sprayed the field."

He suggested that I came to see him and brought the maps. He was very nice and understanding and after showing him the map and explaining how I had flown, I convinced him that I had not flown recklessly. He said he would talk to the CO, having seen me and felt sure he could get the signal cancelled.

It made me wonder if this had gone to a court or an inquiry what chance my word would have had against that of a uniformed Group Captain with scrambled egg on his cap and a row of medals. Although we were both airmen, he knew as much about crop spraying as I knew about operating high speed fighters. Different branches of flying have become much more specialised since the war.

Westwick had many contracts to spray potatoes against blight. This was the disease that devastated the Irish crop in the 19th century, causing starvation among the population and triggered Irish emigration to America. In those days there was no chemical to combat the disease and the farmers were helpless when the crop turned brown and withered before their eyes.

To keep the disease under control, the potatoes were sprayed with a fungicide at 10-14 day intervals, as new foliage grew. This disease flourished in wet, warm conditions, and as the crop could only be sprayed when the leaves were dry, every opportunity had to be exploited when the weather was fine.

A farm in the Fens near Feltwell grew about 700 acres of potatoes every year. It was a favourite with the pilots, as there was a landing strip on the farm, with a drainage ditch on the boundary, giving a supply of water. With good weather and an early start, this farm could be sprayed in a day.

After taking off from Ludham in the Tiger Moth, just before daylight to get an early start, I set course for Feltwell. Flying at about 500 feet, except for the odd street light and the lights from the house of an early riser, the ground was in darkness.

Near North Walsham I suddenly saw a large country house, with all the windows lit up. I could see a large swimming pool, bathed in light, and on the terrace surrounding it stood a large group of people, the ladies in evening dress and the men in dinner jackets. This was at 5 o'clock in the morning! I thought I must be dreaming. Then I remembered that Alex Alexander, the man who started Westwick and was now a director of Imperial Foods, was giving his daughter a 21st birthday party at Westwick House. I don't know who was more surprised, them or me!

On another occasion Barry Riddon and I left for Feltwell in

two Pawnees. The weather was not good, low cloud and misty visibility. We crept along under the cloud, but the visibility got worse so we landed at Deopham Green, a disused airfield. After half an hour it got a little better so we set off again. Visibility once more forced us to land on a strip used by the army on the edge of the Thetford battle area. A short while later, the weather definitely improved so once again we took off for Feltwell.

As we approached the Fens, the cloud lifted, but a ground mist started to form, covering the whole area. By this time I had lost Barry and had a great desire to get on the ground again. I did not think I could find the farm strip in the mist, but I saw the hangars of RAF Feltwell rising out of the mist, which was only about 20 feet high. Feltwell was a non-operational grass airfield, now used as a training school. The grass area had two football pitches on it, complete with goal posts.

Although forward visibility is very restricted in fog, downward visibility through 20 feet is better. Orientating myself from the hangars, I flew low over the airfield to locate the goal posts and any other obstructions. Finding a clear area, I descended into the mist. Just as I was about to hold off, a goal post loomed out of the mist. I pulled up over it and was about to descend again, when I realised that there might be another goal post in front of me. I changed course about 20 degrees and landed. I was congratulating myself on reaching 'terra firma' when there was a loud bang, followed by another and the aircraft lurched to a halt. I got out and looked at the aircraft, which had a crumpled leading edge and a damaged aileron. What on earth had happened? Then I saw a wooden fence, surrounding a baseball pitch, which I had not seen from the air. I had missed the goal-post, but hit the fence!

I walked over to the buildings, but as it was early in the morning there was nobody about. I had to wait until 7 o'clock before the first workers arrived and I could use a phone. In the meantime the mist had dispersed.

Denys flew down with another aircraft, which I took on to the farm strip. Jack Anderson, the engineer came down by road to make temporary repairs so the aircraft could be flown back to Ludham. Barry was able to find the farm strip and with difficulty managed to land. The ground crew said he got out of the aircraft a very shaken pilot!

On another occasion, returning from the Fens in the evening in clear weather, I noticed some high cloud drifting in from the coast. The nearer I got to Ludham, the lower the cloud got. I knew the area very well and felt sure I could reach Ludham under the cloud. It was very low when I got to Wroxham, but I picked up the road to Ludham and followed it. The cloud base got lower and lower, until I noticed that treetops were passing by just under the wing!

I passed a grass field beside the road, and making a quick, low circuit I landed in it. As the aircraft slowed down, there was a bang and it lurched to the right. The right hand wheel had hit the concrete base of a dismantled wartime pillbox, hidden in the grass, and the undercarriage leg was bent.

I was beginning to think that Feltwell had a jinx on me. Once again, returning from the Fens in clear weather, high cloud appeared in the sky, lowering towards the coast. Not to be caught again, I landed in a field near Coltishall, tied the aircraft down and rang my wife to pick me up. When I got home I rang the airfield to tell them what had happened. "What's the matter with you," they asked, "the sun is shining here!"

There must have been a change in temperature or wind, that dispersed the 'sea-fret'. Sometimes you cannot win.

Anglia Television came to the airfield to do a feature on crop spraying for their local news programme. They arrived with cameras and sound equipment and a programme was worked out. I was to fly the Pawnee, and it would start with the aircraft landing, taxying back and stopping in front of the hangar. Then Denys was to be interviewed in front of the aircraft, which would be followed by a spraying demonstration on a field next to the strip.

I took off and lined up for the landing. I concentrated hard and made a beautiful three-point landing. Taxying back, I was pleased with myself, when someone jumped on the wing and said I had to do the landing again. I assumed that something had gone wrong with the camera - maybe they had forgotten to switch it on! The next landing was of my usual standard, right wheel, left wheel, then the tailwheel, with a couple of small bounces. When the programme was over and the television people had left I asked, "What went wrong on the first landing?"

"Oh, as you landed," I was told, "your friend Francois arrived and exclaimed in a loud voice, 'Why can't he always bloody well land like that?' and this was picked up on the sound system." So much for my friends!

Operating from a disused airfield beside a main road in Lincolnshire, the visibility was very poor. The work was about six miles away, and I navigated along the country lanes with my finger on the map. "Over two crossroads, first road on the left, over the stream, second road on the right, then up the first farm track." And the reverse on the way back. After several loads I got familiar with the route and flew back on a compass course. But I must have got a bit complacent.

Coming back for another load I landed and taxied up to the loading area, but there was no lorry! It could not have gone for more water, because the pump, mixing drum and all the other paraphernalia would have been there. The features did not seem familiar. Hastily I looked at the aeronautical map and discovered that there was another disused airfield two miles up the road. I had landed on the wrong airfield!

After several happy years with Westwick, during which another take-over absorbed us into Imperial Foods, I was thinking of moving on. Several things influenced me, some of them quite trivial, but it showed the way things were going.

A directive from Imperial Foods filtered down to us, stating what grade of employee could travel first class or second class on the railway, and what sums they could spend on meals and so on. Pilots normally stayed in modest pubs, but sometimes late at night, with pubs full, they were not inclined to search for accommodation within these guidelines. While at work meals were probably sandwiches eaten while refuelling. A good dinner, with a bottle of wine helped you to relax at the end of a tiring day.

Landing at March late one night, the agent took me to stay in a pub which did not serve evening meals. With no transport the only place I could get a meal was at a night club. Arriving at the club at 10 o'clock, the manager said I was welcome to a meal, but I would have to join the club on a temporary membership of £2. It was that or go hungry so I paid up and had a good meal. I bet that was not allowed for in Imperial Foods directive.

Then Denys Howard left to run a pub. Denys had shielded us from a lot of the bureaucracy of a big company and I felt sure it would not be such a happy place run by a manager who did not know the unique conditions under which aerial crop sprayers had to work.

These circumstances made me consider starting a crop-spraying company of my own. Francois, who had taken a job in the Cayman Islands, was interested in investing some money, initially as a sleeping partner, with a view to joining later when the company was established.

The aerial crop-spraying industry was expanding in England and it seemed a good time to set up on our own. I started talking to banks about finance and looking for secondhand aircraft. It was a challenge, an opportunity to put into practice some of the things I had learnt while working for other companies and a chance to be my own boss.

22

Going Solo Again

Starting your own aircraft business is similar to going solo when learning to fly. I had read books on the subject, talked to many people and seen, as an employee, how some companies worked. Now, with this knowledge, I was going 'solo'. And like going solo in an aeroplane, I had much to learn.

Although, both as a bachelor and as a married man, I lived comfortably, there was never much cash in the bank. My wife and I both enjoyed home life so we put our money into pleasant, comfortable and well-furnished homes. When I was free-lancing on short contracts we lived in Devonshire, but after I started working full-time in Norfolk, we had to move.

We found a dilapidated farmhouse in the country, beside a small lake, a few miles from Wroxham. We were lucky to find a builder, a Mr Norgate, who enjoyed working on old houses. We employed neither a surveyor nor an architect, as Mr Norgate was very experienced and together we modernised the house to our requirements. Walls came down to enlarge rooms, bathrooms were added, extra windows and central heating put in until we had a comfortable home without destroying the character of the property.

Mr Norgate told me that he was seventy years old, had been in the building trade since he was fourteen, and had enjoyed every minute of it. I thought, "What a lucky man." Even at that age, he climbed ladders and chased his men.

The house had no name, and in the early days we directed

visitors and tradesmen by explaining it was "the house by the lake." So this is what we named it. Some of my humorous friends addressed letters to, 'The shed by the pond,' or 'The shack by the ditch!'

When I went to various banks with my ideas for starting my own business and told them I had no money, that all my assets were in my home, they showed little interest. My friend Francois, home on leave from the Cayman Islands, showed interest in the project and was ready to put some money in. It was agreed that I would start the company and he would join later if it got off the ground.

A friend told me that the local Barclays branch had a new manager, a Mr Rushton, whom they found most helpful. I went to see him, told him what Francois and I wanted to do, and what my finances were. He showed great interest and adopted a positive attitude. The bank would only lend us the same amount pound for pound that we put into the business, so he set about rearranging my assets by remortgaging my house, to give me cash. That hurdle was overcome.

Some Piper Pawnee crop spraying aircraft were advertised in *Flight* magazine for sale in America, by a man named John Hawkes. I rang him in Fort Lauderdale and arranged to buy one of the aircraft. I never met him, but he rang me several times about shipping details and always had a long chat about the weather and how he enjoyed visiting England.

This was long distance from America and it amazed me, as I was watching ever penny! Maybe it was how the Americans did business. I heard a lot about him over the years; he was a buccaneer type, buying, selling and ferrying aircraft all over the world. I heard years later that he had been lost at sea ferrying an aircraft.

Jim McMahon from Crop Culture was also most helpful. He put me in touch with Ken Couling, who ran a successful business, I believe, in the 'rag' trade. As a sideline he had an interest in aviation and would arrange hire purchase of aircraft for selected customers. On the recommendation from Jim he agreed to finance our Pawnee.

Ken Couling also financed our second Pawnee. I got a quotation from a national hire purchase company, but their rate was a half per cent higher, so I did not pursue it. They, however, pursued me, and when I told them the difference in rates, came back with an offer a quarter per cent lower than Mr Couling. I did not like such tactics, so stayed with him.

This paid off, because several years later, when we only had six months further payments to make to end the agreement, we encountered cash problems, just before the main spraying season. I asked him if we could waive our monthly payments and settle the outstanding amount after the spraying season, when our financial position would be better. To this he agreed. I doubt if the other company would have been so accommodating, and might even have repossessed the aircraft.

Jim also put us in touch with his insurers, Norman, Butcher and Jones. Keith Jones, the managing director, was aware of the record of both Francois and myself from the time we flew for Crop Culture, so he was able to obtain a favourable rate for us.

Keith, although he insured operators all over the world, took a personal interest in all his customers, and although our account was relatively small, always came to Norfolk every year to discuss our insurance.

Mike Wadia, who looked after the aviation business at the London office, was always available, and minor alterations in our policy could be arranged verbally over the phone without a lot of paperwork.

In the slack season our aircraft could be put on to 'ground risk only', saving us some money. When one of our aircraft went to Miller Aerial Spraying, in Lincolnshire, for Certificate of Airworthiness renewal, I drove Tony Hampton (a pilot who joined us later) to collect it and fly it back to Norfolk. Halfway home, I suddenly realised that it was still on ground risk only. I stopped at a phone box and rang Mike Wadia to put it on flight risk for the ferry. "When is he taking off and how long is the ferry?" asked Mike.

"He took off half and hour ago," I replied, "and is probably almost home by now."

"Right," said Mike. "We'll cover the ferry flight."

No fuss, no bother.

We now had to find a base from which to operate. Nigel Wright, the manager of Arrow Air Services, offered us facilities at Shipdham Airfield. We used this base for some years, until we moved to Little Snoring. It was mutually helpful, as sometimes

Arrow Air Services needed a licensed aircraft engineer, which I could supply.

Westwick were the only agricultural merchants in Norfolk and Suffolk operating their own aircraft. Other merchants would not use them as they wanted to sell their own chemicals. We did not deal in chemicals, being solely applicators, which suited the merchants.

They supplied the agricultural technical knowledge and chemical and we carried out the application. Over the years we did much work for merchants, such as Crop Care Chemicals, in north Norfolk, Sands Agricultural Services at Stalham, Growers Services at Ixworth in Suffolk, Protectacrop, and several others. We also built up a clientele of farmers for whom we worked directly.

I was warned that farmers were bad payers, but we never had a bad debt. In fact, Bill Hawkes, manager of Brancaster Farms, and several others, offered to pay us at the end of the work, instead of waiting until we invoiced them, to help us in the early days.

We were now set up to start and had work on the books, but no aircraft. It was still on a ship in mid-Atlantic. Pat Miller, of Miller Aerial Spraying in Lincolnshire, came to the rescue and hired us a Pawnee and a fertiliser loader. Henry Labouchere, who had been my marker at Westwick, joined us as loader and we had a young student as a marker.

Our first work was fertilising in Bedford for two agricultural fieldsmen, Ian Buchanan and John Tomlin. They had recently started their own company, Topspray, as merchants and ground sprayers. We were both keen to make a success of our businesses and we were kept very busy.

In the meantime our Pawnee had arrived at Felixstowe docks, but seemed to be stuck there. I rang several times, but could not get much sense out of anyone. I complained to my wife, "It takes longer to get from one side of the docks to the other, than it does to cross the bloody Atlantic!"

Eventually, my wife, seeing my frustration and fed up with my complaints when I came back from a long day's flying, rang the docks herself. She found the foreman who moved all the containers around, and chatted him up. She said her husband had just started in business and had had to hire an aircraft at great expense, and was working very hard.

She asked him about his job, remarked how interesting it must be and how his wife must be very proud of him and what lovely children he must have, and so on. After ten minutes, he was won over. "Don't you worry, m'dear." he said. "I have to move some containers tomorrow, and I will look out for your husband's and bring it to the front."

Women are much better at this sort of thing than men. I would have complained that it took longer to pass through the docks, than cross the Atlantic and the container would have been pushed right to the back! Soon the aircraft arrived at Bowker Air Services, who assembled it, did all the paper work to get it registered in this country and issued it with a Certificate of Airworthiness. I collected it from their base at Rush Green and returned the hired aircraft to Pat Miller. We were in business.

The first season of 1973 was quite successful and I was kept busy. As well as flying all day, in the evening I had to organise the next day's work and send out invoices. The aircraft had to be maintained, fuel supplies arranged, staff paid, VAT calculated and so on. I did not find it overwhelming, in fact enjoyed the variety of activities. We had no staff other than the loader and marker and my wife manning the phone.

In September, the main spraying season ended. Henry went back to Australia and the marker started college, which left me on my own. There was not enough work to warrant full-time staff in that winter, so I realised that I had to find a way to work on my own. At times I could get a retired farmer to mark or load for me, but he was not always available.

I decided to use 'static markers' in place of the human one. They consisted of 'Day-Glo' coloured cardboard tubes, attached to garden canes of various lengths, depending on the height of the crop. They were stuck in the ground across the field at a distance to correspond to the swath width. A small 'counter' was mounted on to the instrument panel of the aircraft to record the number of spray runs.

With this system I was able to load the aircraft and spray the field without assistance. The system was only useful at times of light work load, but we did continue using static markers for small or isolated fields, allowing a human marker more time to move from field to field.

During this year we experimented with augers to load the aircraft with fertiliser. The most popular machine for this was a 4x4 ex-army Bedford truck, fitted with a gantry and a bucket. Loading was quick, but the truck was heavy on fuel, difficult to handle, and in wet weather, churned up the grass loading area, which did not please the farmer.

We bought a cheap second-hand dumper truck and a 3 inch auger and got it fitted up by an agricultural engineer. It was not very successful, as the small auger loaded too slowly and we had trouble with the drive; however it proved that the principle was right.

Alan Furness, who had worked for Westwick on the ground spraying side, joined us for the 1974 season and stayed with the company until it ceased to operate in 1985. He made a great contribution to the company in those years and was the mainstay of the ground operations. Alan had an HGV driver's licence, so we looked for a lorry which would transport a dumper truck and aircraft fuel for fertiliser work and a large water tank and aircraft fuel for spraying work.

We found a Ford lorry, with a long, low tray. It had been used for transporting machinery, had a hand-operated winch, sloping back and loading ramps, ideal for our needs. We bought a 30 cwt Thwaites dumper truck which we modified into a fertiliser loader fitted with a six inch auger. This worked very well and would load half a ton into the aircraft in under two minutes, which was acceptable. An added advantage was that the auger broke up any lumpy fertiliser as it wound it up the shaft. It was cheap to run, using little fuel and did not need road tax or insurance.

For the 1974 season we took on a marker to join Alan as the nucleus of our permanent staff. The spring fertilising went well and the spraying season had just started, when in June, I crashed the aircraft.

Taking off on a narrow concrete taxi-way of a disused airfield, I was about to raise the tail, when the aircraft swung violently to the left and off the taxi-way into the field alongside. It continued to swing and skid, the left undercarriage collapsed and it ended up facing 180 degrees to the direction of take-off. It was all over in seconds.

Surprised, but unhurt, I got out of the aircraft and surveyed the damage. It was very bad and the aircraft would be out of service for a long time; and this was the beginning of a busy spraying season.

After recovering from the shock, I knew I had to get another aircraft quickly. When the marker came back, I drove to the nearest phone box and rang Pat Miller to see if he had an aircraft I could hire. Once again, he came to the rescue, and two days later we were flying again.

Examining the wreck I found that the front bolt holding the tailwheel springs had sheared, allowing the tailwheel to turn at an angle and send me off the strip. Subsequently, this bolt was check-tightened regularly and replaced with a new one each year.

I also found that one propeller blade was bent backwards and the other bent forwards. Usually in a crash both blades are bent back. I thought I was clever to do this and kept the blade for several years to show disbelievers my skill.

When the agent told the farmer that the aircraft had crashed, his first words were, "What about my crop, when is it going to be sprayed?"

Usually the first thing everyone asks is, "Is the pilot all right?"

Thankfully, there are not many people like that farmer.

We had another good season and now had enough work for two aircraft, so we bought the one we had on hire. The damaged Pawnee was going to take several months to repair, but it would be ready for the next season.

Francois's contract was coming to an end and he planned to join the company. However, the Mosquito Research Unit in the Cayman Islands was buying a helicopter and offered Francois a conversion course on it if he renewed his contract. Understandably, he found this was an offer he could not refuse, so he postponed joining the company for two years.

Tony Hampton, an experienced crop-spraying pilot, had recently finished a contract in Cyprus, and was living in Norwich and flying for Air Anglia. He was invited to join the company to fly the second aircraft.

After many years crop spraying for various companies, I had developed firm ideas about how operations should be carried out. Operations are affected by many factors, the main one being the weather. If, when the weather is fine, opportunities to spray are missed due to unpreparedness or 'unserviceability' of equipment, those acres that could have been sprayed are lost for ever.

The aircraft flies at a certain speed, the pilot turns at a certain rate and the effective swath width is fixed, so time over the crop is difficult to improve.

Later, however, we were able to improve this by fitting different wing tips. The round wing tips of the Pawnee produced wing tip vortices, which caused the spray to curl up above the wing. In windy conditions this increased the drift problem. By fitting square wing tips, produced by a company in America, the wing-tip vortice was reduced, so reducing the drift. It also gave a greater effective swath width, which increased productivity per flying hour.

We aimed to make improvements in turn round time, to reduce the time spent on the ground loading and refuelling the aircraft. The dumper trucks with an auger could load fertiliser at a satisfactory rate, but the driver had to get down and open the door on the top of the aircraft hopper. We fitted a cable so that the pilot could open the door from the cockpit. This saved time and the energy of the driver.

The spray chemical was pumped into the aircraft hopper through a hose connected to a loading valve in the side of the aircraft. All the hoses were fitted with quick release couplings.

Valves were fitted to the loading pump, so various operations, such as mixing or loading could be carried out by opening and shutting valves, without having to disconnect the hoses.

At first, refuelling was by four-gallon plastic cans, filled from a 44 gallon drum and poured into the aircraft tank through a filter. We had tools made to undo the bungs on the drums. They were easy to make and cheap. Too often I had seen ground crew struggling to remove the bungs with a screwdriver and a pair of pliers, barking their knuckles in the process. Later we replaced the drums with a 300 gallon bowser, mounted on the lorry and fitted with a hand-pump, hose and nozzle, so fuel could be pumped directly into the aircraft tank.

On the lorry we carried a spare loading pump and hoses, as well as aircraft spares such as a spray pump, a main-wheel, brake linings, a tailwheel unit and spark plugs, dope and fabric, a selection of nuts and bolts and, of course, a toolbox.

We had a spare filter for the aircraft spray system and spare spray nozzles. When these became clogged while spraying, they were changed while the aircraft was being loaded and cleaned at leisure.

None of these innovations was expensive and they paid for themselves by greater productivity. It was not possible to cover every eventuality. Once a pheasant flew up out of the crop as I passed over and knocked the pilot head off, which registered airspeed so I had to spray for the rest of the day with no airspeed indicator.

At the back of my house there was a large yard and a long open cart shed. When work was quiet we concreted the yard, built a wall on the open side of the shed and concreted the floor.

We dug an inspection pit to service our vans and fitted a bench and shelving. This made an excellent workshop and store. Every year we dismantled the aircraft at Shipdham airfield and transported the fuselage and wings to the workshop for overhaul.

The water tank on the lorry held 500 gallons, and on a busy day this had to be replenished three or four times. Water was usually drawn from the nearest pond or stream and in some areas this could involve a journey of several miles, causing delays.

On airstrips which we used frequently and had a main water supply nearby, we put a static water tank, fitted with a ball valve, and connected it to the water main. This eliminated the break in operations while the lorry went to refill its tank. Also on some airstrips we had a small hut, where we could store fuel and equipment, and where agents could leave chemical, maps and worksheets.

Our better agents became aware of the economics of our operations and assembled a parcel of work, possibly several hundred acres, around an airstrip before calling us in. Others gave us 20 acres to spray on its own, then the next day called up with another job in the same area. This wasted time and petrol on ferry flights.

When attached to an agent in Lincolnshire, working for Crop Culture, I was sent to spray 10 acres, 15 miles away. I pointed out that this was not profitable for my company, but the agent said it was a very good customer of theirs. They had nothing to lose, they sold some chemical and collected a commission on the work, but the spray company lost money, the operation costing more in petrol than the income.

In our first year an agent asked for a special quotation for a large acreage over the season. Eager for work, and expecting several thousand acres, a competitive price was given. Over the season the work came in dribs and drabs and only amounted to 800 acres in all. I was not caught like that again.

During the spraying season we often worked long hours, seven days a week. I adopted a policy that when there was work to be done, then we worked all the time the weather allowed us. If the weather was bad, then everyone stayed at home until it improved. In spite of this, many hours were spent on desolate airfields, hoping a marginal wind would drop.

Occasionally there was a day when everything went wrong. The marker got his van bogged in a wet field, the loading pump refused to start, a hose burst, the aircraft got a puncture. The more we tried to put things right, the more things went wrong. Everyone got tired, frustrated and bad tempered. Rather than struggle on with more things going wrong, it was better to pack up for the day, have a good night's rest and start again fresh in the morning. As an old engineer I knew, used to say, "Boy, you can't fart against thunder!"

j

23
Avalanche of Work

The winter and spring of 1975/76 brought little work. The spring was dry and most of the farmers were able to fertilise the crops with ground machines. By May there had been little income for almost nine months. Our overdraft was getting high and I was getting worried.

Work started to come in slowly, then it became an avalanche! It was the year of the aphid! Returning home one night my wife said an agent had rung in with 5,000 acres. Over the next few days, agents and farmers rang in with orders, and we had over 15,000 acres on the books, with more arriving every day.

The weather was fine and hot and Tony Hampton and I were flying all day and every day to cope with the work. We were using petrol faster than our invoices were being paid. Shell were strict on the terms of payment for petrol; they had been caught in the past with charter companies going bust owing them money.

Our overdraft was up to our limit, and unfortunately our friendly bank manager, Mr Rushton, had been moved to Norwich and we had a new manager. I went to see him to borrow some money to pay Shell, so we could order more petrol to keep flying. I told him we had invoiced more work than our overdraft, and had orders for many more acres.

He was a cautious type and asked for income and expenditure predictions for the next three years! I was far too busy flying and earning money to sit down and produce such figures, even if it was practicable.

Who can predict what weather will bring what diseases in what crops in two or three years time? Now I was worried again. We were using petrol at a fast rate and could not order more until we paid the last bill.

Once again my wife's charm solved the problem. I came home late one night, tired from a long day's flying, and she told me she had spoken to the bank and we could have the money. We had a very successful season and went from the red well into the black. At the end of the season I transferred our substantial balance to the branch where Mr Rushton was now manager.

In the short term it was good to have all this work, but long term I do not think it did the aerial crop spraying industry much good. We were all overwhelmed with the work and many farmers did not get their crops treated.

Any one of our main agents could have kept an aircraft busy for the whole season, but this would have meant other agents having no aircraft at all. It was very hard but we had to ration the work, working for one agent for two days and then going on to another for two days, and so on, then coming back to the original agent and starting the rounds again. We tried to concentrate on the farmers who used aircraft every year, and the farmers who only used aircraft in an emergency had low priority.

Towards the end there was a shortage of chemicals, as the chemical companies were unable to keep up with the demand. Merchants ransacked their stores for old or forgotten stock and some imported lorry loads from the continent.

In the middle of all this activity, I got marooned at North Creake airfield on the North Norfolk coast. We arrived there late one evening, ready to work the next day. As I was tying the aircraft down, sea-fret drifted in from the coast a few miles away, and by the time we left visibility was bad.

Driving to the airfield the next morning, we ran into the mist five or six miles away and when we got there the airfield was blanketed in fog and visibility was only a few yards. We sat in the van, drinking coffee and chatting, waiting for the sun to come up and burn it off. By mid-morning it was still as bad. Sometimes the visibility got a little better, but it soon clamped down again.

This situation lasted for two days. Sitting on the airfield I could hear other aircraft spraying in the clear, sunny area a few miles inland. The agent was being bombarded by the farmers ringing up to find out why their crops were not being sprayed. Frustration drove me to take off on several occasions when the weather appeared to improve slightly, but as soon as I was airborne more mist drifted in, sending me scuttling back to the landing strip.

The clear weather was only a few miles away, but I had no instruments for flying in cloud, and even if I had, I had very limited experience of instrument flying. From accident investigations it is reckoned that even an experienced pilot will become disorientated after a few minutes of cloud flying without instruments and spin into the ground. I did not consider the urgency of the farmer to have his crop sprayed, warranted me risking my life. On the third day the sea-fret disappeared and we were able to work again.

Over the years many amusing and odd incidents occurred. We operated from an airfield at Nuthampstead where several private pilots kept light aircraft, one being an airline pilot. On one visit he asked if he could look around the Pawnee and sit in the cockpit. When he got out he remarked on the lack of instruments. "What Q setting do you set on your altimeter?" he asked me.

"At the height I fly," I answered, "I don't refer to the altimeter. In fact I usually use it for counting the loads."

He walked away with a disgusted look on his face, as if I was an irresponsible cowboy.

Talking of cowboys, an irate man wrote a letter to *Flight* magazine complaining that he had seen an aircraft land on Holkham beach in Norfolk and demanded that these 'cowboy' pilots should be dealt with.

The pilot was Henry Labouchere, who worked for us in our first season. He replied to the letter, explaining that he had landed his Tiger Moth on the beach to inspect some cattle in a nearby field, that he was looking after in the farmer's absence. He ended his letter, 'which, I suppose, does make me a cowboy.'

My wife had a very basic sense of humour and always caught me out on April Fool's Day. One year I was working away from home and felt safe. I rang in every night to see if there were any messages. On the last day of March, I rang in as usual.

"A farmer from Ipswich rang in today," said my wife. "He wants you to ring him as soon as possible. He seems to have a lot of work and wants to discuss it with you. Here is his number."

I rang the number several times that evening, but got no reply, so assumed the farmer was out for the night. Next morning, during a lull, I took the marker's van and drove to the nearest public phone box. I dialled the number and a voice said, "Ipswich crematorium." This surprised me and I didn't know what to say. "Ipswich crematorium, can I help you?" said the voice again. Then the penny dropped!

"The bitch, she's got me!" I exclaimed.

"I beg your pardon, sir," said the voice. "This is the Ipswich crematorium." I briefly explained to the voice how I came to be ringing, but he did not seem to think it funny. Maybe working in a crematorium is not conducive to a sense of humour.

I am one of those people who, if I go anywhere near an aircraft I get covered in oil and grease. Consequently I always wore old, scruffy clothes while I was working. My wife always urged me to dress a little smarter. "Why don't you dress like Bob Milsom?" she would ask.

Bob was a crop spraying pilot we knew who always looked neat and tidy, even at the end of a day's flying. He wore a collar and tie, had creases in his trousers and his shoes were polished.

One day Alan and I were lying under the aircraft struggling to stop a leak in the spray system. Oil dripped on us from the engine, chemical ran down our arms on to our chests, and the ground was dusty. When we had fixed the leak and crawled out from under the aircraft, we were dishevelled, covered in oil and soaked in chemical. Alan looked at me. "I don't know why you don't dress like Bob Milsom," he remarked. The situation was so incongruous that we both collapsed on to the ground in peals of laughter.

Spraying a field of wheat, my turns took me over a sugar beet field where a group of men and women were hoeing weeds. To amuse myself I did steep, low level turns round them. After I had done this several times, one of the men got fed up, and to show what he thought of me, he dropped his hoe, turned his back, dropped his trousers, bent down and mooned me!

A local flying club put on an air display and asked if I would give a crop spraying demonstration. When I arrived all the participants were briefed on their position in the programme. I was allotted a slot near the end. The Red Arrow display team was taking part, which pleased me as I was one of their fans.

I watched the Red Arrows give their display, which thrilled me as usual. As soon as they had finished, the organiser rushed up.

"There has been a change in the programme, Peter," he said. "Quickly, will you go on now?"

I jumped into the Pawnee, took off, made a steep low turn, and flew in front of the crowd at six feet, spraying out water. At the end of the run I made another steep turn, lining up to do another run. As I passed in front of the crowd, I noticed that many of them were turning away and heading for the beer tent. I tightened my turns and flew lower, but I could not keep their interest. I did not blame them, after the Red Arrows any display would be an anti-climax.

The company seemed to be working efficiently, despite the vagaries of the weather and the unpredictability of the demand for our service. We had good ground crews, Tony was a hardworking and efficient pilot, who could organise his own work. Our equipment gave fast turn-round times and the aircraft gave little trouble, mainly due to the extensive overhaul we gave them in the winter months.

Our main problems stemmed from the increasing interest that the Civil Aviation Authority took in our operations and the aversion some environmental groups took to our activities.

24

Complaints and Controls

For many years the Civil Aviation Authority took little interest in the activities of the aerial crop spraying industry. An exemption from the rule forbidding flights within 500 feet of a person or building was granted to operators when spraying a crop. Action was only taken by the CAA if a pilot blatantly broke the air safety regulations.

Responsible operators - and the majority were - would inform the police where they were operating. The police were able to pacify people who rang them, worried about a noisy, low flying aircraft near their house or village. People living in houses next to the field being sprayed and other sensitive areas, such as schools and hospitals were also informed. One hospital standing on a hill overlooking fields we sprayed would push patients on to the verandah, so they could watch.

As the industry expanded, CAA started to take a more active interest. A small department was formed under Mr Pat Walker, a retired senior RAF officer. Discussions were started with the operators about regulations to ensure safety both within the industry and to the public. The CAA wished to talk to a body representing the operators, so the operators approached the National Association of Agricultural Contractors to form an aerial crop spraying section within that organisation. Nearly all aerial crop spraying companies were owned by pilots, who tended to be individualistic and practical men. They did not enjoy committee meetings and were not well versed nor enjoyed involvement in legal and political discussions.

The operators had several discussions, some of them heated, with Mr Walker about his proposals. We insisted that the operators were consulted before any regulations were put into effect. This was done, but in a very insensitive manner.

In the height of a busy season, proposals would be sent to the operators with a request that they submitted their views and objections within a few weeks, so that the regulation could come into force on a certain date. Pilot/owners were too busy earning a living to stop and have meetings at this time. In spite of our protests this situation only improved slightly. The CAA had months in which to discuss and formulate regulations, but expected us to review them in a few weeks.

These discussions resulted in the CAA introducing a licence for operators, the issue of which was dependent on the operator submitting an operations manual for approval. This manual had to give details of the company organisation and qualifications of staff and specify in great detail how operations would be carried out, such as who to notify, safety precautions, mapping details, calculations of aircraft load, selection of airstrips, training programmes for pilots, safe distances when flying near buildings or roads and many more stipulations covering every aspect of operations.

This was going to involve a lot of work, but luckily a larger operator compiled a manual and had it approved, and offered it to other operators at a modest fee. We bought a copy and it was approved by CAA. A copy had to be available to staff and carried with all operating units. With one kept in the office and one sent to CAA, we had to have five copies.

Inspectors from CAA and the Health and Safety Executive visited units in the field to ensure that we were operating correctly. When these visits were expected we always arranged for them to find a small, unimportant fault. We would discuss the defect in great detail and be suitably contrite at our omission. This would take some time, so the rest of the unit only got a cursory inspection.

It prevented the inspector delving too deeply and finding some additional and probably, expensive requirement. Providing he had something to report it justified his visit, so everyone was happy. Most of the Health and Safety inspectors were reasonable people.

Occasionally an inspector would be aiming for 100 per cent safety, regardless of frequency of risk and expense to eliminate it.

For almost a year we had no visits from a CAA inspector. Everything seemed to be quiet and we naively assumed we were doing things right and would be left in peace to get on with our work. How wrong we were!

A letter arrived from CAA, enclosing a long list of amendments to make to our manual. No wonder we had not seen any inspectors, they had spent the year going through every operator's manual with a fine toothcomb calling for many amendments.

We had over 100 alterations to make. Some were quite minor, such as altering 'should' to 'shall', and 'a climbing turn' to 'a gently climbing turn'. Some paragraphs had a notation beside them, such as 'amplify' or 'expand' but no indication to show what was wanted. Almost every page of the manual was affected, so most of it had to be retyped. Being a 'two finger' typist, I had to pay a typist to do it. When it was finally finished I sent it off to the CAA.

A few weeks later another letter came from CAA, stating that some of the 'amplifications' and 'expansions' were not satisfactory, but still offering no guidance. And there were yet more alterations in addition to the previous list. This now made me hopping mad. The manual, after it had been compiled was never read. The only times it was referred to was when CAA wrote to say they had had a complaint, and we were in breach of a certain paragraph in the manual. The paragraph was then read to see what crime we were supposed to have committed. It all seemed a complete waste of everyone's time.

I could see the only solution to the manual problem was to find out from CAA exactly what they wanted. Correspondence could go back and forth for weeks, or maybe months. I rang the inspector and asked to come and talk over the problems.

Tony Hampton and I travelled to London for this meeting. On the way I said to Tony, "We are not going to leave until all the wording is agreed by CAA." We arrived at the CAA office at 10 o'clock and left at 5 o'clock, exhausted!

Tony and I sat in front of the inspector's desk with the manual and the list of amendments. We went through the list item by item. When the inspector said the paragraph needed amplification or expansion, we asked him how he wanted it worded. As he stated how he thought it should read, I wrote it down and read it back to him. "Do you agree with that?" I asked. When he agreed we went on to the next item. This went on all the morning and into the afternoon. Beer and sandwiches appeared at lunchtime, which we ate while working. Then the inspector got onto other subjects.

"Who supplies the maps for the work?" he asked.

"Either one of our staff or the agent, and sometimes the farmer supplies a farm map," I replied.

The inspector then went on to ask how we marked hazards such as power lines and sensitive areas like houses, roads and hospitals.

"When the pilot comes to do the work, it may have been mapped some days before," said the inspector. "Does he then go and inspect the field himself from the ground before he starts to spray?"

"Good lord, no!" I exclaimed. "He has all the information on the map. Why should he need to do that?"

"Well," said the inspector, "things may have altered. For instance, someone may have put a tall crane in the field."

I was now tired and frustrated. "You know," I exclaimed, "pilots do have eyes!"

Leaving that subject he asked if the aircraft needed a spare part in the field who authorised the issue of that part.

"No one," I said. "If a part was needed that was not carried on the unit, someone, probably the marker, would be sent back to base to collect it."

"The marker would not be very knowledgeable, would he?" asked the inspector.

"They are not idiots, you know," I said. "A marker knows what a spray pump or a main-wheel looks like."

"Yes," answered the inspector, "but who would authorise the issue of the replacement."

"No one," I repeated. "It would be obvious to the crew when a part was damaged or not working. Just plain common sense and someone would go and get a replacement. We are not BOAC, you know, with a storeman and requisitions in triplicate."

Finally the inspector brought out a loading chart. This is a series of graphs and information is fed into them, such as windspeed, temperature, length of the strip and so on, and when you get to the other side of the graph, it tells you what load you can safely carry.

"I would like you to include this in your manual," he said.

"I'm not putting that in the manual," I declared. "Those things are bloody dangerous."

"I would like it to go in," said the inspector. "I think it could be very useful."

"We already have in the manual, a simple, safe and well tried method of assessing a safe load for a particular landing strip. You tell us the manual is a legal document. We are not operating from airports where accurate information is available, we are operating from farmers' fields. If an inexperienced pilot used that chart by estimating the information necessary, it could all be biased one way, and he would take off over-loaded and hit the fence. You could kill someone if you insist that it goes in the manual." By now I was really getting steamed up!

The inspector thought for a moment, then he said, "Well, would you put it in the appendix?"

"All right," I said. "It can go in the appendix, but I shall put a note on it that it is advisory only and is not to be used for calculating loads."

Leaving the building I said to Tony, "I'm exhausted. That was harder than a long day's flying." The amendments were retyped and accepted by CAA.

A new inspector, Jim Mackie, arrived to carry out an inspection of our records for the annual renewal of our operator's licence. After he had finished he said, rather apologetically, "There are a couple of amendments we would like you to make to your manual."

"Oh no. Not more! I've just got over a big battle with CAA about our manual."

"Yes, I know about that," said Jim. "The other inspectors were also fed up with having such a tedious and boring job. I do understand how you feel, but these are very minor, and I would appreciate it if you would put them in your manual."

Jim had been a helicopter spray pilot himself, and knew some of our problems, so I did not make a fuss about it. Many likeable people are in bureaucratic organisations and often have to carry out duties they do not like or are not in agreement with, but the system is bigger than them.

Aerial crop spraying brought complaints from some members of the public. Some were frivolous and some justified, but none of them serious. To my knowledge no person or property was hurt or damaged by aerial crop spraying. Occasionally, due to conditions often beyond the pilot's control, such as a change of wind direction, or the pilot miscalculating the wind strength, gardens or cars would receive some of the spray drift. It is annoying and should be avoided, but the consequences were not serious.

At our meetings with CAA, Mr Walker used to take a serious view of the number of complaints that were received from the public. In fact, he based the standard of our operations on these criteria, and intimated that if the complaints were not reduced, he would introduce further controls.

The operators pointed out that the number of complaints amounted to one in every 15,000 acres sprayed and on CAA's own admission 50 per cent were not significant. Some were from 'professional complainers', people who would complain about anything. Others were people or environmental groups who were against the use of agricultural chemicals, and particularly against aerial spraying. As our operations were visible and audible over a wide area we were easy targets.

None of these arguments convinced Mr Walker, who maintained, "that the public had a democratic right to complain." It made me think that, perhaps, I also had a democratic right to go about my lawful business without being harassed by professional complainers.

We were often accused of bizarre and amazing occurrences. Television sets not working, cars failing to start, cats giving premature birth, chimney pots cracking and headaches being some of our minor accomplishments.

One summer's morning many cars were covered in little spots, which looked just like a spray pattern from an aircraft. Before we had even started up an aircraft, the phone was ringing, people complaining that we had sprayed their cars. Later in the day the radio news reported that severe storms in the Sahara had taken dust up to a great height and the southerly winds had taken it over large parts of Europe. In the night there had been a light shower of rain, which picked up the dust as it fell. When the raindrops dried off on the surface of the car, they left the little particles of sand, which looked just like spray droplets. Only one person rang to apologise.

25

Problems With Fruit

This country is not as air minded as Australia, New Zealand and America, and low flying aircraft cause concern to the public. Because our operations were carried out at a very low height, this gave rise to complaints from some of the public.

Although people will happily drive along a two-lane highway at 60 mph, passing other cars coming in the opposite direction at 60 mph, within a few feet of each other, giving a closing speed of 120 mph, if an aircraft comes within a hundred yards of them, they rush to complain. "He nearly took our chimney off," is a favourite remark.

A letter appeared in the local press, the writer complaining that aerial crop spraying near a main road could distract motorists, causing them to drive into a ditch or other cars. It made me wonder if, while looking at a new model from Lotus Cars, I flew into a tree, I could blame the maker for distracting me!

One of our aircraft covered some cars standing in a sale yard next to a garage with spray drift. The owner rang in the evening. "I know you have a job to do and it was not deliberate," he said, "but all my cars have to be washed and polished again." I apologised and assured him it was a mistake.

"We are not very good at polishing cars," I told him, "but if you get them cleaned and send me the bill, I will send you a cheque." This was a civilised and sensible solution for both parties. On several occasions we recompensed people for inconvenience we had caused.

On the other hand some people react very strongly. I drifted some insecticide over some fruit bushes in a garden. The owner wrote a very strong letter, saying he could not now eat the fruit and went on to say that all agricultural chemicals should be banned as the long-term affects could be dire for the human race.

I rang him up and apologised and suggested that he was exaggerating. I offered to buy the fruit off him if he would pick them, as I was quite happy to eat them. He was most indignant at this suggestion and as I had not time to argue, I sent a cheque in compensation.

His attitude annoyed me, so I wrote to him, pointing out that whether he liked it or not, this was the modern method of farming. I went on to say; 'We all benefit from modern innovations, many of which have side effects on other people. Every time you drive your car, you pollute the atmosphere. When you turn on a tap and get clean water, it is because miles away a valley has been flooded to make a reservoir and villagers and farmers who have lived there for years are displaced.

'Every time you use electricity it is possible because miners working in unhealthy and dangerous conditions, supply coal to the power stations and the national grid system spoils the countryside to bring the power to your house. If some people objected to these modern benefits we enjoy and succeeded in banning them, we could still be living in caves.' He wrote back to say maybe I had some points, but he still thought agricultural chemicals should be banned!

We received a complaint from a woman who claimed she had been affected by spray from one of our aircraft, while working in a field nearby. I rang her doctor to find out the symptoms as the spray consisted of both an insecticide and a fungicide. He said his patient had come out in a rash on all parts of her body that were exposed.

"I am convinced that her symptoms have been caused by the spray," he said. "This woman has worked in the fields for years and the only difference this time is that aerial spraying was being carried out nearby."

The symptoms were not those of insecticide poisoning, and as the fungicide was a new product that year, I informed the manufacturers. I also informed our insurers as the woman was making a claim for compensation with the backing of her union. The matter then passed out of our hands, but I did some investigation.

I found the field the woman was working in, which was half a mile away from the nearest field sprayed. I also wrote to the weather office at Bracknell and asked if they could supply me with wind speeds and directions in that area that day. The winds were light and did not blow in the direction of the woman. I passed on this information to our insurers.

The chemical company again carried out skin reaction tests with the chemical. Some of their fieldsmen complained to me that for weeks, when arriving at the office, they had to bare their backs and suffer a sample of the chemical being applied to their skin.

The investigation dragged on for almost a year. Eventually our insurers rang up to tell me that the rash the woman experienced was the side effects from medication supplied by her doctor! The assessor went on, "We have negotiated a small settlement on her without admitting liability."

"Why are you paying compensation when it was nothing to do with us? That village is very militant about aerial spraying and it will only encourage other people to make silly claims." I exclaimed.

"This woman has the strong backing of her union," he explained, "and if it went to court, it is likely she would be awarded a larger amount for the stress she suffered, believing it was the spray which caused the symptoms."

"You are not serious, are you?" I asked.

"I can assure you from our experience, this could be most likely," he replied, "and although I sympathise with your view, from our point of view it is the cheapest way to settle the claim."

I could see his point, but I thought it was a funny old world.

There was a group of cottages near Ludham airfield, where Westwick Distributors was based. When any aerial activity took place near these cottages, the occupants complained of headaches, nausea and sore throats. The local farmer got the same complaints if he sprayed his crops with a ground machine. The local doctor got so concerned at the regular attendance of the cottage dwellers at his surgery, that he referred the matter to the County Medical Officer.

However, the complaints stopped after the local farmer, getting fed up, hitched his spray machine to his tractor, filled the tank with plain water and sprayed his fields. When he got home the phone was ringing and the cottagers were complaining of headaches, nausea and sore throats!

I could never understand how a person who had momentary contact with spray drift should suffer headaches and nausea, when operators of aircraft and ground spraying machines who were in contact with the chemical daily for long periods, both in its diluted and undiluted state, did not suffer these symptoms.

Some people complained that they had been 'drenched' in spray. I conducted a small experiment. The most commonly used insecticide was applied at the rate of 6 fluid ounces in 2 gallons of water spread over one acre. I generously calculated the area of the human body and worked out how much liquid a person would receive if he stood naked under the aircraft when it was spraying.

The figures I got had lots of noughts after the decimal place. Going to the local chemist I asked him to measure these amounts. The total liquid amounted to a desert spoonful, and the chemical content was so small he had not the equipment to measure it.

"If I put one drop from an eye-dropper into your bottle, it will be several times too much," he said.

No one stands under the aircraft, naked or clothed. Drift would be about 25 per cent of the total liquid, and even in summer, unless you are on a beach, clothing covers 75 per cent of the body. The contact is minute. Unpleasant, yes. Annoying, yes. But hardly dangerous.

A Royal Commission on Environmental Pollution investigated the polluting effects of agricultural chemicals. One of their recommendations was that prior notification of aerial spraying operations should be extended beyond the properties immediately adjacent to the field.

At discussions with CAA the operators pointed out that this could cause more complaints. In fact this did occur. People complained, not of the operation, but that they had not been informed. The operators also pointed out that if the notification area was increased it would be necessary in a busy season to employ extra staff, with a van, to carry out this requirement, which would add to the operator's cost. "Well," said Mr Walker, "you will have to increase your charges."

The number of people and organisations lobbying to be given prior notification of our operations was increasing monthly. As well as the police, there were householders, schools, hospitals, civil and military airfields, broiler houses, turkey houses, racing stables, beekeepers, bird sanctuaries, The Nature Conservancy and other conservation areas.

This was in addition to the normal operational contacts the company had to make to agents, farmers, landing strip owners, the local weather station and staff. It was a wonder that any crops got sprayed at all.

When the operators protested at yet another notification being added to the list, Mr Walker remarked, "It's only a phone call."

This was before the advent of mobile phones. Public telephone boxes were not situated on the corner of every farm landing strip. Arrangements for the next day's operations had to be made in the evening after a day's flying. Many of the organisations requiring notification worked a 9 to 5 day, 5 days a week. Mr Walker, no doubt, had a secretary, who got him his phone numbers while he got on with other work.

After leaving one of these meetings a pilot remarked, "I think we should take up some respectable occupation, like drug dealing or running a brothel!"

After spraying a field of potatoes, having previously notified houses nearby, a man rang me to say the tomatoes in his greenhouse were wilting.

"I'm sure the chemical would not harm tomatoes," I told him.

"The roses in my front garden are not looking too good, either," he added.

"I'll contact the chemical company and see what they say," I told him.

"No harm at all," said the chemical company, "in fact we recommend this chemical for tomatoes and roses."

When I passed this information to the man, he did not believe me and asked for the name and telephone number of the chemical company.

Beekeepers suffered from the effects of crop spraying as insecticides also killed bees feeding in the crop. Bee warning schemes were set up in various parts of the country. I do not know how effective they were in other areas, but in our region the beekeepers were not co-operative. In one county we were sent the names and addresses of 600 beekeepers. As there were only four operators in this area, it seemed more sensible for the beekeepers to liaise with the farmer and the operator rather than the operator try to find out where the bees were. But the beekeepers maintained it was our responsibility to find out where their bees were kept and inform them if we were spraying nearby. This was impracticable because the beekeeper might not have his hives where he lived, but many miles away.

Some beekeepers were sensible and co-operative, and when the farmer was going to spray his crop, got in touch with us. We would arrange to spray the crop when the bees were not active or the keeper would delay releasing the bees from the hive for a few hours in the morning. We, in turn, promised not to spray when the bees were out. Sometimes this caused us minor inconvenience but it saved the bees. At the end of the season appreciative beekeepers left pots of honey on my doorstep.

I sympathise with many of the aims of the environmentalists and conservationists, but I do find that they are sometimes ignorant of the wider implications of their actions and suffer from tunnel vision. Some organisations encouraged their members to protest about all aerial crop spraying, although only about forty per cent of the treatments involved poisons in a dilute form. The chemicals we were allowed to spray were very restricted by the Ministry of Agriculture and had been passed by the Pesticides Safety Precautions Scheme.

A farmer told me that a large group of bird watchers, coming from all over the country to sight a rare species reported in the area, had trampled down half an acre of his corn.

On television one night a Kent apple grower was protesting about the importation of French 'Golden Delicious' apples. He was interviewed against the background of his orchard. When the interview ended he got into his Renault car and drove away!

At the time of the Sizewell 'B' inquiry, I was discussing the use of nuclear energy with a man who opposed the building of this power station and had signed petitions against it. During conversation it transpired that he was unaware that there had already been a nuclear power station at Sizewell for over 20 years!

The Health and Safety Executive appeared at a meeting with CAA, to introduce requirements for protective clothing for markers and loaders. The markers were required to wear overalls with tight cuffs at wrist and ankle, gloves, a hat with neck protection like a French Foreign Legionnaire and a plastic face visor.

"For years markers have not worn this gear and have not been harmed. They don't stand under the aircraft, but to one side, so have little contact with the chemical," said one operator.

"But this is a poison you are spraying," replied the HSE official.

"If the markers have to wear that gear," said another, "standing for hours in the middle of a corn field and running from field to field on a hot summer's day, they will faint from heat exhaustion before they are poisoned."

Our protests were of no avail and we had to supply the equipment. But the markers still preferred a pair of shorts and a bottle of 'Ambre Solaire!'

For a time I, along with many other pilots, became conscious that our activities might bring about more complaints and started to fly looking over our shoulders.

This tended to make me apprehensive and distract me from the job in hand which, when flying at low level, could be dangerous. If a motorist stopped and watched me out of interest I immediately wondered if I was upsetting someone. I soon realised that this attitude could be dangerous, so dismissed it.

There was no standard to judge the public's reaction. Sometimes spraying near a village early in the morning I had the feeling that someone might complain, but nothing happened. On the other hand spraying some fields on marshland near Gt. Yarmouth, without a house in sight, a woman walking her dog, whom I did not see, complained.

Pilots are restricted to flying not more than 100 hours in 28 days, to ensure they do not suffer from stress or over-tiredness. I never found flying stressful or over-tiring. After a long day's flying, a shower, a gin and tonic, a meal and a good night's sleep, saw me fresh for the next day. What did cause me stress and raised my blood pressure was dealing with CAA, Health and Safety, the Vatman, and similar authorities.

A short time before I retired, I attended a meeting between CAA and the operators. Mr Walker had moved on to the Air-crew Licensing Section and was replaced by a man I had not met. Also attending was the newly appointed Director of CAA.

Whether Mr Walker enjoyed or dreaded the tempestuous meetings with the operators I never knew. Probably he took them in his stride as part of his job. When I went to see him, in his new department, about the validation of the licence of a New Zealand pilot we were employing for a season, he was most helpful.

The agenda for the CAA meeting covered the usual subjects, complaints and prior notification. Complaints remained at about the same level, 100-150 a year, of which only half were significant.

"My previous appointment was Commandant at Heathrow Airport," said the new Director, "and we dealt with about 5,000 complaints a year."

That, I thought, put the matter in the correct perspective.

The meeting went on to discuss prior notification. Mr Walker's successor, who had not entered the discussion, suddenly spoke.

"What concerns me," he said, "is a situation where an old age pensioner might be standing on a step ladder, painting his ceiling and is frightened by a low flying aircraft, falling down and breaking his leg."

There was a long silence. No one else spoke, so I could not let this remark go unchallenged.

"How many cases have there been," I asked, "of old age pensioners, up a step ladder, painting the ceiling, being frightened by a low flying aircraft, falling down and breaking a leg?"

There was another long silence, finally broken by the chairman saying. "We'll now move on to the next item on the agenda."

The scope and form of prior notification was still being discussed between CAA, NAAC, the Ministry of Transport and other bodies long after I retired.

26

A Tragic Accident

During the late 1970s aerial crop spraying appeared to be well established, and operators hoped that aircraft would be used by the farmers for routine treatments and not just in an emergency. New chemicals to combat disease in crops appeared almost every year. Some of the granular formulations were applied at very low rates, only a few pounds per acre and there was no ground machine capable of applying it accurately, so aircraft were used.

There were now some forty operators with about 150 aircraft operating in the United Kingdom. The majority were fixed-wing aircraft, including some like the Ag-Cat powered by prop-turbine engines. Some companies operated helicopters, which under certain conditions were more effective operationally, but expensive to operate.

The helicopter operators claimed better coverage due to the down-wash of the overhead rotors, and used it as a sales point. However the down-wash from the helicopter rotors was similar to that of the down-wash from a fixed wing aircraft when flying at 80 mph.

New chemicals extended the season. The spreading of granular herbicides and slug bait to winter wheat and sowing of turnip seed extended the season to the end of the year. As these chemicals are applied at such a low rate, sometimes only a few pounds per acre, calibration is tricky.

Turnip seeds are sown into a standing barley crop a few weeks before harvest. The seeds drop to the bottom of the crop, safe from birds and in the wet, warm atmosphere, germinate. When the barley is harvested, the turnip plants are exposed to sunshine and rain and grow quickly. This supplies winter feed for sheep.

The seeds are small, round and hard, similar to shotgun pellets and flow very fast. Just a twitch on the calibration handle can double the application rate. A pilot, unfamiliar with the work, setting what he thought was a small opening, spread 20 acres of seed in one run!

A virus appeared in the sugar beet crop, which turned the leaves yellow and reduced the yield. The treatment was to spray powdered sulphur mixed in water. The timing for this treatment was after cereals had been harvested, but before the fields had been ploughed. It was therefore possible to find a landing strip in the middle of the farm, so eliminating ferry flights and speeding up the operation.

The problem with using human markers is the delay while they get to the fields, especially if they are widely spaced. The Americans developed an automatic flagman, which enabled the pilot to mark the field himself. This consisted of a tube fitted on to the wing, which housed cardboard discs to which were attached two long streamers. A disc was released by a plunger operated electrically by the pilot pressing a button on the joystick. The disc fell beneath the aircraft and the streamers spread out, showing the pilot where his last run had been. As the flag is made of paper, it is biodegradable and environmentally friendly.

When the first automatic flagman was fitted, Tony and I did some trials on Shipdham airfield. The aircraft, on the next run, had to be positioned in relation to the flag to give the correct swath width. It was interesting that Tony's swathes were too narrow and mine were too wide. After some practice we got the swath widths right. The flagman was also useful for dropping cryptic messages to the marker, such as 'Delay of one hour, stay where you are', or 'Out of cigs, get 20 Players when you come back to strip'.

When the CAA heard that operators were using static markers and automatic flagmen they were not happy that there was no man on the ground when fields were sprayed. As the operators had gone to the expense of installing this equipment to increase their efficiency and also satisfy the Health and Safety Executive by removing human markers from contact with chemical which they considered dangerous, it seemed pointless to have a man standing around doing nothing.

Francois was due to join the company in the summer of 1978, when his contract in the Cayman Islands finished. We now had three Pawnees and three ground support units. This seemed to be a manageable size for a small company, but big enough to give our customers a good service. Francois also being a licensed aircraft engineer meant we were in a good position to maintain and overhaul our own aircraft.

We operated with the minimum of overheads. The directors were operational pilots. They ran their own units, invoiced their customers and acted as a small company within a bigger one. Accounts, banking, payments and salaries were carried out at the main office. Our permanent ground staff assisted with the aircraft maintenance and equipment repairs in the winter and became very proficient.

Alan Furness, as well as doing motor and equipment repairs, became a useful aircraft engineer. Being endowed with a large amount of common sense, we could leave him to work on an aircraft unsupervised, knowing that he would not do anything stupid. If he came across a problem he could not solve, he would leave it until Francois or I returned, or telephone another engineer for advice. With experience over the years he was capable of many jobs, such as changing wheels, brakes, spark plugs, tailwheel units, spray equipment and also became a good fabric worker when we recovered mainplanes and control surfaces.

Just as we appeared to be nicely set up, Tony was killed while spraying cotton in the Sudan. I never found out what caused the crash but he was a skilled and careful pilot, so it must have been something beyond his control; perhaps a momentary distraction at a critical time or an engine failure. A tragic death, leaving a wife with two young children.

Francois was not coming back until the summer, so I had to find a pilot for the fertilising season which was to start in a few weeks time. Due to a shortage of experienced spray pilots in England, several companies employed pilots from Australia and New Zealand, our busy season being their quiet time.

I was recommended a New Zealand pilot, Colin Green, who agreed to come at short notice. People from the Commonwealth were now subject to immigration laws and could only work and reside in England if they had a work permit. If, however, their grandparents were British born, they were exempt. I thought this applied to Colin, but as I was not sure I thought I had better do the right thing and apply for a work permit.

It was with great difficulty that I found where to apply. The local labour exchange and the Department of Labour were not able to help me. Eventually I found that I had to apply to a department of the Home Office in a London suburb.

I wrote, explaining the situation, that one of our pilots had been killed flying overseas and we had contracts with farmers to fulfil, starting in a few weeks. We needed another pilot urgently and there were none available in England. I also added that I did not think that Colin was subject to the immigration restrictions, but was applying anyway to make sure that I was not breaking the law. This was a bad mistake as it gave the officials an opportunity to postpone making a decision.

They wrote back asking for Colin's birth certificate and the birth and marriage certificates of his parents and grandparents - originals, not copies. This could take months and Colin was already on his way. Thinking about this for a few days, I decided to use a bureaucratic ploy back on them, writing to say the matter was in hand and I would contact them when I had the necessary documents.

In the meantime Colin got his New Zealand pilot's licence validated and was flying. Many months later the Home Office wrote to ask if I had the documents they required, but I was able to tell them that Mr Green had returned to New Zealand. Going to the British High Commission office back home, he found that he was not subject to the immigration law, anyway.

When Australian and New Zealand pilots started to arrive in England in the early 1960s and went to the Ministry of Civil Aviation for validations there were many fierce arguments. The pilot would present his documents to a clerk at the counter who took them to an official in the depth of the building, who decided on the requirements for validation. Different officials gave different rulings and as they only dealt with the applicant through the clerk, tempers sometimes ran high and the poor clerk got some rough treatment from the 'wild colonial boys!'

When I came back from Australia, my Australian licence was validated after taking an Air Law examination. I asked what examinations I would have to take to obtain a British licence and was given a list. As I was going overseas I did not pursue it. Later, on sending my licence back to Australia, it was renewed, but I was told that it would not be renewed again as I was not living in Australia and flying Australian registered aircraft. This put me in a spot and on asking again what examinations I would have to take to obtain a British licence I was given a different list.

It looked as if I would have to take time off and study for the British examination. By good fortune, as so many overseas pilots were coming to work in England due to the expansion of the industry, Crop Culture persuaded the Ministry to issue British licences to overseas pilots, endorsed for crop spraying only. This suited me very well, and I forgot about sitting the examinations. A few years later the format of the commercial pilot's licence was changed, and I was issued with a new one without the restriction. Whether this was policy or a mistake, I never enquired!

It was pleasant coming back every night to home comforts after spending so much time on short overseas contracts. I even became a tourist and took holidays on the continent with my wife. Previously, coming home from overseas, where I lived in hotels, rest-houses and 'bachelor' messes, the last thing I wanted to do was to stay in another hotel.

I got to know our customers. One farmer who had a small vineyard gave us a couple of bottles of his wine when we worked for him and some of the estates which had a shoot would send a brace of pheasants. Francois was sometimes invited for a day's shooting on a farm.

Peter Thomas farmed at Lyng in north Norfolk, a long way from the nearest airstrip. He appreciated our problems in a busy season and gave us plenty of notice. "If you find you can fit me in," he said, "fly over the house and I will come out and mark for you." However, we put in static markers and as his farm was on the route when I flew out from our new base at Little Snoring in the morning, I sprayed a load then and another when I flew back at night.

Over two or three days I sprayed all his crop. He always gave the ground crew a few pounds for a beer and wrote and thanked us for the service at the end of the season. Needless to say, we gave him the best service we could.

During a busy fertilising season I treated some fields on an estate in Suffolk. There was a church nearby, screened by trees. When we were busy, working seven days a week, Sunday did not register. If the surroundings had been more open, I would have seen signs of activity and realised that a service was in progress and avoided the church.

A few days later I got a letter from a church warden, saying that the noise of the aircraft had upset the service and all aerial spraying should be banned. It was an unpleasant letter, so I ignored him and wrote to the vicar apologising. He never replied. Perhaps when I told him I did not realise it was Sunday, he thought I was beyond redemption.

The annoying part was that a week earlier, expecting to spray a field on a Sunday which had a church in the corner, I went to a lot of trouble to locate the vicar and find out when he was holding a service.

Being a small industry, all the operators knew each other. Although in many cases business competitors, they would help each other out in trouble. Maybe the battles with CAA bonded us together. When I had an unserviceable magneto while operating in Bedfordshire, Bill Bowker let me have a replacement from his store which was only just down the road. On another occasion needing a replacement for a damaged rudder, Pat Miller flew it to our working strip in his Piper Cherokee.

After I left Westwick Distributors to start my own business all contact ceased. Soon after I crashed my Pawnee, Westwick badly damaged a wing on one of their Pawnees. They decided to let bygones be bygones and asked if they could borrow or hire my undamaged wing until they got a replacement from America. My aircraft was going to take some months to repair and the wing was sitting in the hangar, so I agreed. What the hire charge for a wing was I had no idea, but as it had to have a spar modification incorporated, I said if they did this I would accept it as a fee. Barter is sometimes better than cash.

I enjoyed flying over the East Anglian countryside in the various seasons. In summer the green woods, the corn turning from green to gold, and the splashes of yellow from the oil seed rape. Winter was so different, bare trees and brown fallow fields. When it snowed the whole character of the countryside changed. Many of the familiar landmarks disappeared or changed - it seemed like a different country.

From the air I often saw deer, and flying back along the North Norfolk coast I would circle and watch seals basking on the sandbanks off Brancaster. In a wood in Suffolk I came across a heronry, with about 20 nests, a sight I could never see from the ground.

I used to house-hunt from the air. If I spotted an empty house or a derelict cottage, I marked it on the map and then my wife and I went to view it from the ground. After we had found a house, I wanted to pave a yard. While spraying a field I saw a heap of broken paving slabs. The farmer let me have them, so I loaded them onto the lorry and took them home. Over a period I spotted several other heaps, large and small and collected them. The ground staff got a bit fed up with my loading the lorry or marker's van with lumps of concrete, but they humoured me and eventually I had enough to pave my yard.

Work came from a farmer in an area of Suffolk which was short of landing strips. However it was near the disused airfield at Stradishall. All the land had been returned to farming, except for a beautiful long runway, which came under the jurisdiction of the Property Services Agency. I rang the area office and asked an official if I could use it to spray some crops nearby.

"Have you got permission from Air Traffic Control?" he asked.

"I don't need to," I replied. "It is non-controlled airspace."

"Well, there is no control tower there, or any fire or rescue services," the official went on.

"That's all right," I replied. "We carry our own safety equipment on the lorry and this is approved by the CAA."

"Why can't you use Cambridge Airport," said the official, "it's not far away."

"It's over 20 miles from our work," I replied. "You don't seem to know much about aerial spraying, so perhaps I could speak to your manager."

"The manager is not here," he replied.

"Would you give me his name so I can contact him later?" I asked.

With reluctance, the official gave me the manager's name and added, "I can assure you, you will never get permission to use Stradishall."

I wrote to the manager, explaining our needs and received a contract for me to sign, valid for one year, stating the conditions for the use of Stradishall airfield. The conditions were not suitable to our needs; they wanted 48 hours' notice, we could not use it at week-ends and the landing fees were high. However, if I signed the contract and sent a fee of £15.66 (how do they arrive at such a figure?) we could use the airfield. It was unlikely we would use the airfield under these terms, but just to confound the unhelpful official, I returned the contract with a cheque. Why is it, if you ask some officials if you can do something, they immediately adopt a negative attitude? Rather than help, they think up reasons why it cannot be done.

Turning over a field next to the one I was spraying, I saw several goats tethered in front of a small building. They were jumping about and showing signs of distress, so I pulled up and circled around. A man came out of the building and started to lead the goats away. I thought this was helpful of him, and waited until the goats had been removed before I continued. After a few more turns over the field I noticed a man walking with a gun under his arm, who seemed to be following me. On one of the turns he pointed the gun at me and I saw a puff of smoke as he fired. I was well out of range, but I took a dim view of this. I was able to keep well out of range by widening my turns, but he still followed me.

When I got home I reported this to the police and a constable came to take a statement. He then asked me, "Do you want to prosecute this man?"

"No, I don't want to prosecute him," I answered, "I just want a policeman to give him a good talking to, and tell him not to be so foolish. Give him a good scare and threaten him with the loss of his gun licence." Whether this was done I do not know, but later the representative of another company, which had work in the area, was warned by the farmer that he would shoot at any aircraft that came near his property.

Three months later I had a letter from the Air Safety Enforcement branch of the Civil Aviation Authority. It said:

> 'The Authority has received a report from the police of a crop-spraying incident. Briefly, it appears that your crop spraying activities were conducted without warning and in such a manner as to so annoy the occupants of the farm as to arouse them to fire a shotgun in the vicinity of the aircraft.
>
> You should be aware that whilst the Authority does not intend

to take action against any of the parties concerned in the incident, it nevertheless takes a very serious view of the matter and should there be further such reports it will not hesitate to take appropriate action.

It is for the purpose of avoiding conflict between crop-spraying aircraft and the community at large that your Aerial Applications Manual contains requirements for you to notify the occupants of buildings, etc, near to the intended target area in order to minimise nuisance to third parties.'

I read this letter in amazement. The farm referred to consisted of two Nissen huts in the middle of a field. After some thought I replied as follows:

'I refer to your letter regarding the shooting incident. To say that I was both amazed and shocked that you should take such a lenient view of the action of a person who shoots at an aeroplane to express his annoyance, is indeed an understatement.

I suppose you realise that this action could have caused the aircraft to crash and injure or kill the pilot. Such a crash could in turn endanger innocent third parties.

At no time was the operation conducted outside the requirements of the company's operations manual. Every crop-spraying pilot is concerned to conduct operations at minimum danger and annoyance to the public. In turn, he expects the public not to act in such an irresponsible manner as to endanger his life.

This industry has a good safety record in relation to third parties. In over 30 years of aerial crop-spraying in this country there has been no incident of serious damage or injury to third party property or persons.

Since this incident, another aerial crop-spraying company had work in this area and their representative was warned by the farmer that he would shoot at the aircraft if it came near his property.

It would appear that there is a danger to Air Safety in this area and I would like to know what action the Authority intends to take.'

My letter must have caused the official to have second thoughts. He wrote back to say that as I told the police I did not intend to prosecute the farmer, he assumed I did not think the incident to be very serious.

To prosecute the farmer would take up my time and time of the police and the court. As I had no witness, it would be my word against his and he would probably get a caution. I thought it would be more effective if he had a warning from a policeman, and cheaper, too.

27

Enforced Retirement

Every year had its highlights. There was the aphid year when we had so much work no company could cope with it all. There was the fertiliser year when a wet spring brought much work, but the weather made flying difficult. There was the bean year, when we spread so much granular insecticide that holes were worn in the spreader vanes. And there were the sugar beet years, which extended the season into the autumn.

The hope that farmers would use aircraft for routine treatment of their crops did not materialise. There were many reasons for this, but they all added up to less work for aircraft.

Some of it was due to pressure from environmental groups and individuals. Several of our customers ceased using aircraft because as soon as one appeared on the farm he was harassed by some of his neighbours complaining.

Farmers now had to enter some of the crop five or six times to carry out various treatments, so a system of 'tramlining' was introduced. When drilling cereals, a number of the drills were blanked off, so an unsown path was made, equal to the width and position of the tractor wheels. In turn these were spaced to correspond to the swath width of the ground machines. With this method the crop was not damaged when treated and the 'tramlines' allowed accurate coverage of the crop and did away with the need for a marker to guide the tractor.

Agricultural machinery manufacturers were producing more sophisticated machines giving wide swath coverage; specialist machines to spread granules at low application rates, high clearance machines to treat high crops and low pressure vehicles with balloon tyres making it possible to work on wet fields without crop damage or the machines bogging down.

The farmers had had many profitable years and it paid them to invest in machinery rather than pay tax. Moreover the chemical manufacturers had gained more knowledge and experience and found that if treatments were not carried out at a certain time in relation to plant growth or level of infestation, they were less effective. This concentrated the work into a narrower time span.

The decrease in work was slow and imperceptible. Where previously we worked off one airstrip for a whole day, now we would have several moves. I suppose I should have recognised the signs earlier, but as my brother-in-law, who was a bank manager, pointed out to me, to many small businessmen the business is not just an income but a way of life. Consequently they are reluctant to give up, even when the bottom line on the accounts warns them that they should.

We took one Pawnee out of service and Francois and I operated two units for a time, but it soon became apparent that the company could only just support the two of us. Francois was offered a contract back in the Cayman Islands and decided to take it. He and his wife, Jenny, had spent most of their married life living and working in the tropics and did not enjoy the harsher northern climate.

From three units and nine staff, the company was now reduced to Alan Furness and myself. With the use of static markers and the automatic flagman, Alan and I, with a seasonal human marker, operated successfully for two years. Then, on my six monthly pilot's medical, an irregular heart beat showed up on the ECG. I was called to the CAA medical branch for further tests, including wearing a portable ECG machine to monitor my heart over 24 hours. The end result was that I could no longer hold a pilot's licence. After an examination by a heart specialist at the Norfolk and Norwich hospital he told me that many people had this heart irregularity, but as they did not have routine ECGs, they were not aware of it and lived happy normal lives.

The specialist told me there was nothing seriously wrong with my heart and could not recommend any treatment. He did his best for me and wrote to the CAA with his views, but naturally enough, a sixty year old pilot with an odd heartbeat is not a good risk. So after thirty years and 12,000 hours my life as an aerial crop-spraying pilot had come to an end.

Alan and I were now out of work. Alan had worked for us for over ten years and was almost part of the family, beside being the backbone of the ground side of the company. He joined a company making windows for boats and found a great contrast. All his life he had worked in branches of agriculture, working irregular hours in the open air. Standing at a work bench in a factory came hard. He found his fellow workers had a different view of life.

He told me: "It's amazing, when the whistle goes at 5 o'clock, whatever tools they are using, they open their hands, drop them on the bench, grab their coats and are gone. One evening when the whistle went I had a few screws to fit to finish a window. It took me about three minutes, but when I left the factory was empty and the only car in the car park was mine." His employers soon realised his worth and he now has a section of the factory to run.

I was too young to retire, and I could not afford to, anyway. I decided to go back to engineering, but after thirty years on the fringe of aviation, I came in for a shock. Seeing that a new company making a light aircraft was advertising for service engineers, I drove down to the factory in the south of England. Entering the building I found myself in a reception lounge with a pretty girl behind a desk. It could have been the foyer of a hotel. I told her I had come about the job and she called the personnel manager. I explained to him that I had driven down from Norfolk about the job they had advertised. He gave me a form to fill and told me to post it in.

I was quite disconcerted by this attitude. I could see the manager's office two doors down the corridor, but it might as well have been miles away. After the war, if I called on a company about a job, the Chief Engineer or Chief Inspector would see me and have a chat, even if he had no job to offer. We would know other people in the industry and had probably worked on the same aerodrome or with the same company at various times.

The form only had a small portion relating to experience, but much of it asked about schooling, 'O' levels, national insurance number, what sports I played and my grandmother's maiden name. I did not fill it in. Things had certainly changed. Chief Inspectors are now Quality Control Managers, Chief Engineers are now Engineering Managers and Chief Storemen are now Supply Officers or Purchasing Officers. Even the CAA area surveyor is now a Regional Manager. And we used to laugh when rat catchers became Rodent Control Officers!

Eventually I joined a branch of a large company maintaining aircraft for small charter companies and third-level operators. I found myself back on DC3s after thirty-five years and was surprised how much I still remembered about this aircraft.

Many things had changed, but other things were familiar. The stores still had a drill but no chuck key, a pop rivet gun that did not work, and ran out of popular sizes of bolts and washers. The engine stands, trestles and ladders were government surplus from the war, big, heavy and awkward. They had certainly been built to last!

I saw an engineer having trouble starting the motor of a DC3. When he had no success, he removed a cowling and tapped the side of the carburettor, after which the engine started. I can remember doing the same thing in Jersey, years ago, when the metering valve stuck. That had not changed either.

However, what used to be the technical records office had changed out of all recognition. It was now part of quality control with progress charts on the wall, computers, copying machines, electric typewriters - and the paperwork!

There was a saying amongst the engineers in the late nineteen forties. 'When the weight of the paperwork reaches the weight of the aircraft, it is safe to fly.' Now they would have to say, 'When the weight of the paperwork is five times the weight of the aircraft it is safe to fly!'

Getting into a small, four-seater, modern aircraft, I turned on the master switch. The instrument panel lit up with coloured lights, some static, some flashing, horns sounded and behind the panel electric motors started to whirl and hum. It was like a Wurlitzer organ! I was used to aircraft where if you put the petrol and magneto switches on and pressed the starter button, the engine went and if the oil pressure registered, you were ready to go!

Much of the work was for third-level operators who had mail contracts with the Post Office. They operated obsolete aircraft on hire purchase and ran them into the ground. They slowly got behind with their maintenance payments and when 'lifed' items such as engines and propellers needed overhaul, they applied for an extension. After they had squeezed everything out of the aircraft, all the components out of life and perhaps an expensive inspection or modification was due, they went out of business and the hire company repossessed. The cost of making the aircraft airworthy again was probably more than what it was worth. They made the old type of secondhand car dealer seem like paragons of virtue!

After about 12 months the company shut down so I free-lanced, looking after light aircraft for private owners and I did some fabric work for Air Atlantique, a company that still made a profit from operating DC3s.

While I was at their Coventry base, recovering DC3 control surfaces, they had a problem on a DC6. They contacted Douglas Aircraft in America for advice and Douglas sent their European service engineer. He stood in the hangar, a man of about forty years of age, and said, "Do you know, I have never seen a DC6 before." I realised then that I was getting old!

I lived in the final era when the industry was run by aviators and not businessmen. No one made much money but life was varied, interesting and fun, with plenty of 'characters'.

The advance in aviation since the Wright brothers first flew in 1903 has been phenomenal. Aircraft are now built by international consortiums and designed and flown by computers, a highly technical and serious business. The 'characters' have gone and so has a lot of the fun. I expect the present generation will be expressing the same sentiments when in turn, they retire.

When my engineer's licence became due for renewal I thought I might not renew it. Owners of wood and fabric aircraft persuaded me to carry on. Engineers coming into the industry are not interested in the older aircraft; it is jets, pressurisation and electronics for them. To find an engineer who can and is interested enough to refabric an Auster wing is becoming more difficult. I know my limitations and restrict my activities to the simple aeroplanes, Tiger Moths, Austers, Jodels and Piper Cubs.

It provides me with a glass of wine and a pipe of tobacco while I remember the happy times I had in aviation, the interesting countries I visited and the variety of people I met. There is a saying, "It's better to be born lucky, than rich." I concur with that sentiment.